LIVE AT JACKSON STATION

LIVE AT JACKSON STATION

Music, Community, and Tragedy
in a Southern Blues Bar

DANIEL M. HARRISON

THE UNIVERSITY OF
SOUTH CAROLINA PRESS

© 2020 University of South Carolina

Published by the University of South Carolina Press
Columbia, South Carolina 29208

www.uscpress.com

Manufactured in the United States of America

29 28 27 26 25 24 23 22 21 20
10 9 8 7 6 5 4 3 2 1

Library of Congress Cataloging-in-Publication Data
can be found at http://catalog.loc.gov/.

ISBN 978-1-64336-206-9 (hardback)
ISBN 978-1-64336-145-1 (paperback)
ISBN 978-1-64336-146-8 (ebook)

To my students—may you each find
your own Jackson Station.

One often finds courage and principle in unexpected places.
  —Benjamin E. Mays

Contents

Illustrations

Acknowledgments

"Tell me about Jackson Station," Walter Salas-Humara said one morning over breakfast. With the help of Nike Hyduke and Jon Holloway, I had brought Walter to Greenwood for a concert. Salas-Humara, a singer-songwriter and founding member of the Silos, was in Atlanta the night before having dinner with Jeff Calder of the Swimming Pool Qs. Calder had been raving about Jackson Station. Walter wanted to know more about the place. Since that fateful moment in May 2014—which triggered the beginning of the research that undergirds this book—I have been thinking (or talking or writing) about Jackson Station, at least a little bit, almost every day of my life.

Sadly, I never went to Jackson Station. I did not arrive in Greenwood until 2005—fifteen years after Jackson Station had shut down. Most of what I know about the place I have learned from many interviews with people who were kind enough to speak to me about it. The names of these folks are listed in the pages that follow. I am tremendously grateful for their time and stories. I sincerely hope that this book does justice to their memories of Jackson Station. It could not have been written without them.

There are many other people in the greater Greenwood community (and beyond) who have chatted with me more informally about Jackson Station over the years. At the risk of leaving anyone out, I will not attempt to name them here. You know who you are. Your interest and encouragement have been enormously helpful. I am grateful to each of you.

I would like to give special thanks to the following people who helped with this project in substantive ways. The late Reggie Massey (who passed away while I was working on this book), was an early cheerleader of the project and shared with me many of the archival materials in this work. He knew the magic of Jackson Station and the importance of keeping its spirit alive. I am sorry Reggie did not live to see the final product, but I know he would be happy to see the book finished. Reggie introduced me to Cora Garmany, who hosted a delightful dinner for us in Pomaria, which led to contact with Teddy Roberts. I am very appreciative to Claire DeLune for arranging an interview with Drink Small. I am also grateful to George Singleton who put me in touch with some important initial contacts. Early interviews with Jeff Calder, Glenn Phillips and Bob Margolin validated my hunch that Jackson Station was a place of significance. Ben Hawthorne and Harris Bailey eagerly assisted from the beginning, providing crucial input at key junctures. Angela Rowland was kind enough to share Jackson Station memorabilia and put me in touch with Linn Johnson. Russ Fitzgerald generously offered expert musical knowledge and a firsthand account of working at Jackson Station. Phyllis Free has been a great supporter of the project, a keen reader, and hooked me up with David Truly. Bill Postman gave warm feedback on an early draft. Bill Danaher offered encouraging and helpful feedback on a later draft. Charlie Geer suggested how to start the book as well as great advice about how to improve the writing. I thank the Greenwood *Index-Journal* for their superb coverage of Jackson Station over the years. David Goldman has been a wealth of information and enthusiastic supporter of the project since the beginning. Tinsley Ellis graciously introduced me to Dave Schools of Widespread Panic, who was kind enough to grant me a telephone interview. It was after that conversation that I realized the story of Jackson Station resonated well beyond Greenwood County. Welborn Adams helped me get to the bottom of the Strom Thurmond connection to Jackson Station. Mark Cline and Armistead Wellford provided important last-minute details and a reminder that, at the end of the day, Jackson Station was indeed all about the music.

A sabbatical at Lander University provided release from teaching duties during the fall 2018 term, which gave me the time to write an initial rough draft. I am thankful to those who made that award possible. I am grateful to Richard Cosentino, Scott Jones, Lucas McMillan, and Ashley Woodiwiss for their continuing support of my work. Lisa Wiecki and her staff at Jackson Library did an outstanding job getting me access to books, articles, and other materials in a very timely manner. Keith McCaslan converted old cassette tapes of shows at Jackson Station into digital format. Bonner Abercrombie and Stacey Hart in the Lander Print Shop helped me format and scan the final images in this book. Lawrence Hazelrigg continues to be an important advocate and ally. Ehren Foley, acquisitions editor at the University of South Carolina Press, has done a terrific job shepherding this book through the publication process. Virginia Dumont-Poston read the entire manuscript during the summer of 2019 and provided outstanding recommendations about how to improve the narrative. Two anonymous readers at the University of South Carolina Press gave extremely helpful comments and constructive criticism on the penultimate draft. I hope they will see the book is now better because of their efforts. Finally, my deepest appreciation goes to my wonderful wife, artist Rebecca Salter Harrison; and our two extraordinary daughters Liliana and Mirabel, for allowing me the time and space to work on this project. They are my pride and joy.

Daniel M. Harrison
Greenwood, SC
July 29, 2020

INTRODUCTION

Yeah, I'm going back
to that shack way across the railroad track.
Uh huh, that's where I think I belong.
        —The Grateful Dead[1]

Throughout the 1980s, Jackson Station[2] Rhythm & Blues Club of Hodges, South Carolina, was one of the liveliest places to be. The remote music venue, which was housed in an old railway depot about eighty miles due east of Athens, Georgia, was "one of the premiere hotbeds for rhythm and blues"[3] not only in the state, but also across the Southeast. The club advertised a "comfortable, relaxed, really laid-back atmosphere."[4] It brought a cosmopolitan sensibility to the South Carolina backcountry and a stage for local celebration. For about a decade, Jackson Station buzzed with eccentric, effervescent people who came together to socialize and appreciate live music.

Mattie Phifer, erstwhile guitarist and singer for the all-female blues band the Sensible Pumps,[5] describes the scene this way: "Packed, full, fun, everybody partying, dancing, real eclectic mix of people. Jackson Station didn't know class or race; it was just a place [where] people from all walks of life came late at night."[6]

On Friday nights, folks flocked to Jackson Station from across the region to see "southeastern blues artists and national touring acts on their southern circuits."[7] Bands would often play their music until five o'clock in the morning. Such operating hours were not the only scandalous thing about the place. Jackson Station was owned by two openly gay men—Gerald Jackson (1946–2010) and Steven Bryant (1952–2012). These men may or may not have been called "queers," "faggots," or "pole smokers" behind their backs by less tolerant members of the tiny, conservative, Christian town they lived in. In 2020, South Carolina still lists "buggery" as a felony offense under its Code

Jackson's Station Rhythm & Blues Club, ca. 1986.

of Laws.[8] However, Jackson and Bryant operated Jackson Station in the 1970s and '80s, many years before the United States Supreme Court ruled in *Lawrence v. Texas* (2003), that state laws criminalizing sexual relationships between individuals of the same sex were unconstitutional.[9] In such an historical climate, it seems quite remarkable that it was through the impassioned, enterprising efforts of these two individuals—as well as Gerald's mother, Elizabeth Jackson (1922–2001)[10]—that Jackson Station developed the distinction of being one of the South's best blues bars.[11]

"It was like *Smokey and the Bandit* meets *Boys in the Band* in outer space," said the Reverend Billy C. Wirtz, the avant-garde piano bluesman and one of the first professional musicians to perform at Jackson Station.[12] "It was like no place on the planet you had ever seen."[13]

Jackson Station was "part church, part carnival, and part diner,"[14] recalled Atlanta-based guitar legend Glenn Phillips, one of the top guitarists in the nation, who played the club many times during its years of operation. Other regular performers at Jackson Station (and who will be discussed later in this book) include the New Wave band the Swimming Pool Qs (1978–present), famed rhythm and blues singer Nappy Brown (1929–2008), and jam band giant Widespread Panic (1986–present).

"I loved playing there," said Widespread Panic bassist Dave Schools,[15] of Jackson Station. "We would play until we would either ran everybody the hell out of the room or they were tired of serving those drunks. I do recall the sun coming up at least once or twice."[16]

Jackson's Station Concert Calendar, April 1989.

Jackson Station was the embodiment of the best in the American honky-tonk/juke-joint/roadhouse/blues-bar tradition. The fact that the club had once operated as a railroad depot made it even more unique. Of course, as Georgia Blues guitarist Tinsley Ellis notes, "There were places like Jackson Station in other states. That wasn't the only place in the world like that. Musicians like myself and Delbert McClinton and all, we've been playing places like that our whole career. [Jackson Station] was just the epitome of it."[17]

Like the best blues clubs, like the One Knite bar in Austin, Texas, Jackson Station offered "swinging, crotch-grinding rhythm-and-blues and soul music, stuff that would keep the crowd dancing and drinking, hot and horny."[18] From 1970 to 1976, the One Knite was the "unofficial home of the blues in Austin"[19] and an old Stevie Ray Vaughan (1954–1990)[20] haunt. A few years later, Jackson Station would emerge in Hodges, South Carolina, hoisting its own tent as a part of a larger blues revival across the United States. The One Knite was a "dark, dank, wonderfully forbidden place. Patrons entered the old stone building . . . by walking through the frame of an upright coffin. Once inside, the smell of stale beer, yesterday's smoke, and puke immediately filled the nostrils. The cluttered *objets de junque* hanging from ceiling—old kitchen sinks, bicycle tires, mangled appliances—sent up warning flags that this was not a joint for the meek or faint of heart."[21] Jackson Station was probably not as quite as malodorous as the One Knite, and the décor was likely much more fabulous, but there was certainly a family resemblance between the two venues. Tipitina's, the iconic New Orleans music club (also a product of the 1970s) provides another point of comparison.[22] On the West Coast, Jewel's Catch One in Los Angeles had similarities to Jackson Station in that it also provided a safe space for gay and lesbian people to congregate.[23] In South Carolina, one might find a scene approximating aspects of Jackson Station at the Garden & Gun Club in Charleston of the late 1970s and the early 1980s.[24]

Despite such likenesses to these other musical establishments, however, Jackson Station was in a class of its own. The place was a "haven for blues fans, wanderers, lost hippies, beat poets, and anyone else seeking a good time."[25] For many musicians and patrons, Jackson Station embodied the "coolest blues bar and music scene the SC upstate has ever seen."[26] For more than a decade, that old railroad depot in Hodges was a beacon for blues and alternative music across the southeast. It breathed life into the careers of old musicians and nurtured younger talent on their way to success. However, the magic ended in April 1990. A horrible crime was committed at the club. Jackson Station shut down.

This book tells the story of Jackson Station—the people who owned the place, the folks who worked there, the patrons who drank there, and the musicians who played there. Jackson Station was a key institution in South Carolina's upstate and was an essential part of its community. In the pages that follow, I explain how Jackson Station came into being in the first place, how it flourished as a music club, and how it has faded into oblivion.

Research for this project began in earnest in May 2014. The resulting text is a mixture of cultural sociology, ethnomusicology, social history, and literary nonfiction. The mode of inquiry is historical and qualitative. The historical part of the research process involved the study of primary historical texts such as old newspapers, police reports, court transcripts, Jackson Station pamphlets, band posters, photographs, and live recordings from the club itself.

The qualitative part of the research process involved conducting about sixty-five in-depth interviews (either in person or over the telephone) with various individuals who—in their capacity as patrons, friends, or musicians—had important information or stories about Jackson Station.

Jackson Station functioned as both destination and waystation for music lovers in the area. It provided a space for social action that created memories that live today. Jackson Station's reputation as one of the more significant blues bars in the Southeast has been long been recognized by touring musicians of that era. It is rightly noted as being exceptional by Emily Edwards in her excellent study of Southern drink houses.[27] While there have been a number of previously written partial accounts of Jackson Station, the whole story of this legendary Southern blues bar—from its inception to its tragic finale—has yet to be told.

ONE

CAROLINA DRAMA

A bar is just a church where they serve beer.
—Jim White[1]

Parents in Greenwood County warned their children to not go to Jackson Station.

"My Daddy would not let me go up there," said Taylor (Wilson) Tucker, owner of Thayer's Boutique in uptown Greenwood, South Carolina.[2]

The worry was that their otherwise respectable sons and daughters might get into trouble up at Jackson Station (or "Jackson's," as the locals called it),[3] a music club with a reputation for being a gay bar, drug den, and place for wild parties lasting until the sun came up.

"Nothing good ever happens on the streets after midnight," was the collective old timer wisdom, and ever thus, advice shrugged off dismissively by a generation used to late nights suffered without too many consequences other than a lack of sleep and the occasional hangover. But what happened in the early hours of April 7, 1990, was a reckoning, of sorts, suggesting that maybe the elders had been right after all. This is what their parents had been warning them about. Something sinister, and even quite evil, was in the woods of the South Carolina backcountry that night.

South Carolina blues legend Drink Small[4] had just finished his last set of the night when he was approached by the piano player in the Legendary Blues Band.[5] Along with Drink Small, the band had been sharing the billing at Jackson Station with saxophonist Fats Jackson and singer Sweet Betty, both from Atlanta, Georgia. The musician Grady "Fats" Jackson told Small that someone had jumped Gerald Jackson in the parking lot.

"Gerald is out there lying on the ground," the man said to him.

Drink Small went to the front door of the club, walked down the ramp, and out into the parking lot. He saw Gerald on his back.

Concert Flyer for April 6, 1990.

It was a "bad blow," remembers Small. He says, "blood was gushing" from Gerald's head.[6]

About a dozen people soon circled forty-three-year-old Gerald Jackson, who was gurgling, grasping for life, and coming in and out of consciousness. It was a horrible, chaotic scene. It was 3:30 on Saturday morning. Jackson Station was an all-night club, often staying open until 5:00 a.m. or later. Even at this hour, there was still a crowd of about 150 people at the club. Late-night partiers and blues enthusiasts had driven to the rural town of Hodges (located in the northwest portion of South Carolina) from places like Charleston, Columbia, and Greenville to see the show. Ten minutes earlier, they would have been ordering beer, doing shots, wolfing down a Spur Burger,[7] or trying to get the phone number of the person at the end of the bar.

"Ain't no more playing that night," reflects Drink Small.[8] People were confused, angry, and upset. Manic revelry quickly gave way to collective trauma. Inebriated customers wandered around aimlessly, buzzes suddenly killed, trying to figure out what had just happened, who was responsible, and what to do next.

At 3:34 a.m., an emergency call was placed to the Greenwood County Sheriff's Office. There has been an assault and battery at Jackson Station.[9] Sergeant Randy Miles, who was attending to an incident in Ware Shoals, South Carolina (about ten miles up the road) told the dispatcher he was on his way. He sped south on US 25, pulling into the Jackson Station parking lot at 3:47 a.m. Officer Miles "found [the] victim lying on [the] ground severely bleeding with [a] large laceration to right side of [his] head."[10] Miles saw about fifteen to twenty-five people in the parking lot, "all gathered around in a little huddle over someone."[11]

Dirk Armstrong, a bartender at Jackson Station and a close friend of Gerald and Steve, was one of the first to get to Gerald. He had run out of the club at the very moment a white pickup truck was peeling out of the lot.[12] Armstrong knelt beside his injured friend. He tried to staunch the flow of blood coming from the deep gash in Gerald's head.

Originally from Tampa, Florida, Armstrong was a recent graduate of Erskine College in Due West, South Carolina, a tiny town ten miles northwest of Hodges. Dirk had attended Erskine from 1984 to 1989, graduating with a biology degree. He started coming to Jackson Station "within a month or six weeks of first going up to Erskine." He appreciated the "very welcoming environment" and its impressive selection of beer. He swiftly became friends with Gerald and Steve. Soon he was working at Jackson Station on the weekends. He started by spinning records in the DJ room and then "wormed [his] way into the kitchen." From there, Dirk further "inserted himself into the whole organization." Before long, he was "working behind the bar," and later would host a New Wave night ("Dirk's Night Out") every Tuesday. Dirk also helped Gerald book bands.

"It was kind of a 24/7 thing," Dirk says about working at Jackson Station. "Always keeping up the yard, and trying to keep the fence up to keep the cows in."[13]

Yet such memories would be years away from where Armstrong was at that moment, sitting out in the dirt parking lot at Jackson Station with a bloody T-shirt in his hand trying to keep Gerald Jackson alive.

: TWO :

GERALD JACKSON

The entrance to hell is not far from Hodges, SC.
    —Gerald Jackson[1]

The tragedy was that Gerald got along with everybody. Gerald Thomas Jackson was born in Greenwood, South Carolina, on October 10, 1946, and raised up the road in the small town of Hodges. A Vietnam veteran and openly gay man, Jackson was a bit of an anomaly, even for the rural South Carolina upstate of his time.

Gerald's parents were Matthew Edgar "Ed" Jackson (1903–1959) and Elizabeth Davis Jackson (1922–2001). Born in Bamberg, South Carolina, Matthew Edgar Jackson had graduated from Greenwood High School and briefly attended Clemson College. He had moved to Hodges in 1939.[2] His parents were Arnold and Mary Ellen Smith Jackson.

Jennie Anna Elizabeth Davis was originally from Whitmire, SC. The daughter of Clarence and Alma Butler Davis, Gerald's mother was twenty-one and living in Greenwood when she married thirty-nine-year-old Ed Jackson on September 4, 1943.[3] Gerald's sister, Ellen, was born in 1944. The family lived at 4113 Moorefield Street, at the intersection of SC 178 and US 25. It was a good location. The Jackson family "had been merchants in the area for several generations."[4] Gerald Jackson's grandfather, Arnold Jackson (1876–1946),[5] had opened a general store in Hodges in 1919. "We had a general store that was known as Jackson Station," Gerald Jackson later told his friends and customers. "There was an electric trolley running from Greenville to Augusta,[6] and it had a stop right here."[7]

After Arnold Jackson passed away, Gerald's parents started running the general store themselves. Hodges resident John Sanders recalls that Ed Jackson was a "big, overweight guy."

Sanders remembers the Jackson general store this way: "He ran a bar. They had draft beer and barstools . . . He sold chicken feed to candy. They sold gas. Out to the side, he had a garage; he had an old Black guy do mechanic work."[8] The Jackson business was one of the larger general stores in the area. "It had everything. They had gas pumps . . . They had a meat counter. They sold fresh meat out of a cooler."[9]

The small town of Hodges had been named in honor of Major George Washington Hodges (1792–1876). Gerald Jackson would boast, "In earlier days, Hodges was a thriving railroading center and farming town."[10] Although today Hodges appears rather sedate, in the late nineteenth and early twentieth centuries, it was known as a rough place with a reputation for drinking, gambling and other mayhem. Gerald claimed that Hodges was "often referred to as a 'Hell Hole' [with] 5 bars[11] (saloons) and only 4 stores. There was a time when a person could get off a train and drink in any of several bars, watch a horse race and witness a cockfight before the next train came along."[12]

"The town gained the nickname of Hell because of the frequent shootings and cuttings,"[13] Gerald had said, which led to one of his infamous tales. This was "a story about a drunk who got on the train at Columbia without a ticket. When the conductor checked him and found he did not have a ticket, he asked him where he wanted off. The drunk is said to have muttered drunkenly, 'I want off at Hell.' The conductor then replied, 'In that case, we'll have to let you off at Hodges.'"[14]

Gerald would often jokes to his patrons: "The entrance to hell is not far from Hodges, SC!"[15] Hodges resident and local historian James "Butch" Emerson Riddle remembers his grandfather, Guy Emerson, telling him that the town's two churches had come into Hodges after the Civil War to clean up the apparent immorality. Due to their efforts, he says the town adopted a one-hundred-year moratorium on selling alcohol within city limits.[16]

Starting in the mid-1800s and lasting for over one hundred years, Hodges was an important node on the regional railroad network. The railway was so central to the town's identity that in its early years, the town was referred to as Hodges Depot, and even earlier as Cokesbury Depot.[17] Cokesbury—an even smaller village (now known mainly for historic Cokesbury College) two miles to the east and established in 1824—was the settlement originally served by Hodges Depot.[18] Later the "Depot" part of the name fell away and the town simply became known as Hodges. Before long, Hodges started developing as a town in its own right.

On November 2, 1871, the *Abbeville Press and Banner* reported that "Hodges Depot, as is known to our readers, is one of our most thriving railroad villages—located at the junction of the Abbeville Branch with the Greenville & Columbia Railroad and taking its name from Gen. G. W. Hodges, the head of a large and influential family, and himself one of the best representatives of man and citizen. A new impetus has been given to the business prosperity of the place since the war."[19]

The Hodges train depot was the hub of the community, offering "jobs as well as entertainment for the people of Hodges."[20] As Vicki Thomas wrote in the Greenwood *Index-Journal* in 1975, "Day and night clerks were needed for the depot seven days a week and someone was hired to keep train engines fired up each weekend when train crews would go out of town."[21]

Eventually, automobiles and eighteen-wheeler tractor-trailers replaced the trains. The Jackson Station general store became a Gulf filling station.[22] Ed Jackson took over the business from his father in 1946. He and Elizabeth "put a café in the store and sold hot dogs and hamburgers, because so many truck drivers were stopping here." Gerald would say that, "at the time, ours was the biggest country store on that part of Highway 25."[23] A Greyhound Bus stop and ticket counter allowed easy access to travel across the country.[24]

As a boy, Gerald went to West Hodges Elementary School (now Hodges Elementary).[25] He was twelve when his father died of a heart attack on the morning on January 17, 1959.[26] Ed Jackson also left his widow, Elizabeth, who was thirty seven years old. Daughter Ellen was fourteen.[27]

John Sanders said, "After Gerald's dad passed away, his mother couldn't deal with," running the store by herself, and so she rented out the space. A family moved in and lived in the back of the building. The business did not do well, and "the store eventually went down the hill."[28]

Despite his father's death, Gerald was successful at school, excelling in music and art. He was a soloist in the Boy's Chorus in the fifth grade.[29] In April 1960, he played Father Bear in the spring production of "Goldilocks Adventure."[30] In 1961, Gerald, now a student at Northside Junior High School, earned second place for selling $26 worth of tickets to the Pancake Jamboree, a fundraiser for new uniforms for the marching band.[31] When he was fifteen, Gerald won third place in a poster competition about traffic safety awareness and had his picture featured in the Greenwood *Index-Journal*.[32]

Gerald continued to shine at Greenwood High School, then located in downtown Greenwood. During Christmas 1963, seventeen-year-old Gerald organized a "Carol Sing" on the Hodges Town Square. The event featured the Greenwood High School Marching Band and choirs from Hodges churches.[33] About two hundred people showed up for the holiday cheer before heading to the Methodist Church for refreshments.[34]

In the spring of 1964, Gerald was an editor and reporter with the Greenwood Trade and Industrial club with an expressed interest in woodworking.[35] At, Greenwood High, Gerald was the leader (Drum Major) of the marching band.[36]

"That's the queen out there prancing," laughs old friend and Greenwood native Linn Johnson, who went to high school with Jackson. Linn first met Gerald when they took a literature class together their sophomore year. They would become lifelong friends. Linn first remembers speaking to Gerald in the school lunchroom.

"He and I just hit it off," she says. "We were just good buddies. That was the beginning of a fabulous relationship."

In the spring of 1965, Gerald worked as a school AV (audio-visual) assistant[37] and provided technical support for the Greenwood High School Talent Showcase.[38] He was on the Decorating Committees for the Junior Prom in April 1966[39] and the Midwinter Ball in January 1967.[40]

After graduating from Greenwood High in the spring of 1967, Gerald enrolled at the Greenwood College of Commerce, and earned a junior accounting degree in 1968.[41] He also attended Lander College.[42] It was around this time that he decided to join the armed forces. In the summer of 1969, Gerald completed a fourteen-week Hospitalman Apprentice training course at the Naval Training Center in Great Lakes, Illinois, where he received instruction in "patient care, the study of anatomy and physiology, minor surgery, the nature and prevention of communicable diseases, and the administering of medicines."[43] Later that year, Gerald underwent additional training at the Marine's Field Medical school at Camp Lejeune, North Carolina. In that course, he was taught "field first aid, preventative medicine, sanitation and weapons orientation."[44]

In the fall of 1969, Gerald shipped out to Vietnam. During his tour of duty, he worked as a Navy Corpsman. This role is essentially that of a military First Responder. The main job of the Corpsman was to attend to wounded marines on the battlefield. Six hundred and forty-five Navy corpsmen would die during the Vietnam conflict.[45] The motto of the corpsman was: "To hell and back for a wounded marine." They would be called to the field of battle with the command: "Corpsman up!" As Lieutenant Chesty Puller explains it,

Gerald Jackson, ca. 1969.

the Navy Corpsmen were "the Marine's doctors[—]There's none better in the business than a Navy Corpsman."[46]

Bill Coleman, of South Carolina, who was a close friend and neighbor to Gerald and Steve, says Gerald "was attached to a Marine Company. He was the only one out there to give the last rites to a Catholic Marine. He gave them morphine, stuff[ed] their 'you know what' back into their body cavities, [and] was there to administer, well, his last breath. Gerald had that experience."[47]

Being a Corpsman would turn out to be a prescient calling for Gerald Jackson as he spent so much of his life taking care of other people. Jack Mc-Connell, a bartender at Jackson Station while a student at Erskine College in from 1978 to 1982, says, "Gerald's whole background was not fighting people in Vietnam, it was trying to save people. A lot of the skills he had from that time he carried over into his bar business."[48] In the navy, he had received valuable training as a "neuro-psychiatric technician."[49] Years later, Gerald would refer to his status at Jackson Station as part "nursemaid."[50]

However, Gerald did not talk about Vietnam much.

"He probably saw a lot," says old friend and Jackson Station regular Roland Tranter, "since he didn't talk about it. Most of the ones that kind of had it rough don't talk about it, and the ones who didn't do anything make up a lot of stuff."[51] Another close friend, Anita Clinton, says that what Gerald saw and experienced in Vietnam haunted him. "You could tell in his eyes," she said. "To be there at such a time of pain and anguish, at the end of so many lives as they crossed over, and not being able to help them."[52]

Somewhere along the way, Gerald realized he was gay. David Goldman, Gerald's longtime friend,[53] suggests that there are two main options facing people who know they are gay: they run from it or choose to accept it. "From what he told me," Goldman said, "Gerald embraced it from a young age."[54]

In his prime, Jackson stood about six feet tall. He had expressive blue eyes and blond hair. In middle age, he developed a paunch but is said to have worn it well. Despite his committed relationship with Steve, Gerald would have regular liaisons with other men, some of whom were half his age.[55]

High school friend Linn Johnson says she knew that Gerald was gay early on.

"I had a gay cousin, so I knew what gay was in 1962," Johnson said. "I knew what was going on." Johnson thinks Gerald did not have any boyfriends in high school, but that he "probably was infatuated with 15 boys."[56]

Gerald's manner and appearance did not always signal his sexual identity. Many people who met Gerald for the first time did not realize he was gay. "You would never know," that Gerald was gay, says friend Bonnie Capps, a Jackson Station regular. "He looked like Uncle Bob down here."[57]

Yet Gerald Jackson never denied his sexuality, which is remarkable given the cultural norms of his geographic location. Musician Billy Wirtz says that Gerald "was totally out"[58] when he met him in 1982. He said Gerald joked with him that there wasn't a whole lot to do in Hodges other than "fuck some of the farm boys every now and then."[59] It would have been difficult being openly gay in any part of the country in the 1970s and 1980s, let alone the conservative South. Yet Gerald was quite integrated into, and in some ways at the center of, his rural Southern community. Perhaps Gerald's experience in Vietnam and his status as a veteran mitigated some of the stigma (whether self-imposed or applied by others) that his sexual orientation may have caused him.

"When he came back [from Vietnam], he was out," said Linn Johnson. "He didn't care. He was never one to push it in your face, but he was just a gay man. He'd seen war." Johnson says Gerald's attitude was, "I'm coming back and this is who I am and you like it or lump it."[60]

David Goldman says that Gerald taught him many lessons over the years. The most important one was that "being gay has nothing to do with being weak or getting walked on."[61] In a time when the dominant representations of gay men in America were very limited (the media portrayed gays either as sissies, monsters, or as objects of ridicule),[62] Gerald and Steve taught people that not only is there nothing wrong with being gay, but that gay folk can be anywhere, even in Hodges.

Brand Stille, erstwhile bartender at Jackson Station and now an administrator at Wofford College in Spartanburg, South Carolina, remarks that Gerald and Steve were "very courageous. [They were] probably the first openly gay couple I ever knew."[63] As Roland Tranter says, "It was the South, and it is really, the rural south, and South Carolina. And people, they accepted them. There was never, ever, that I know of, any problem, about them being gay, and being there, and all that stuff."[64]

John Sanders admits that some people did occasionally talk smack about Gerald's sexuality. "You know how people are," he says. "It's just like school . . . It bounced off his ear. He didn't hear it. Gerald didn't hear a negative. He was pretty much like that."[65] Acclaimed Southern author George Singleton— who grew up in Greenwood and has written stories about the area—has the following memory of attending Jackson Station one evening with his father. He writes:

> One time, when I was about 22, my father and I went up the road (his little textile supply business was a couple miles south on [Hwy] 25) to get a beer or two. This was early afternoon, maybe four or five o'clock. Steve and Gerald were there, waiting for a heifer of theirs to give birth in the pasture out back. It did. They named the baby bull George, after my father. Steve was working on the giant chalk menu board, and he said he was going to add a "PLT" for the evening's offerings, which would stand for Placenta-Lettuce-and-Tomato. My father—a gruff, slightly crazy, hard-working man—loved Gerald Jackson. He said, "I don't care that he's got a boyfriend. That's one hard-working man."[66]

"It was known, but it didn't seem to matter," suggests Joe Cabri, the famed Lander University tennis coach, about Gerald's sexual orientation.[67]

"Nobody really thought about Gerald being gay, they just thought he was a bitch," jokes Tommy Kidd, who grew up with Steve Bryant in Liberty, South Carolina, and with his good buddy Roland Tranter, frequented Jackson Station extensively.[68]

Personally, Gerald Jackson had a warm, welcoming demeanor with a "calm presence."[69] He had a keen sense of humor and a barman's ability to strike up a conversation with anyone. Gerald was "intuitive, empathetic, and sensitive to others."[70]

"He had the manner," says Joe Cabri, "of a Southern aristocrat in ordinary clothes. He just made people feel at ease. No matter what."[71]

Jeff Calder, lead singer of the Southern New Wave band the Swimming Pool Qs[72] remembers that Gerald had a "button down Ivy League" sort of fashion sense. He exhibited a "well-dressed presentation,"[73] Calder says. Jackson struck him a consummate Southern gentleman with a great "love of life."[74]

David Goldman says that Gerald Jackson treated everyone with "courtesy and respect." He dealt with people using the old outlaw biker code: "Treat me good, and I'll treat you better. Treat me bad, I'll treat you worse."[75]

Deborah Milling, who attended Lander College in the late 1970s and is now a psychiatrist in Charleston, South Carolina, remembers Gerald as being "friendly, personable, very observant," and wholly dedicated to the success of his business.[76]

Greenwood local historian Harris Bailey, who also attended Lander during what he calls the school's "Golden Age,"[77] spent dozens of evenings at Jackson Station. He remembers Gerald well. "Gerald was a card," Bailey says. "He was always telling a story . . . or lies."[78]

Gerald would often tease people in a genial kind of a way. For example, buxom women would be described as "corn fed." "She's corn fed," Gerald would chuckle, "corn fed."[79] He would pepper his conversation with sexual allusions and double entendres, dishing one moment while trying to seduce his obviously heterosexual (and uninterested) friends in another.

"It was just sort of like a kidding, good natured, ribbing kind of thing,"[80] says Jack McConnell, who observed such banter in the bar frequently. And on occasion, Gerald's customers would give it right back to him. McConnell remembers one funny story when he was tending bar one day: Another Erskine student, Gary (who, like McConnell was also straight), was one of a number of people drinking at the bar. McConnell says Gerald had been hitting on Gary for years, since he had been a freshman. He said, "Gerald walked by . . . And [Gary] was from New Jersey and maybe more forward than the Southern kids were. And when he walked by, [Gary] pinched Gerald on the ass, in a quick way and then turned so Gerald couldn't see who pinched him on the ass. So, Gerald turns around and looks, and I could see this expression like, 'Who the hell was that who did that? Then it dawned on him that it was Gary who did that. It was maybe one of the first times I saw Gerald blush. Gerald just kind of blushed, and smiled and turned away, because he knew that the guy was kind of messing with him and wasn't serious about it."[81]

Jeff Calder of the Swimming Pool Qs has a story about Gerald Jackson's sense of irony. He says, "We actually have a photo of loading our van. J.E. [Garnett] our bass player, who is kind of a tall, handsome guy. He's got [a] classic, sort of, punk looking character. Somewhat rockabilly punk hairstyle and so forth. He was a handsome guy. He was bent over, loading a piece of gear into the back of the truck. And Gerald said, 'J.E., you don't want to do that around here. The gates to hell are in Hodges, SC.'[82] [*Laughing*]. We roared with laughter when Gerald said that."

Gerald would impishly flirt with his dear friend (and accountant) Anita Clinton. "He would always joke and tell me if he were straight he would 'chase me' or if Steve ever left him, or he had met me first." Clinton says, "It was a big joke between all of us for decades."[83]

Brand Stille remembers showing up at work one Friday night and complimenting Gerald on the tie he was wearing. Gerald thanked Stille for the compliment, then took off the tie and gave it to him. Stille was puzzled. He said, "Gerald, I said I liked your tie, I didn't say I wanted your tie." However, Gerald would not take the tie back. He said, "My father told me that if a man ever compliments another man's tie, he should take it off and give it to him."[84]

Bonnie Capps says Gerald Jackson was "so generous hearted. He would do anything for you. Everybody loved him. He was so giving, charitable, and accepting."[85] She says Gerald and Steve "cared you were there." They would "remember your name, remember your drink."[86] If people were too drunk to drive, Gerald would give them a ride home. If someone really needed to stay the night, they might sleep on the porch, or even under the deck.[87] Gerald and Steve would just lock the club up and leave them be.[88] Then they would go on home to crash out, often sleeping until two or three in the afternoon.[89]

Karen Miller Johnson, a student at Lander in the 1980s and now owner of Greenwood Nursery, also has poignant memories of Gerald Jackson. She remembers one evening driving with a friend back from Greenville. The car overheated in Ware Shoals. It was nighttime. Unable to reach anyone else to help her, Johnson called Jackson Station. Gerald told her to stay where she was. He arrived ten minutes later with three cold beers and two gallons of water. They each had beer while the engine was cooling. Gerald filled up the radiator. He told Karen to drive home carefully and get the car looked at as soon as possible.[90] Karen and her friend made it home safely.

Ralph Campbell, of Shoals Junction, South Carolina, similarly remembers Gerald's generosity. Campbell spent many an evening at Jackson Station in the mid-1980s when he was home from the Citadel. On one occasion, he was broke and hungry yet still hanging out at the bar. He wanted a hot dog but did not have the cash on him. He explained his plight to Gerald.

"Go ahead and get yourself your hotdog," Gerald told Ralph. "You can pay me tomorrow."[91]

"Gerald was born to stand behind that bar," declares David Goldman.[92] He says Gerald was a "really unique individual" who he describes as "part proud Southern redneck, part hippie, and part queen."

To refer to Gerald as a hippie is to highlight his peaceful manner in dealing with the world, which was often facilitated by nature. On his way back from Vietnam, Gerald had smuggled a few marijuana seeds out of the country in the bottom of a tube of toothpaste. When he got back to Hodges, he planted them in his mother's flower garden, telling her they were tomato plants.[93]

As to other substances, while he would enjoy beer from time to time, Gerald was not a heavy drinker. "Gerald was not drunk every night the way we[—]his loyal customers[—]were, but he was certainly not a teetotaler,"[94] says David Goldman.

Famed Georgia blues guitarist Tinsley Ellis recalls that "Gerald had a real good connection with moonshine. He wasn't a bootlegger, but his clientele gave him some moonshine and he ended up giving me a bottle. It was the first time I ever had moonshine. It was made out of blueberries yet it was crystal clear." Ellis says he took the jar of moonshine on tour with him. "We were on tour at the time with Stevie Ray Vaughan and took it and offered some to him, but he didn't want any," Ellis says, chuckling. "He didn't want it."[95]

It seems that the inertial power of being a Southern redneck (in addition to having military service) allowed Gerald to get by, most of the time, just being Gerald. People generally left him alone. He was unafraid. Gerald was a white man with property who had deep roots in the area. He was also a churchgoer,[96] a mason, and a member of the local Bascomb Lodge.[97]

"Gerald was a well-respected person around town," recalls friend Reggie Massey, who had known Gerald since they had gone to Northside Middle School together. "Everybody knew the other side, that he was different from the rest of them, from most of them. [But he was] just the kind of guy that would laugh right along with you, when you're around him."[98]

Massey said he asked Gerald one day about what being a mason meant to him. He says Gerald would talk "a little bit about it because I would ask, but he wouldn't give up its secrets." One day Massey said Gerald took him to the Masonic Lodge in Cokesbury. He started asking Gerald questions like, "Why this? What does this mean? Trying to get some kind of handle on why you're here. I wouldn't put you in a Masonic Lodge, you know, just right off the street." Yet Gerald would remain silent.[99]

Reggie says that when Gerald was not at the club, he was working on various projects. Occasionally, he and his friends would head to Athens, Georgia, or Columbia, South Carolina, to see music shows.[100] Gerald fished at local ponds around Hodges,[101] or just liked to hang out with Steve and their two dogs, Max and Bogart. In Jackson Station pamphlets, these creatures would be described as "Gerald's friendly, but highly protective dogs (one-half Doberman, one-half German Shepherd). They bite, so don't tease them."[102]

Musician David Truly, a blues guitarist and the leader of the Truly Dangerous Swamp Band[103] says, "dogs were always welcome" at Jackson Station. Truly would bring Swamper the Wonder Dog—a white, "short-haired mongrel pup with one blue eye and one brown,"—with him whenever his band played at the depot.[104]

In addition to his other identities, Gerald Jackson was a proud product of the South. Gerald was "incredibly proud of his Southern heritage," says David Goldman. He "delighted in being a Southerner." Goldman says Gerald was "from one of the last generations of people whose first national love was for the South. First you were a Southerner, and then you became an American."[105] Politically, Goldman says Gerald was "libertarian," in that he "thought people should not be interfered with, that they should be able to do what they want to do."[106] Jackson Station patron Benjamin Hawthorne places Gerald's politics as "slightly left of center." He says he was "not liberal, but not very conservative either."[107]

A red, white, and blue, "FUCK COMMUNISM" banner written in "beautiful, patriotic letters,"[108] and which for years adorned the top of the bar at Jackson Station, would have appealed to democratic socialists as much as right-wing Republicans. "Gerald was not a liberal, in the conventional sense," explains David Goldman. "He was on the left side of issues like the legalization of marijuana and gay rights, and he definitely believed in a fair shake for everyone, regardless of race. But on some issues, he leaned conservative." For example, Gerald was not always on the same page as his environmentalist friends. Goldman remembers talks about "some proposed dam project that was opposed by environmentalists because of its potential impact on an endangered fish called the Snail darter [*Percina tanasi*]." Goldman said that "[w]hile most of us reflexively lined up against the project, Gerald argued for it, saying basically, 'Who's ever heard of this fish, and who cares?' I remember a late-night party in Abbeville at which our host, a female lawyer, was positively shrieking at Gerald because he didn't get it about the Snail darter."[109]

Gerald was extremely strict when it came to one's work ethic. He insisted on people earning their daily bread. According to Goldman, Gerald "believed emphatically that everyone should work." "He had no sympathy for those who weren't pulling their own weight." One evening at the club, when Goldman was temporarily out of work and looking for a job, Gerald took him to task. "'What are you doing up here at 3:00 in the morning?!" Jackson scolded him. "When the hell did you think you were going to get that job?'" Goldman said, "He would crack you on the head if you needed it." He also says Gerald could not cope with people who were "overly needy." "You couldn't be a mess," around Gerald, Goldman said. "He wouldn't stand for it."[110]

THREE

STEVEN BRYANT AND ELIZABETH JACKSON

Every time I think of you
I feel shot right through with
a bolt of blue.
        —New Order[1]

Steven Bryant—Gerald's "special friend and devoted companion"[2]—was shorter, thinner, and seven years younger, than Gerald Jackson. The two men were in a committed relationship together for over thirty years. In his description of the "The Help" on promotional flyers for Jackson Station, Gerald lists Steve as "barkeeper, confessor, janitor, assistant nursemaid."

"Steve was an incredible guy," remembers musician Glenn Phillips.[3]

"I am not really sure," how Gerald and Steve first met, admits Hazel Bryant, Steve's mother, in an interview at the family home in Liberty, South Carolina. "I think [Steve] met Ellen[4] first."

"They made a good team," Hazel says of Gerald and Steve. "Because both of them were real . . . come up with some real comments. They made a pretty good comic strip. They were both a lot of fun."[5]

Steve Bryant was born and raised in Liberty, South Carolina. He graduated from Liberty High School in 1970.[6] His father was Austin Earl Bryant (1930–2012). He had two younger sisters.

"Steve was a little guy," notes Hazel Bryant. "He wasn't big like Gerald."

Friend Tommy Kidd, who also grew up in Liberty, says Steve was a "country boy, he lived on the outskirts of Liberty, in Flat Rock. Went to Flat Rock Baptist Church." He says Steve was a "real smart kid" and "really quiet." Kidd remembers that Steve "was gay, but he was absolutely not publicly gay. He was just feminine. He definitely was not out of the closet in high school."[7]

Steven Bryant, ca. 1986.

Steve Bryant's brother-in-law, Terry Pierce, also says that Steve kept his sexual orientation under tight wraps: "I never saw Steve act stereotypically gay except when he was around Gerald."[8]

Despite his diminutive stature, Steve was surprisingly not picked on or bullied at Liberty High School. Kidd remembers that "the guys that lived in that same area were some of the biggest rednecks, [and were among the] worst people in the county." Yet, Kidd says, "They just looked after him. They would mess with everybody but not Steve because he grew up right down the street from them. They knew him, so they kind of took care of him."[9]

Steve's father, Austin, worked in a textile mill in Catateechee, South Carolina. He would later help out at his brother-in-law's television repair shop. Steve would work at the shop on Saturdays.[10] After high school, Steve moved briefly moved to Atlanta to study computing at a private technical college. He had carefully saved up for the school's tuition, which he paid in advance. Steve was crestfallen when the computer school only "lasted about four weeks," before unexpectedly shutting down.

"He went to school on Monday morning and the sign on the door said, gone, closed," says Steve's mother. Steve "lost every dime, never got a penny back. Nothing. They took the money and left." Hazel Bryant says the experience "threw [Steve] for a loop and he ended up in Marshall Pickens[11] for a while. And that's where he started smoking." After a few weeks at Marshall Pickens, Steve enrolled at Greenville Technical College, where he took courses in mental health.

"He said that helped him a lot in working at the depot," Bryant says, chuckling. "Because he had to learn a lot of psychology in that."[12]

Steve was very personable and loved music. Like Gerald, Steve could pass at being straight; he would just give more hints away. But most of the time, as with Gerald, people just did not think too much about his Steve's sexual orientation. It was a nonissue.

"Steve was just working," remembers Tommy Kidd. "He was working the bar and running the place."[13]

Old friend Bonnie Capps remembers Steve as "very affectionate, very compassionate," but also says he had a serious side. "You didn't want to make Steve mad," she says.

Steve Bryant's brother-in-law, Terry Pierce, suggests that Jackson Station, as a business, "was not a profitable enterprise and that Gerald ran it on a shoestring. I know Steve wasn't paid a salary."[14] Pierce says that "in a traditional [heterosexual] relationship, [Steve] would have been the wife that supported her husband's dream."[15]

David Goldman describes the nature of Gerald and Steve's relationship in the following way. He says: "Gerald was definitely the more butch of the two, but he could camp it up when he wanted to. Steve had a femme vibe, but he could hold his own with a toolbox or a fishing pole. Gerald always referred to Steve as 'my buddy' because he thought 'my lover' sounded 'too sissy.'" Goldman says that although Steve was native to South Carolina, "he did not have a Southern accent like Gerald. He had a sort of dry, 'TV' accent that didn't suggest he was from anywhere in particular. He often related stories with one eyebrow up, and gestured with his menthol 100 to make a point."[16]

"Steve was a gentle soul," says the great blues guitarist Bob Margolin, "but always rose to the occasion if someone got a little too wild in the bar."[17]

Brand Stille was fond of Steve but remembers him as being slightly more "prickly" than Gerald. He says Steve was "more uptight and into the business side of things."[18]

Gerald and Steve had "wonderfully playful" personalities, recalls Anita Clinton.[19] She says the three of them were great friends and "always told each other we loved each other and hugged a LOT. We were all huggers."

Clinton says, "We called each other 'Girlfriend' all the time. For example, *'Girlfriend, you don't need to wear that color,'* or, *'Girlfriend, I think you need to check yourself,'* or, *'Girlfriend, you really need to get behind that bar and make me a sandwich.'* If one of us did not agree with something, it was *'Girlfriend, PLEASEEEEEEEEE . . .'*"[20]

Elizabeth Jackson, Gerald's mother, was the prima donna of Jackson Station Depot. Mrs. Jackson is listed as the "White-haired lady" on Jackson Station pamphlets and concert calendars. David Goldman says, "Gerald always referred to [Elizabeth Jackson] as 'Mother,' not 'Mama' or 'Mom.' Or perhaps 'Miss Lib' if he was pointing out some of her foolishness."[21]

After becoming a widow in her late thirties, Elizabeth Jackson raised Ellen and Gerald as a single mother. She was fifty-five years old when Jackson Station first opened for business. For years, she would work the door of the club collecting the cover charge (which ranged, throughout the years, from $3 to $10) on band nights. No one could enter the club without going past her station.

Elizabeth Jackson had a major financial stake in Jackson Station. "As the night went on, it became more expensive to get into the club," says Catherine Brickley, piano player in the Sensible Pumps. Benjamin Hawthorne, a friend of Gerald and Steve and part-time DJ at the club, says Mrs. Jackson "was the source of the money."[22]

"All this is mine," Elizabeth Jackson declared to David Goldman as he waltzed through the front door of the club one evening.

"Gerald got the bar money," Hodges native John Sanders explains, "but when they had a band, [Elizabeth Jackson] paid the band and took all the proceeds. She made money from the bands."[23]

At times, the money was difficult to manage. Jackson Station regular Lee Rush recalls one tragic story: "I do remember once when we were there, Gerald was upset because he burned a stack of cash. I don't know how much. He had hidden the cash in the back of a toaster oven and forgotten about it. He later went to toast himself a sandwich and burned the cash. One of the Lander professors we were friends with told Gerald that the government would replace the cash if it wasn't too badly burned. Gerald didn't want to talk about it at the time, and I don't know if he ever got the money replaced or not."[24]

"She came down and took care of all that," says Hazel Bryant, definitively, referring to the cash money made at the door of Jackson Station. "And she took it. She did not divide. She took it all."[25]

Mrs. Jackson's presence at the club was one of the more peculiar characteristics of Jackson Station. Patrons would find themselves at Jackson Station —as if they just awoke from a dream—stumbling out of an automobile, to find themselves in a godforsaken hinterland. They would get in a queue, trying to gain admittance to the nether reaches of a massive ancient train depot. They would be wanting to see some music, get tight, looking for some action.

And the first person they would encounter would be a fierce old white woman intent on assessing their appearance and demeanor. It was impossible not to engage with her. Mrs. Jackson demanded deference and recognition.

"Who has their mother running their door at the club, from eleven o'clock to four in the morning?" laughs Sensible Pumps musician Catherine Brickley.[26]

"Nobody messed with her," recalls Bonnie Capps. "She was feisty and loud." She says Mrs. Jackson would "tell you to get the hell off the property" if she did not like the look of you. Ben Hawthorne remembers Mrs. Jackson being "mean as a snake, really critical." He says, "She would ride Gerald all the time."

Steve's mother, Hazel, agrees that Elizabeth Jackson was "very mean" to both Gerald and to Steve. "She hated both of them. She did," Bryant said. Steve in particular "couldn't do nothing right. Nothing." She said Gerald would often say to her, "Boy, I wish my mama was like you [*laughing*]. I heard that quite a few times."[27]

At the club, Mrs. Jackson would exert absolute control over the door. "She decided, pretty much, who got in and who didn't," says Roland Tranter. "And there were people who she turned away. If she thought you might get in here and cause trouble, she sent you home, wouldn't let you in."[28]

"She was very tough at the door," says Jack McConnell.[29]

"She didn't take any crap from anybody," says Catherine Brickley. "I was really kind of afraid of her, but she was always very nice."[30]

"Not many people could deal with her," says John Sanders.[31] "She tried to guide Gerald by the nose. She hated Steve. She hated Steve because they were so tight. She didn't want Gerald to have any close friends. She wanted Gerald all to herself. She wanted to tell him everything to do, and what to do, and how to do it. I hate to say it, but it's true."[32]

Sanders claims Mrs. Jackson would not allow Steve to stay with Gerald in the family home (directly across the street from Jackson Station) while they were fixing up the depot. He says Gerald bought a small camper and put it behind the house for Steve to live in. Steve "had to sleep out there," Sanders says disgustingly. "They treated him like a yard dog."[33]

Mrs. Elizabeth would not hesitate to make her opinions known to the musicians who played Jackson Station. The Reverend Billy Wirtz remembers that Mrs. Jackson once took him to task over the risqué songs he had performed during a previous appearance at the club. Wirtz says she gave him a "lecture one time as I was walking in the place. 'Don't come in hear singing that dirty music!'" Wirtz says Mrs. Jackson told him. "Oh Mama, he's fine," Gerald shot back at his mother.

Despite Mrs. Elizabeth's difficult nature, Gerald would often joke about his mother.

"Gerald, just how old is your mama?" someone would ask him. "Hell, she ain't old enough," he would retort, sardonically.[34] He would feign romantical interest in his clearly straight and platonic friend Anita Clinton to boost Mrs. Jackson's hopes for a heterosexual union. Clinton laughs, saying the theatrics "used to make her day. She used to try to fix us up back then." Even after decades had passed and knowing full well that there was no way anything would ever happen between Anita and her son, Mrs. Jackson "still would wink and tell me that her little Gerald would make some pretty babies."[35]

Gerald celebrated Elizabeth's iconic status at the club and recognized her role in Jackson Station's success. "This place wouldn't have been possible if it hadn't been for the support of my mother,"[36] he told the *Greenville News* in 1983.

David Truly, who ran his own music club—the Old Post Office Emporium—on Hilton Head Island in the 1980s, remembers "the power of his mom." He says one of the first things Gerald would do when musicians would arrive at the club would be to introduce them to Mrs. Jackson. "You need to meet my mother," Gerald would say. "You need to meet my mom, here she is."

"That didn't happen at other nightclubs, that's for damn sure," Truly comments. "That's the only club I've ever known where the first priority is to meet the mom."[37] Truly believes that Elizabeth Jackson's stature at Jackson Station contributed to the club's success. He says, "There was a certain respect for mothers in the South. Even though Gerald's behavior was certainly not particularly accepted, there was a respect for the mom and her boy." Truly says, "When [Mrs. Jackson] came around, man, everybody was saying 'Hi.' There was a certain amount of respect among everybody, from Congressmen to fucking bikers to everybody, when mom came around."[38]

Famed blues guitarist Bob Margolin[39] has positive memories of Elizabeth Jackson. He said he "always spent time talking" with Gerald's mother when he was at Jackson Station. Margolin said it was rare to meet "many Southern women of her generation." In his view, Elizabeth was "socially graceful, insightful, and fascinating."[40]

"I loved Miss Jackson," relates Cora Garmany, widow of the famed rhythm and blues singer Nappy Brown (1929–2008), whose career was resurrected in large part because of his shows at Jackson Station.[41] "I really did.

We got along real good." Garmany contradicts the people who found Mrs. Jackson disagreeable. "She was just bossified," Garmany suggests. "As long as everything went her way, you were all right with her," she says. Yet Garmany admits Mrs. Jackson "could go to fussin' at Gerald."[42]

Phyllis Free (a.k.a. the Swamp Mama), drummer with the Truly Dangerous Swamp Band, also remembers Mrs. Jackson warmly. One evening in the early 1980s, the Swamp Band had just finished an energetic second set of music at Jackson Station. Free headed to the bar to get a refreshment, wearing her normal drumming attire of a T-shirt and nylon running shorts. She waited at the bar to get a drink.

Then, suddenly, Free found that her shorts had been yanked down below her bottom. She had been "depantsed"! Free quickly pulled up her shorts, whirled around, and found a "Southern good old boy" grinning at her. Never one to be intimidated, Free shook a matronly finger in the face of the cretin and told him that he should know better than to pull such a stunt. The offender slinked away.

Later that night, Free was approached by Mrs. Jackson. She had witnessed the incident from across the room. She apologized for the man's boorish behavior. She asked if Phyllis was all right and told her she was "worried you wouldn't want to come back."[43] Graciously dismissing the incident with good humor, Free thanked Mrs. Jackson for her concern and said she was fine.

The triad of Gerald, Steve, and Gerald's mother formed a powerful social ensemble at Jackson Station that would befit a Southern Gothic novel. There were many other people of course, who played a more-or-less important role over the years—friends and acquaintances who worked as bartenders, cooks, DJs, security people, and so on. All of them, in their own way, would contribute to the identity of Jackson Station. But without Gerald, Steve, and Mrs. Elizabeth, there would have never been a club in the first place.

: FOUR :

THE EARLY YEARS

It ain't me, it ain't me
I ain't no senator's son, son
      —Creedence Clearwater Revival[1]

After Gerald completed his service in Vietnam, he returned to Hodges and moved in with his mother in the family home on Moorefield Street. His official discharge date from the Navy was October 30, 1975.[2] Gerald intended to carry on the mercantile business that had been established by his grandfather and carried on by his father and mother. However, he "came back with no store to carry on the family tradition."[3]

While Gerald had been away, the old Jackson General Store, which had been located across the street from the Jackson household, had been lost in a fire.[4] Gerald claimed that a train had been pulling into Hodges from the South and had applied the brakes too quickly. This caused a "brake fire" with sparks spraying from the train wheels. The sparks "set the woods on fire and burned the store to the ground."[5] John Sanders says that "[once] that got cleaned up, the lot was just bare, and that's when Gerald got the idea to put the Depot there. He had the location."[6]

Yet he also had to pay the bills. Gerald's first job after Vietnam was at Whitten Village, a state facility for people with special needs in Clinton, South Carolina, about thirty miles east of Hodges. Gerald worked with "developmentally disabled children,"[7] making "a positive difference in those young lives daily."[8] He enjoyed the work, but his main dream was opening a blues bar in his hometown.

In the American South, affection for music runs deep. One of the most emblematic forms of Southern culture is the blues. Blues music emerged out of the social conditions and relations of the U.S. Deep South in the late nineteenth and early twentieth centuries. As noted by famed blues musician

Bonnie Raitt, "And you have to remember; all the great blues-rock that we love came about as a direct result of what was created in the Mississippi Delta."[9] From the Delta, the blues branched out like the massive Tree of Life in New Orleans—north to Chicago, west to Texas, east to Georgia and the Carolina Piedmont, south down to Florida. And of course, even earlier, the origins of blues music can be found in the drums of West Africa.

As the great American poet Langston Hughes argued in 1932, blues music must be understood in relation to African American spirituals:

> The blues, unlike the spirituals, have a strict poetic pattern: one long line, repeated, and a third line to rhyme with the first two. Sometimes the second line in repetition is slightly changed and sometimes, but very seldom, it is omitted. Unlike the spirituals, the blues are not group songs. When sung under natural circumstances, they are usu-ally sung by one man or woman alone. Whereas the spirituals are often songs about escaping from trouble, going to heaven and living happily ever after, the blues are songs about being in the midst of trouble, friendless, hungry, disappointed in love, right here on the earth. The mood of the blues is almost always despondency, but when they are sung people laugh.[10]

Writer and poet Richard Wright also considered the relationship between spirituals and the blues, emphasizing the historical mode of production that created each musical form. Wright claimed that spirituals "came from the slaves who were closest to the Big Houses of the plantations where they caught vestiges of Christianity whiffed to them by Southern Whites' crude forms of Baptist or Methodist religions." Blues music, on the other hand, developed out of field slave culture. Wright wrote, "Field slaves were almost completely beyond the pale. And it was from them and their descendants that the devil songs called the blues came."[11] Contrary to the angelic spirituals, blues songs related to the profane. They told stories of the "migrant, the rambler, the steel driver, the ditch digger, the roustabout, the pimp, the prostitute, [and] the urban, or rural illiterate outsider."[12]

In a phone interview, blues piano player Reverend Billy Wirtz suggests, "Blues is the Black populist existential fuel of life. Gospel is what should be. Blues is what is. Gospel is the way things should be in a perfect world. Gospel says no matter how fucked up life gets, no matter how bad, with a little bit of prayer, a little bit of faith, it will get better. Blues says, don't count on it."[13]

At one time (and perhaps for some this is still true today), listening to blues music might have been considered kind of opiate for the masses, a way of thinking about misfortune that would help people triumph over tragedy. Indeed, Georgia blues guitarist Robert Lee "Chick" Willis (1934–2013) once described blues music as a "soothing device." As he put it:

> It was a soul searching device. Blues was something that . . . your mother could die; you could use the blues to lighten the burden on you. Your wife or your husband could leave you—and you could use the blues to light the load on your heart. Know what I'm saying? You could be mad, pissed off at somebody. You could use the blues to keep you from going out and killing up somebody.[14]

Blues songs also allowed one to articulate sentiments critical of the status quo through a different, more oblique, media. Willis notes:

> And if you were a slave back in the day and your master was treating you bad, you couldn't walk up to the master and say, "You gotta leave me alone," you know, but you could sing about it. And the other slaves could relate to it and say, "Man sure is treating Chick bad over there. You heard what he just sang?" But the Master is saying, as he is clapping and clapping, "Hey, that's a nice song. Sing that again. Sing that song again."[15]

Blues music opened work, religion, politics, intimate relationships, and home life for analysis, celebration, and critique. The blues offered insight into the way things are, reflection on past mistakes, and inspiration for the future.

Of course, someone like John Fahey might suggest that the real impetus behind an embrace of the blues is simply the search for emotional connection. Fahey argues that this was the ultimate reason behind the Blues Revival in places such as Berkley, California, in the early 1960s. Fahey's comments about what he calls "Berkeley people," could apply to other parts of the white, bourgeois, music-consuming public (then and today). As Fahey writes in *How Bluegrass Destroyed My Life*: "They know that emotions exist because they have read about these curious oddities. But since they cannot locate them in themselves, they assume that they exist elsewhere. And where better than in the bosoms of country blues singers, who they have noted exhibit a wide range of affect, mostly incomprehensible to themselves."[16] The question about white appropriation of Black cultural forms, such as the blues, is of course an important one, but one that cannot be explored here. Relative to matters at hand, the crux of the debate hinges on whether the blues (like, e.g., reason) is a universal aspect of the human condition that should be accessible to anyone or if it is a distinctly African American form that whites should leave well enough alone.

With the advent of the electric guitar, blues songs' lyrics became secondary to the sound. Making the blues electric not only amplified the sound, and thereby made the blues a sonic force to be reckoned with; it also afforded listeners an opportunity to more completely "rock out" when listening to music, to get immersed in the sound. We have the great blues musicians of the 1950s like Muddy Waters[17] and Lil' Walter to thank for this. As Rolling Stones guitarist Keith Richards, (who, it is worth pointing out, would have been not much of a musician were it not for the blues), comments: "Anyone who can make a sound like that is alright with me. The power of the blues was a mind blower."[18]

Blues guitarists as diverse as Eric Clapton, Stevie Ray Vaughan, Bob Margolin, Tinsley Ellis, and Jack White are all descendants of this electric blues tradition. Electric blues takes the elemental structures of old blues songs (for example, I-IV-V chord progressions), and couples them with wild guitar riffs, as well as distortions, and the sounds of other amplified instruments. The resultant concoction is a very primal, loud, and in many cases, quite long, jam session. It is this kind of music—perfected by artists like Jimi Hendrix, Led Zeppelin, and the Allman Brothers—and still played today by acts such as Widespread Panic, which captivated so many patrons at Jackson Station, giving them the energy to stay awake until sunrise.

Bluesman Taj Mahal expresses well the power of the blues as a force of liberation. He discusses concerts for Black sharecroppers at Dockery Plantation in Mississippi in the early 20th century. "People worked there all week long, no radios, no music, no entertainment," Mahal says. "But on the weekends, the musicians came out. It served as a bond for people who were in bondage. And it gave you a way out. You played that music, you could be outside of yourself, you know. You could take everybody else out . . . outside of their selves."[19]

Blues musicians are akin to shamans holding forth over a sacred gathering. They are carriers of the trickster tradition. They have power and spells that the masses do not understand. Through their wizardry, they make noises with their bodies and machines that are not normally found in nature. Relatively few individuals know how to make these sounds. Through such efforts, blues musicians are capable of generating profoundly powerful emotions in people, both individually and collectively. Music venues like Jackson Station, where such music was found, can be seen as hallowed ground, as a kind of *axis mundi*.[20] Jackson Station was an enchanted space where spirits were unleashed unto the world.

As a blues club, over the years Jackson Station developed a style of its own that, as Tinsley Ellis says, is "often imitated; never duplicated." Ellis argues that contemporary corporate music venues like House of Blues are but a pale simulation of Jackson Station. He says Jackson Station is "what the House of Blues family wants to be like. In their restaurant, you go in their restaurant, and it looks like a Southern roadhouse. They're copying what Jackson Station was."[21] As Greenwood music promoter Nicholas Hyduke notes, Jackson Station "mirrored the blues and blues culture,"[22] which gave it credibility. While the blues are not as central to the culture of the South Carolina Piedmont relative to other places in the South, the history of blues music is not complete without considering contributions from the Palmetto State.[23]

For example, Pink Anderson (1900–1974)—for whom the rock 'n' roll band Pink Floyd was named—was from Laurens, South Carolina, thirty miles northeast of Jackson Station. Anderson was known for a style of music known as the "Piedmont Blues." Harmonica player Freddie Vanderford describes Piedmont Blues as "more acoustic type stuff. It's more up tempo, humorous, that sort of thing."[24] Vanderford says that Pink was just one of the tremendous blues talents to emerge from the area. He also mentions Peg Leg Sam, Baby Tate, Cootie Stark, as well as Henry "Rufe" Johnson (a.k.a. Union County Flash). Many of these artists were recorded on Trix Records, a company founded by ethnomusicologist Peter B. Lowry. Other famous South Carolina musical artists include Dizzy Gillespie (who was from Cheraw, near the North Carolina state line), and James Brown (born one hundred miles southeast of Hodges, in Barnwell, South Carolina).

Gerald's military service in Vietnam had exposed him to many different cultures and worldviews[25] that he wanted to share with the people of Hodges. Opening a nightclub on his family property would allow him to do just that. Gerald "recalled some of the wild and crazy clubs he'd seen in places like Okinawa, Singapore and Bangkok—sites that amazed a country boy from Hodges, SC—and set out to build Jackson Station, down home honkytonk roadhouse deluxe."[26] As Steve Bryant said in a 1992 interview, "At the time, he was working for the Whitten Company, but this station was his all-consuming dream." Gerald had "seen these great clubs" overseas. "You have to realize it's an awesome experience for a country boy from Hodges. Well, it occurred to him that these places were nothing more than oriental versions of down-home honky-tonks."[27]

Gerald already had three acres of property at his disposal. The next step would be constructing a venue. This problem was solved in early 1975 when Gerald had a fortuitous encounter with the Southern railway company. One day Gerald saw some railway men milling around the old Southern Railroad Depot.[28] This was the original Hodges Greenville & Columbia Depot that had been built in 1870, right in the center of town. It was situated perpendicular to Godfrey's Grocery Store[29] and about seventy-five yards from the brick-built Piedmont & Northern Railroad Depot (built in 1920) across the way. For years, Gerald had pondered the fate of the wooden Southern Depot, which had been out of commission as a freight train depot since 1965 and had not seen any passenger service since 1957.[30] He said he "been looking at this this old depot since I was a little a boy and wanted it."[31] For ten years, it had just been "sitting back up the road, abandoned and run down." Jackson "wondered what [the railroad] had in mind for the old building."[32] Gerald asked the men.

"They told me they were going to burn it down or tear it down, because they wanted it off the tax books," Jackson said.[33] The railroad company originally wanted $500 for the depot. However, the men told Gerald that he could have it for "a dollar if you really want it," but only if it was moved within six months.[34] Gerald said, "They were just going to tear it down if didn't buy it and move it, and I'd always wanted to own a nightclub and saw and opportunity, so I took them up on it."[35]

The depot, built in 1870, was "constructed with 2 inch pegs" and "built on 3' x 11' heart of pine timbers."[36] The structure was notable for being an "all-weather depot," which provided an escape from the elements. In many small towns, railroad depots were "no more than open sheds."[37] It should be noted that there is disagreement about the age of the depot. Evidence uncovered during research for this book suggests 1870 as the best guess, which would place it in the Reconstruction Era.[38] Gerald proudly proclaimed antebellum provenance for his depot. On Jackson Station flyers, membership cards, and in other literature Gerald claimed that: "The G&C [Greenville & Columbia] Railroad built this building in 1852." Eighteen fifty-two would have been a good initial estimate, since this is indeed the year when the railroad first went through Hodges. However, as Hershey and Graves[39] note, it would have been unlikely that an investment in a building the scale of Jackson Station would have happened immediately after tracks were laid.

Hodges Southern Railway Depot, ca. 1970.

Gerald's dating of the depot to 1852 was twenty-eight years before that of local railway expert James H. Wade (1993, 32), who took a picture of the Hodges Southern Railway Depot in its original location in 1970.

Wade claimed the depot had been built in 1880. However, Wade did not explain how he arrived at this date.

In June 1965, the *Greenville News*[40] reported that the Hodges train depot was shutting down after almost a century. Reporter Mike Ellis interviewed Southern Railway Freight Agent Harold Salley, who had been working at the Hodges Depot since 1957. Salley told Ellis that the depot had been built ninety-five years earlier. While it is true that there are mentions of "Hodges Depot" in the historical record prior to 1870—some of which were announced or exaggerated by Gerald Jackson himself—the term was used to refer to the broader community or town of Hodges and not the station building per se.

Train service first came to the area (which was then part of Abbeville County) in 1852 with the Greenville & Columbia Railroad.[41] The railroad linked the South Carolina upstate to the state capital, and from there to the rest of the country.[42] The small train stop in what is now Hodges, initially served the neighboring Cokesbury community two miles to the east. Gerald was correct to say that the name of Hodges was "originally Cokesbury Depot,[43] and was later changed to honor George Washington Hodges."[44]

As the settlement of Hodges started to grow, it attracted problems associated with larger towns and cities. On July 19, 1866, there was a murder in Hodges. Amaziah Peyton, "a free negro formerly residing in this place and generally esteemed by the citizens," was brutally murdered at Hodges Depot. According to the *Intelligencer* (Anderson, South Carolina), Peyton "got out of the train and went to the dinner house, where he was met by one Reuben L. Golding, a notorious and desperate character, demanding to know his business. The negro responded that he wanted to get something to eat, when Golding said to him he could not get it, and asked him the time of day; the negro pulled out his watch, which Golding attempted to jerk from him, and did succeed in getting a piece of the chain. Both then stepped back a few paces, when Golding drew a pistol and deliberately shot the negro, the ball entering just above the left groin. The reckless wretch then walked leisurely away, while spectators gave the wounded man assistance." The newspaper reported that "[t]here was no provocation on the part of the deceased," and argued that Golding, "this vile offender against the laws of God and man," should face "punishment for his dastardly, cowardly act."[45]

There also have been at least two assassinations in Hodges. On March 31, 1866, the *Keowee Courier* in Pickens, South Carolina, reported that "[a] Federal soldier was shot at Hodge's Depot, Abbeville District, on the 23rd instant, by a stranger, without provocation. The assassin escaped."[46] Two years later, on October 16, 1868, Benjamin Franklin Randolph, one of the state's leading African American politicians, was also assassinated in Hodges.[47] Originally from Kentucky, Randolph moved to Ohio when he was young and went on to attend Oberlin College.[48] Randolph, who was a Methodist minister and a member of the Freedman's Bureau, "arrived in Hilton Head in 1864 as chaplain of the Twenty-sixth United States Colored Troops."[49] He would later serve as assistant superintendent of schools for the Freedman's Bureau in South Carolina. In January 1868, Randolph had participated in the South Carolina State Constitutional Convention, a pivotal event of the Reconstruction Era. Randolph served in the South Carolina Senate, representing Orangeburg, and was Chairman of the South Carolina Republican State Committee. He was canvassing for the Republican Party in Abbeville County when he was shot to death at Hodges Depot.[50] The *Edgefield Advertiser* reported on October 28, 1868, that Benjamin F. Randolph, "mulatto Senator from Orangeburg, and author of certain incendiary harangues in the up-country,"[51] was killed by members of the Ku Klux Klan (KKK).[52] According to the *Lancaster (Penn.) Intelligencer*, Randolph "was standing on the platform of a first-class passenger car when he was approached by three

White men, supposed to be strangers in the neighborhood, as they were never recognized, each one of whom fired a ball into him."[53] While some witnesses believed Randolph had been murdered because he was "riding in a first-class car," others said it was Randolph's "incendiary" speeches that advocated "the destruction and property of all the White men in the state,"[54] which were responsible for his demise.

In 1869, the *Abbeville Press and Banner* published vivid testimony by one of the assassins, W. K. Tolbert, about the murder and its aftermath. Tolbert explained why the KKK had targeted Randolph: "The object of the Klan was the regulate the Republican party; break it up if they could, add strength to the Democratic Party. To do so they were to kill out the leaders of the Republican Party, and drive them out of State . . . It was understood that Randolph was the man that organized the Union Leagues in South Carolina, and that was one of the reasons why he was killed."[55] Prior to his death, D. Wyatt Aiken, Abbeville planter and editor of the *Rural Carolinian,* had publicly called for Randolph's assassination.[56] According to the *Charleston Daily News,* South Carolina governor R. K. Scott, condemned the attack in a speech to the General Assembly. He referred to the shooting as "most revolting" and to Randolph as "a man of enlarged views, of great force of character, and exercised and extensive influence on public sentiment.[57] In February 1871, a memorial was established for Senator Randolph in Columbia.[58]

Gerald Jackson knew a lot about the history of Hodges and the trains that used to come through the depot. He said that the "size and the width of the old train depots was determined by the intended uses of the building." The Hodges depot

> was intended for freight as it is mostly warehouse [*sic*]. The large sliding doors were used to move freight . . . This depot served two cotton mills as well as all the area farmers and merchants . . . Hodges was one of the few towns to have a turntable (which was located behind Godfrey's Market.) This device literally turned the train around so that it could go back where it came from. There were two trains to lay over in Hodges: the upper and the lower train. The upper train went to Greenville and the lower went to Columbia.[59]

By the late nineteenth century, Hodges had turned into a thriving township. On July 20, 1888, "Ben Tillman, leading developer of Clemson College and Winthrop and Converse Colleges, gave his first political stump meeting at the Hodges Depot."[60]

"Pitchfork" Ben Tillman is one of South Carolina's most infamous characters. Racist, bombastic, and master politician, the one-eyed Tillman (1847–1918) had a huge impact on state, regional, and national politics. He served as governor of South Carolina from 1890 to 1894 and as U.S. senator from 1895 to 1918. Armed with his absolutist belief that "[t]his is a White man's country and always will be a White man's country,"[61] Tillman arguably did more to maintain racial inequality in South Carolina than any other individual. An occasional advocate of lynching, and with a style and rhetoric that at times bears an uncanny resemblance to that of another well-known figure, Tillman used his speeches to divide the electorate.[62] He abhorred the federal government and instilled a hatred and fear of African Americans in the minds of White farmers. He spoke at Hodges Depot just as his star was rising on the South Carolina political stage. After the event, Tillman gave stump speeches later that summer in "Greenville, Chester, Sumter, Florence, Charleston, and Blackville."[63]

Hodges Depot was the site of another grisly murder in November 1895 when a white woman, twenty-five-year-old Narcissa Bagwell, was kidnapped while walking to the train station. She was traveling to Atlanta. Bagwell had sent her trunk to the depot ahead of her, but it was stolen along the way. The *Intelligencer* of Anderson, South Carolina, reported that two local African American men, John Mitchell and Wash Ware, were taken into custody. It was alleged that Wash Ware "took the trunk to Hodges and tried to check it to Florida, but the agent would not check unless he had a ticket." Ware's acquaintance, John Mitchell, robbed Miss Bagwell of $30 on her way to the station, killed her, "mutilated the body, cutting off the legs and arms and placing the remains in an outhouse filled with fodder to which fire was set."[64] The paper noted, "Large crowds are gathering in the neighborhood of Hodges" in anticipation of a possible lynching. However, it was subsequently reported that the two men "landed safely in the Abbeville jail and no trouble is expected."[65]

While these are, as far as we know, true stories related to Hodges Depot, others are inaccurate. For example, Gerald Jackson would incorrectly claim that, during the Civil War Hodges Depot "was somewhat of a mini-mall." He said, "Watches[66] were repaired here, rags collected, hoop skirts sold and repaired, cotton and dry-goods as well as groceries and liquor dispensed by the Federal Post Office!"[67] Gerald also was fond of stating that, at the end of the war, "Jefferson Davis and his war cabinet parted in Cokesbury before going to Abbeville, SC, to sign the papers of surrender of the Confederate States of

America to the Union army." Gerald said that Davis "stopped in this railroad depot"[68] on his way out of town, "before going on sign the surrender papers in Abbeville."[69] If the 1965 reporting (mentioned above) by Mike Ellis is correct, then there is no way this could have happened. It might be correct to say that Jefferson Davis had passed through the town of Hodges, South Carolina, but he could not have stopped in the depot because it would not have been built for another five years.

FIVE

SETTING UP SHOP

Sugar Plum Fairy came and hit the streets
Lookin' for soul food and a place to eat
Went to the Apollo
You should have seen him go, go, go
     —Lou Reed[1]

Perhaps Gerald can be forgiven his conflation, at times, of the town of Hodges Depot with his own train depot. The town and the railroad were, of course, in many ways, inseparable. Railways put places like Hodges in contact with modern civilization. They made the United States into an industrial power. Railroads gave people an alternative to travel by "wagons, stages and river barges."[2] People in Greenwood could now get to Columbia in five hours, whereas it used to take two days. A trip to Charleston that once took a week could now be done in a day.[3] For over a century, passenger (coal-fired, and then electric) trains connected residents in Greenwood County to destinations both near and far.[4]

Segregated waiting rooms for white and Black customers, which had not previously existed, were added to the Hodges Depot in 1912.[5] By 1914, eight times a day, trains would leave Greenville, South Carolina, and would arrive in Greenwood two hours later. Along the way, they would stop at various small towns such as Belton, Shoals Junction, and Hodges.[6] The railroad brought people together. Guy Emerson remembers that in the 1920s, "[o]n Sundays, everyone would go out to meet the train because it was the only thing we had to look forward to."[7]

Yet soon motor cars on the highways would eclipse the trains on the railways. By the 1960s and 1970s, the railroad industry was dying out across the United States. Eighteen-wheeler tractor-trailers now transported much of the freight across the country. People flew on airplanes and drove their own

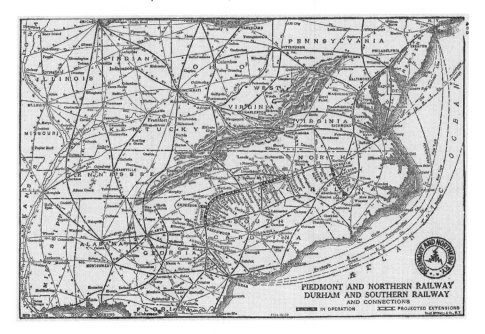

Piedmont & Northern Railway Map, ca. 1940.

vehicles instead of traveling on trains. There ceased to be as much of a need for railways, their assorted artifacts and infrastructure. Questions were raised about how to dispose of old railway buildings. Rather than being destroyed, in many cases "former depots and railway cars" were converted into "restaurants, nightspots, [and even] police stations."[8]

After he bought the Southern Depot, Gerald started devising plans to relocate the 105-year-old structure. It would not be an easy task and took over a month of planning.[9] The building measured ninety-seven feet long and was twenty-eight feet wide. Although the *Greenville News* reported at the time that the depot "weighs over 1,000,000 pounds,"[10] this seems to have been an over-statement. An estimate of fifty tons (or 100,000 pounds) seems more likely. The depot had to be moved very carefully a distance of seven-tenths of a mile from the center of Hodges out to the Jackson family property on Highway 25, across from Gerald's childhood home. Like the best blues clubs, Jackson Station would be located at a crossroads.

With the help of some friends, Gerald "built a 120-foot trailer out of steel and put it under the depot." Then, on June 5, 1975, it was very slowly moved through town and out to the highway. Moving the depot cost Gerald $5,400, a considerable amount of money in those days (over $20,000 in today's dollars).[11] He hired Bill Wright out of Anderson to help with the job. It was not so much the weight but the length of the building that made moving it particularly difficult. Wright said, "When you get something that long you just almost can't handle it. You can't turn it, you can't back up. You have to do what it wants you to do."[12]

"It was an ordeal to get it moved," remembers Bonnie Capps. Jim Sheehan, a reporter with the Anderson *Independent-Mail* wrote that "numerous utility poles and signs" in Hodges had to be taken down.[13] Once the depot had arrived at its new location, Jackson and his friends settled the building on fifty foundation posts made out of mason bricks. By the end of the day, Gerald Jackson declared, "It took six trucks and a bulldozer to move it, but we got it here in once piece."[14] He said he and "his mother were delighted."[15]

Jackson Station Depot was now located just fifty yards away from another Hodges landmark, Otis Harvley's "Waterhole." John Sanders says that Harvley's used to be called "Burroughs'" back then. Otis Harvley had bought the business from Ralph Burroughs. John Sanders said, "Otis married his daughter, Betty. Otis raised his family downstairs in that store . . . Otis bought that store in the fifties. Burroughs at the time didn't do the mechanic work, oil changes, that type of stuff, they sold gas and had general merchandise, vegetables, [and] canned goods."[16]

Otis Harvley would turn the store into a little bar. In 2016, the Waterhole celebrated its fiftieth anniversary in Hodges and claimed the distinction of being one of the oldest (if not the oldest) drinking establishments in Greenwood County. Situated in what is now a small country store with two pool tables and a jukebox, the Waterhole is still known as having "the best and coldest beer in the county."[17] Run by the proprietor, eighty-four-year-old Otis Harvley, this tavern is about as unique as it gets.

Today the bar is mainly frequented by hardworking country folks who have been coming to the Waterhole for years, bodies distorted by decades of hard living and bad eating. Smoking is still allowed in the place, as nicotine stains on the ceiling can attest. Greenwood musician Nic Massey jokes, "Even the pickled eggs are yellow from all the nicotine."[18] Despite its idiosyncrasies, the Waterhole delivers a refreshing beverage, the pool tables are clean with new felt, and newcomers are welcomed.

Otis Harvley had been in business for over a decade when Gerald moved his depot next door. Otis did not bear any animus to his new neighbor. At times, the Jackson Station crowd would wander down to Harvley's for a change of pace. The Waterhole was much smaller. It was an afternoon and evening place and shut down early by 1:00 a.m. Otis says he never went inside Jackson Station, but he did business with Gerald in other ways. One year, Gerald sold Otis a calf. If Gerald was short on beer, Otis might loan him stock from of his own inventory until the beer truck arrived later in the week.[19] On one occasion, Otis helped Gerald put a fence on his property. Gerald was using a post hole digger and was about to make a deep cut in the ground when Otis suddenly stopped him. Gerald was about to tear into a gas line.[20]

Initially, there was little mention of the depot being used as a music venue. Indeed, it was not entirely clear if Gerald had any definitive plans for the building. He told the press, "If anyone reading the paper has any ideas on what to do, get in touch with me in Hodges."[21] Gerald had simply told the railroad company that he wanted to buy the depot so he could restore and preserve it. Whatever plans he did have for the building involved turning it into "something like a museum."[22] Soon after the relocation, however, Gerald started to talk about opening a music club. Doing so would have several advantages. It would let Gerald fulfill his dream of opening a honky-tonk. Gerald and Steve could quit their day jobs. This could move out of Gerald mother's house and live in one of the depot's old waiting rooms. Perhaps they might build a loft.

Jackson Station would feature live blues, Gerald's favorite kind of music, performed by acts from all over the world. Gerald would book the bands, host, and mingle with the patrons. He would use his old Navy medic's cross as a handstamp to mark people who had paid to get in. This would honor his Vietnam experience and, as Anita Clinton says, serve to "remember all those he felt he had let down and lost." Clinton continues, "The medic stamp was personal for him. And I think it also made him feel better. His stamp was now on lively, happy people expressing fun and joy."[23]

Steve would manage the place, tend the bar, and run the kitchen. It is likely Elizabeth Jackson loaned them money to get started. Turning the Reconstruction Era train station into a club would take a tremendous amount of work. The idea was not perfect, but it did not need to be perfect. This was a blues club, after all. Blues clubs aren't "supposed to be flawless." They should be "dirty, low-down, greasy. Anything but perfect."[24]

Moving the depot was just the first in a few arduous series of steps toward opening Jackson Station Rhythm & Blues Club. Gerald and Steve spent three years, from 1975 to 1978,[25] renovating the entire building. "They worked on that depot for years before they got it open," says Steve's mother, Hazel Bryant.[26] Gerald and Steve did much of the work themselves and got help with the rest from friends and local tradespeople. Reggie Massey says Gerald taught himself plumbing, carpentry, and masonry from *Time-Life* do-it-yourself books.[27] The building's "12-inch pine floor planks" had "cracks from a half to two inches wide." Gerald put "slats under the big cracks," filled them with wood filler, and then sanded the floor to "bring out its long-hidden splendor."[28] John Sanders did the wiring and electrical work. Steve assisted when he was not working his job at his job at a local manufacturing plant. Other friends would stop by to chart Gerald's progress, drink a beer, and lend a hand.

One day, Steve had some trouble at his job at the plant. "He was one minute late one day and they told him, 'OK, if you're late again, you're fired," his mother remembers. "So he was one minute late again, and they fired him. So, he never had a job after that. He helped Gerald one hundred percent on that depot."[29]

Gerald and Steve breathed new life into that old building. Gerald built a sixteen-foot wooden bar using doors off another depot he had purchased in Edgefield, South Carolina. "I can use all the original materials for the renovations,"[30] Jackson said of the work. "The Hodges depot is so old it is put together with wooden pegs and I want to preserve the atmosphere of the building." He said he wanted people to "think they are in an old railroad depot."[31] Gerald built an enormous deck that wrapped around the building and added a front ramp and walkway. He told a reporter from the Greenwood *Index-Journal* how he wanted to use "bright railroad colors in the interior and exterior paint schemes" and "original woodwork or fixtures and lumber from the old Southern Depot in Edgefield."[32] In addition to taking care of the basics, such as bringing plumbing and electricity to the building, there also were a number of structural changes that had to be made. Gerald said that "[t]he former ticket office will become the lobby and restrooms and the old freight warehouse will become the bar and cocktail area. The nightclub will be arranged like the former freight section, with tables grouped under the names of former shippers and their commodities."[33] Gerald had a professional design for the club drawn up by Mark Garber of Development Concepts.[34]

The project called for "cutting an entranceway through the old ticket office," "building a stained-glass, arched doorway where the agent's window was," and putting "stained-glass windows in the upper quarter panels of the four freight doors and building ramps to lead to the entrance."[35] In December 1975, Gerald shared his updated vision with the community. He declared, "It's going to be just like you drove up to the train station to take a ride, except the

ride you are going to take is my trip!"[36] Jackson Station would feature rock
'n' roll shows, theatrical productions and film showings.[37] He said the club
"would have something for persons of all ages." Gerald was optimistic about
his club's potential success. He thought if he could "build something neat
like one of those clubs I'd seen in Asia, I'd surely make some money." Gerald
knew he could "fix this building up right cool."[38] Over time, he would indeed
transform "the old train station into one of the most unique night spots in the
South."[39]

Eventually the depot became made habitable enough for Gerald and Steve
to host some of their closest friends at the club. Then they gradually opened
the place to the broader Greenwood community. There was something exciting and transgressive about heading up to Hodges for the evening. The fact
that Jackson Station was said to be a gay bar made the excursion even more
tantalizing.

Social classes in the greater Greenwood area are—as they are everywhere
—delineated by the politics of place. As a young woman growing up in
Greenwood County in the 1960s, Gerald's friend Linn Johnson says she was
told to never to associate with any classmate who lived north of Northside
Drive (near what is now the BI-LO grocery store on the northern side of
town). While Hodges, five miles north of this location, did not have quite the
violent reputation as Ware Shoals (an even-rougher town further up the road)
any establishment in Hodges would initially have been considered *déclassé* by
the old Greenwood gentry.[40]

Nevertheless, eventually, brave, pioneering souls made it up to the club.
Approaching Jackson Station, a newcomer would be surprised by the club,
unaware of what was inside. At the exterior of the building, one encountered
a large, gray, ramshackle structure, made from rough-hewn timber. The building had huge sliding wooden doors, a wraparound porch, chimneys, and a
metal roof. Thorny thistle bushes—planted for aesthetic as well as repellant
purposes—grew tall in the southeast corner of the deck. They stopped people
from climbing over the railing and sneaking into the club.

Jackson Station resembled Dr. Who's TARDIS, in that its outer appearance
conveyed little about the interior. At first, Jackson Station looked just like
a rundown shack in the middle of the country. Closer inspection, however,
revealed a world of sensual pleasures. "I'd never been to a place that was that
unique in terms of the roadhouse," comments Michael Rothschild, owner
of Landslide Records and producer of Widespread Panic's first album, *Space
Wrangler*.[41]

Initially, Jackson Station operated almost as a kind of speakeasy. To gain entry, one had to be friends with Gerald or know someone who knew him. Jackson Station membership cards were handed out to those in the inner circle. Lee and Susan Rush remember, "The clientele was largely gay at first, but Jackson Station was soon a place for everyone."[42] Knocking on the front of the club, one would hear people laughing and talking on the inside. Someone would come to the door. "I'm Gerald Jackson," a voice would say. "Who are you? Who sent you up here?"[43]

If Gerald liked the response, he would let the guest in. If not, he sent the supplicant packing.

"It was like being at somebody's house," recalls David Goldman. Musician Glenn Phillips likens Jackson Station to those "one or two homes," well known to every child growing up, where "you knew you were really welcome." He says Gerald and Steve were like the cool parents who would have all the neighborhood kids over to "let them go nuts, keep them out of trouble for a while."[44]

Before they opened to the public, Gerald and Steve hosted private parties at Jackson Station. One such event was hosted Walter Grady Bishop and his wife Ann Bishop, for none other than the U.S. senator Strom Thurmond (who was Walter's uncle) and his wife Nancy. Knowing what we do not only about Jackson Station but also about Thurmond (who was one of the most historically controversial characters in Southern politics), it seems quite remarkable that Thurmond would have ever gone to the place. He did so, of course, long before the club developed the identity for which it would come to be known. Ann Bishop says the party was held at Jackson Station because "there weren't that many places" to have private parties at that time in Greenwood.[45] She remembers that the guests of honor had "good time" at Jackson Station. She said Gerald and Steve were "nice people" who were "a big help."[46] Although it was a private affair, Gerald let his friend David Goldman attend the party. Goldman remembers the event vividly. He recalls that "Nancy and the Senator stood in the foyer and everyone who came in was introduced to them, old school. Lots of hard liquor was served. At one point a couple of professional dancers, a Black man and a white lady, danced for our amusement."[47]

Jackson Station opened to the public on Halloween night of 1978.[48] The debut was not without its intrigue. Two days earlier, at 1:00 a.m. on October 29, the club had been raided by "ABC agents and Greenwood County Sheriff's deputies." Gerald had been arrested and was charged with "unlawful storage of liquor and refusal to permit inspection of the premises."[49] He was quickly bonded out and would pay a $100 fine the following January for each charge.[50]

The interior of the depot was a fabulous spectacle of lights, signs, and railway kitsch. On the left as one entered the building, one passed a giant, 10 × 10-foot mirror with a gilded six-inch frame. There was no heat in the winter and no air-conditioning in the summer. Two Baron wood-burning stoves were the only sources of heat during the colder months. They were ensconced by metal exoskeletons to stop drunken patrons from scalding themselves. In the summer, Gerald opened up the huge wooden freight doors, which, with the help of ceiling fans, created a cross breeze through the depot.[51] Vast quantities of chilled beer kept people cool and were stored in enormous "wooden ice-boxes in the kitchen."[52] The giant bar was backlit by another huge mirror. Counter stools that had once been used in the Jackson general store were installed along the long bar.[53] A raised platform on the floor behind the bar afforded the bartenders height and authority in their dealings with customers.

"Behind the bar you were a good two feet higher than anybody in there," said John Sanders. "You got an overview."[54] Jack McConnell said it was important for the bartender to have this kind of stature. "You had to have that. Because by the time people got to Jackson's they were already 'fucked up.'"[55] On the south end of the depot past the restrooms were the old segregated waiting rooms adorned with detailed woodwork on the walls. These private spaces were reserved for musicians, staff, and close friends of Gerald and Steve. A screen door behind the end of the bar accessed a small kitchen. Two half staircases went up to the loft (where Gerald and Steve lived in the winter) and down to the basement (where they lived in the summer). Somehow, they made it through the entire year without any electric (or gas) heat, or any air conditioning. John Sanders says that there was a "full bath upstairs, a full bath downstairs. Showers . . . commode, the whole nine yards."[56] Catherine Brickley, piano player in the Sensible Pumps, said that, "It was like a little apartment upstairs." She says the band "would go up there and hang out," readying themselves to go on stage.[57]

A division of labor developed at Jackson Station. Just as they had planned, Gerald was the indefatigable host and Steve was the tireless manager. Steve "did most of the work," says his mother, Hazel Bryant. "Gerald was always busy on the phone or taking care of business, and Steve was doing all the work."[58] Of the atmosphere of the club, Jackson said he "wanted it lively." When he was a boy, he said he "used to love to go to the [Greenwood County] fair and watch those Black burlesque shows. That attitude sort of stuck with me, and that was the format I wanted for this place."[59] The aroma of strawberry incense often lingered in the air. An old row of movie theater chairs lined the west wall of the building, giving people a spot to sit down, take a break from dancing, and watch the show. Gerald painted a huge South Carolina Palmetto tree and crescent moon on the north wall of the building, behind the stage.[60] Artifacts of various kinds—"a visual feast of old paintings, rock posters, street signs"[61]—embellished the walls and ceiling. Most of these were curiosity pieces that Gerald—a self-proclaimed "inheritance freak"[62]—had collected over the years. Particularly noteworthy were Gerald's Navy Corpsman back-pack from Vietnam, a huge photograph of George Wallace (the segregationist Alabama governor who later recanted his racist views), a large moose head,[63] and a vintage Coors beer sign with an illuminated waterfall running through the middle of it.[64]

"I have a lot of friends who bring things in to put on the wall," Jackson told Columbia's the *State* newspaper in 1989.[65] "A lot of what's in here are just old things that built up over the years that my family had stored in one place or another." He joked, "I'm not only a product of my environment, but I am living it."[66] Reggie Massey said Jackson displayed the Wallace photograph "not because he liked George Wallace, [but because] some guy and his Dad had seen it on the side of the road somewhere, took it down, [and] just offered it to him."[67] Dave Schools, bassist of the jam band Widespread Panic, was highly impressed by the décor at Jackson Station. He said, "You don't go to some restaurant supply place and get that stuff. That stuff builds up over time like change on the mantle-piece. The whole thing was surreal."[68]

Railway iconography and memorabilia filled the space. Until 1990, trains still lumbered along through Hodges, south toward Greenwood, and north to Greenville. Jackson Station was in operation just fifty yards away. "We'd hear that train go by while we were playing," remembers Dave Schools.[69] Gerald would give a twenty-five-cent discount on beer every time a train would go by. Failure to act quickly meant that one missed the discount and had to wait for the next train. "When the train has passed, so has the special," Gerald declared.[70] Some patrons passed up the drink discount to go outside and cheer on the train. "They all used to run out back and wave, when the trains were going through," remembers Bruce Cobb.[71]

A huge mason jar filled with water was another attraction at Jackson Station. It sat on the corner of the bar. In the bottom of the jar was a highball glass. According to David Goldman, "If you could drop a coin through a slot in the top and sink it in the glass, you got a free beer!" While that may sound easy enough, Goldman said, "many tried but few succeeded."[72]

Gerald celebrated the historical significance of the depot by printing pamphlets he called "Action Jackson Station flyers." They usually consisted of one-page memoranda photocopied on colored paper with the iconic image of Jackson Station at the top of the page. Gerald made these flyers periodically to share "little tidbits of news" with his customers. He aimed to make the series "informative and enjoyable to read." He urged people to "take the time and ask for it,"[73] when they were in the club.[74]

Across from the bar, two pool tables were illuminated by low hanging chandeliers. A large television hung from the ceiling in the northeast corner of the room. In the spring of 1989, Gerald announced in a flyer that "the miracle of cable television has finally made it to Hodges . . . and Jackson's has it! Both sets (in the main bar and in the reading room) are equipped with it, so if there is something you want to see, just ask. Available channels include HBO, Cinemax, ESPN, MTV and more."[75]

Bands played on the short riser stage at the north end of the building that spanned the length of the wall. Wooden barrels on either side of the stage supported large speakers.[76] The building was the perfect size for a blues bar. It was small enough for intimate sets, yet large enough to accommodate a crowd. "There was plenty of room to dance, if you wanted to dance," said Reggie Massey.[77]

Cattycorner from the bar was a tiny space known as the Music Room. This space housed a turntable and the entirety of Gerald's record collection. Gerald was a keen music lover. Reggie Massey said Gerald had "hundreds and hundreds of albums . . . [A] little bit of everything."[78] Dirk Armstrong described Gerald as "definitely a Rhythm & Blues fan, a big Soul fan." Gerald corralled friends like Jack McConnell, Ben Hawthorne, and Will Holloway to work for him as DJs. Holloway, who grew up in Greenwood and later attended Davidson College in North Carolina, has great memories spinning records at Jackson Station. He worked there in the early 1980s when he was home from college for the summer. For his efforts, he received "free beer and twenty bucks."[79] A number of people worked at Jackson Station in such a capacity. They would be given a free cover charge, some drinks, and a small stipend. Not a lot of scratch to be sure, but not bad for a night's work. Jackson Station was a decent side-hustle for many.

Holloway was impressed by Gerald's music collection. He said Gerald had classic blues records by Son House and Howlin' Wolf and a good selection of

Jackson Station Bar Pamphlet, ca. 1985.

New Wave music, such as early R.E.M. Though Jackson Station was mainly known as a blues bar, its role as a New Wave or counter-culture establishment should also be remembered. Tim Bradshaw, who went to Jackson Station while he was a student at Erskine College in the early 1980s, remembers a significant countercultural presence at Jackson Station. This was reflected in the sorts of bands brought to Jackson Station on Friday nights, as well as the music played more informally at the club during the week.

On Tuesdays in the fall of 1988, Dirk Armstrong hosted "Dirk's Night Out." This was basically "alternative rock" night, featuring music by: PIL, the

Cure, the Alarm, Talking Heads, Dead Kennedys, Grateful Dead, the Smiths, the Sex Pistols, U2, and R.E.M. Greenwood musician Russ Fitzgerald says that "If you were in Greenwood, SC, in the early eighties and you identified yourself as" a "creative" type, you would be at Jackson Station. "That's where your tribe would show up."[80] Will Holloway remembers changing up the playlist as the night progressed. Gerald would tell him to start playing classical music at about 4:00 or 4:30 a.m. to get people to go home. "It is amazing how early Beethoven string quartets can run away bikers," Holloway jokes. Ben Hawthorne said Gerald would not allow certain songs to ever be played at the club, especially not late at night, due to the possibility of a fight breaking out. "Sweet Home Alabama" was one of the blacklisted tunes.[81]

Another unique characteristic of Jackson Station was that the party often spilled beyond the confines of the depot proper and into the space behind the building. A large back deck on the structure's west side, which faced a small cow pasture and the railroad tracks, was often a popular place to congregate. In the winter months, customers would often gather around a fire in an old oil drum.[82] Occasionally, neighborhood kids hiding in bushes across the tracks would rain down bottle rockets on the heads of bemused hippies.[83]

Porches (front and back) are integral to Southern architecture and are undoubtedly one reason why Southerners have the reputation for being more social than people in other parts of the country. Back in the days before air-conditioning, large porches were some of the only places to escape the summer heat. Porches are celebrated in song by many musical artists, including bands such as Widespread Panic, who played at Jackson Station nine times in the 1980s. Widespread Panic recorded the track "Porch Song" in 1990. As the lyrics state:

> From here I watch the world go by
> Working in the moon-time bar and grill
> The word from Earth-my time is up
> But here upon the moon time stands still
> Got no telecommunications
> Cables haven't gotten out this way
> Havin' a good time, here today
> Watching the sun shine
> Matinee
> Never the wrong time
> Time we stay

In many respects, this song could easily have been written about the social scene at Jackson Station. There was a carefree attitude toward time, a life not dependent on technology, and enjoyment of the little things—just sitting in the sun on the back porch. Another great porch song that might capture some of the culture at Jackson Station is Uncle Tupelo's[84] "Screen Door," which includes the following lyrics:

> Down here, where we're at
> Everybody is equally poor
> Down here, we don't care
> We don't care what happens outside the screen door.[85]

The 1970s and early 1980s were indeed a time when many people in the South were "equally poor," and in that equality of poverty took solace in the company of others. Unlike today when so many young people are victims of predatory lending practices and up to their ears in credit card, automobile, and student loan debt, a generation ago, it didn't take a huge income simply to cover basic expenses. People didn't have as much, and they didn't need as much. Housing was half as expensive as it is today. College tuition was a pittance compared with today.

Outside the screen door at Jackson Station, in the spot of land between the back deck and the train tracks, Gerald kept two cows—Florence and Nicki—a Holstein and a Jersey. The cows were useful to him for several reasons: as commodities, quasi-pets, and as a tourist attraction. It was always a treat to go out to back and watch Gerald feed and talk to the bovines.[86] Many people have interesting memories of the cows at Jackson Station.[87] Tinsley Ellis says, "I remember one time we got there and Gerald was walking across the back area there carrying a cow, a calf." Gerald would often keep the public abreast of news about the cows in the Jackson Station pamphlets. In the spring of 1989, Gerald wrote a "Barnyard Birth Announcement," which stated: "Most of you know about Florence and Nicki, our two resident bovines in the pasture behind the station. Both Flo and Nicki have recently been blessed with calves—both little bulls—named Spot and Red. Plus, two more calves, Frank and Ernie, have been imported to Hodges by some good friends in Saluda. Will we soon have to change our name to Jackson's Animal Farm?"[88]

Spot turned out to be bartender Dirk Armstrong's calf, which Gerald awarded him that year as his Christmas bonus. Armstrong says it was "one of the nicest things," Gerald ever did for him. He says Gerald had "actually had overfed Florence, so she was having difficulty giving birth." Intervention was necessary. "I helped pull Spot out," Armstrong recalls. However, he said, "That's the last time I got to touch him, the guy would have nothing to do with me . . . I have pictures of me chasing him around the pasture out back. And then we had them processed." Armstrong made good use of the money. He said, "I actually paid off a year of my student loan [debt] with my Christmas bonus of the calf."

The back deck was the place to catch a more illicit buzz than what could be found inside Jackson Station. "There were a lot of things that went on up there, like, out in the open," said regular Roland Tranter. "Walk out there on the deck, you know, do what you was gonna' do." Tranter says you could find people "[s]moking a joint, snorting cocaine, taking pills, whatever people had, uppers, downers . . . It was the Eighties. Everybody was doing everything, you know?"[89]

Before long, word got out that a new late-night bar had opened north Greenwood in Hodges. The club began to get more popular. "It was a midnight [']til morning bar,"[90] says Tommy Kidd. People were intrigued and soon made pilgrimages to the club. As Lou Reed wrote in a song that was surely a fixture at Jackson Station: "Hey babe, take a walk on the wild side."

David Goldman says that, "It was astonishing to walk through the door [of Jackson Station] for the first time." He compares it to "waking up in the morning and finding a circus in your backyard."[91]

Many of the early Jackson Station patrons would turn out to be a few years younger than they initially appeared to be. From 1935 until 1984, the drinking age in South Carolina for the consumption of beer and wine was eighteen years of age. The state raised the drinking age to nineteen years of age in 1984, and then to twenty-one in 1986. As such, during its first years of operation, the number of potential patrons who could legally drink at Jackson Station was quite large. Not only did this population include the eighteen-and-up crowd, but also many even younger people—fifteen-, sixteen-, and seventeen-year-olds with fake IDs. These were the days when lamination alone was often enough to provide a stamp of legitimacy—or one might beg for a castoff ID from an older friend or relative. Today many bars and restaurants routinely use QR codes to establish the authenticity of a driver's license. In the 1970s and 1980s, just showing any form of identification was normally enough to get in. When Gerald would discover the real age of someone who had been drinking at his bar for years, he would "almost have a heart attack," said Will Holloway. However, "No one was really worried. It was a very different time."[92]

Nonetheless, Gerald would be and remain concerned about underage drinking. He reminded his patrons (this was most likely in 1980): "The legal age for drinking is 18 years of age—not 16 or 17. PLEASE do not bring your friends, brothers or sisters who are under 18 years old! This is an adult bar—a place to rid yourselves of children—so let's keep the youngsters at home or at the local Y."[93] Gerald used a cup color system to distinguish legal from underage patrons. On some nights, his bartenders would put alcoholic beverages in red plastic cups, for example, while nonalcoholic beverages would be poured into the blue ones. The next night, they would switch the colors. This allowed Gerald to quickly scan the bar to see if his patrons were behaving themselves. It was not a foolproof system, of course, but it did allow him to keep better track of who was legally of age.[94] By 1986, the drinking age in South Carolina increased to twenty-one. For a place like Jackson Station, which drew heavily on college-aged populations—especially students from Erskine College and Lander College (later Lander University)—the higher drinking age put a serious dent in the club's clientele and potential revenue. According to Russ Fitzgerald, after the drinking age in South Carolina went from eighteen to twenty-one, "[t]here was a lot less live music all around."[95]

The holidays were a special time of the year at Jackson Station. On New Year's Day, collard greens and black-eyed peas would be cooked on the potbellied stoves in the depot.[96] Reggie Massey remembers how "Gerald would cook up some meats, and everybody that came would bring a vegetable or a dessert." On one occasion, a prankster brought marijuana-laced brownies, which were stashed out of reach behind the bar. Gerald would tell anyone who wanted a brownie to go behind the bar and get one. After a while, Gerald's mother, Elizabeth Jackson—who at this point would have been approaching seventy—started wondering why all these people were eating brownies. Unbeknownst to Gerald, she ate one herself. Mrs. Jackson disappeared for a while, only to be discovered later on riding a bicycle in circles in the parking lot.[97]

Reggie Massey remembers a couple at this same event who had made drive from the Columbia. They were having an extramarital affair together and Jackson Station was their illicit rendezvous location. They stayed at the gathering until early evening, enjoying the party. Soon after, they left the depot and returned to Columbia. About three hours later, Gerald got a phone call. "It was the brownies, wasn't it?" a voice asked. Not surprisingly, the brownies had interfered with the couple's navigational ability and they had gotten completely lost on the way home. They had made it to Georgia before realizing they were driving in the wrong direction.[98]

Gerald Jackson with wood stove, ca. 1983.

In the cold and damp winter months, people basked in the warmth of the wood-burning stoves. Jack McConnell expresses well the essence of Jackson Station in its prime. He writes, "I will never forget surveying the room from the antique shoeshine chair with that old pot-bellied stove glowing white hot on a cold winter's night.

The train rolling by shook the building and sounded its whistle calling the Erskine Kids to the bar for another Foster's at Jackson Station served with the kind smile of a good man."[99] The mention of the "Erskine Kids" was a reference to the students of Erskine College, the private Presbyterian college ten miles up the road from Hodges in Due West, South Carolina. Due West is an even smaller town than Hodges. Otis Harvley's "Waterhole" had been the local hangout for Erskine students for years. Jackson Station provided another option for entertainment without traveling too far from town. Similarly, Lander College students, faculty, and staff would also frequent Jackson Station. Lander University president Larry Jackson (1925–2017) could be found at Jackson Station, along with various administrators. Faculty members such as Branko Rieger, Bob Poe, Bob Phillips, and Leonard Lundquist were also often there. David Goldman comments, "It was not unusual to see your professor cabareting [*sic*] there one night, then teaching class the next day. This, too, was a big part of the appeal."[100]

Lander University music professor Lila Noonkester celebrated her twenty-ninth birthday at Jackson Station in 1989. She says, "The guest list included Lander faculty, at least one Lander VP, and some Lander upperclassmen." Unfortunately, the young professor had her tires slashed that night. As Noonkester tells it, "one of the students had gone out to use the pay phone in a phone booth out front. It was drizzling rain. We discovered that cars had had [their] tires slashed." She said that they "found out later that the guy who slashed the tires had actually stolen one of the cars on which he had already slashed a tire! He was apprehended on his way back to Greenwood."[101]

The crowd at Jackson Station was a "social collage of the citizenry of Greenwood and the surrounding area."[102] There were "good 'ol boys, frat daddies, bikers, spandex-clad hairdressers, suits, preppies, punkers, tie-dyed nuevo hippies and coeds—even people in formal attire, fresh from a wedding reception."[103] As Jeff Calder of the band the Swimming Pool Qs notes, "You wouldn't get that level of diversity in Atlanta in 1984. It was wild."[104] Calder said, "[A]ll the outsiders from the area," came to Jackson Station. "Every type of person. Every kind of person."[105] Phyllis Free describes Jackson Station as "a remarkable intersection of different cultural groups."[106] Widespread Panic bassist Dave Schools remembers "button-down, fraternity and sorority people from this place; and motorcycle people from that place; and just hard drinkers from somewhere else. And that's when shit got weird. It was great."[107]

"Nobody told me the club changed after midnight on Friday nights," said blues guitarist and music producer Scott Cable, laughing. "When it got real late there, it changed over. It would still have blues and live music, but the crowd was much more diverse. Nobody told me."[108] Bob Margolin says there were "all kinds of people, from serious music lovers to wild partiers," at Jackson Station. Sometimes he says it would be "the same person at different times of the night."[109]

: SIX :

PLAYING AT THE STATION

Feeling weak in the Itta Bena hot sun
Crawling to the station we were foamin' at the mouth
Sippin' on a tall boy, sippin' on a tall boy
Just looking for a place to shed our skins
  —Widespread Panic[1]

In the spring of 1982, Jackson Station transformed itself from a libertine redneck salon into a true Southern blues bar by offering extraordinary live music shows at the weekend. Gerald opened Jackson Station, not just because he wanted to open a business, but because of his love of music, especially the blues. If Jackson Station had been just another country bar in the middle of nowhere—even if such a venue was housed in a Reconstruction-era train station—there would be little more than local significance to this story. One reason Jackson Station was such a compelling place that warrants attention today is the important role it played in the careers of professional working musicians.

There was tremendous diversity in the types of shows at Jackson Station.[2] But generally speaking, the artists who played there were working class men and women—guitarists, bassists, vocalists, saxophonists, pianists, and drummers —most of whom survived, by and large, by finding the next gig. Music was their livelihood. Their existence dependent on by making records and being plugged in to the touring circuit. Gerald had deep admiration for the people who made the music happen. It was their full-time job; they were used to living on the road. Gerald booked talented performers who took pride in their craft and knew how to put on a show.

Jackson Station was one stop on a Southern touring circuit that included venues such as the South Main Café in Blacksburg, Virginia; the Double Door in Charlotte, North Carolina; Blind Willie's in Atlanta, Georgia; and

Sliders[3] in Fernandina Beach, Florida.[4] "You could do Jackson Station on a Friday night," says Billy Wirtz, "and then you could play Atlanta, Charlotte, Columbia, Charleston. There was a whole number of places. Asheville, Hickory. Any number of places you could get to on Saturday and have a good weekend."[5]

"Gerald did all kinds of stuff there," remembers Tinsley Ellis, referring to the music played at Jackson Station. "In terms of blues, he did the real traditional stuff like Bob Margolin was playing. And then I'm more blues rock or Allman Brothers kind of music. Then he did it right up to the Panic Tour, the jam band thing."[6]

Yet Jackson Station was baffling, at first, to the musicians who graced the stage there. David Truly and his Swamp band spent many a night at Jackson Station. Truly says that the club was in the "middle of almost nowhere, just at this little weird junction." This perplexed him. "It just seemed like you walked into a little bit of the Twilight Zone," he says. After arriving at Jackson Station for the first time, he turned to his bandmates and asked, "Where are we?"[7]

The following eyewitness account, written in 1984 by freelance reporter Guran Blomgren—who was then touring the U.S. East Coast with *Tottas Bluesband*—was likely shared by many musicians when first setting eyes on Jackson Station: "We arrive before noon in the bright sunshine at what appears to be a very old train station with a semaphore on the roof. Outside, a sun-bleached flag is waving, and there are two dogs and two skulls on the giant porch. There doesn't seem to be anyone around, but after a phone call the place's owners show up and let us in."[8]

David Truly (who in addition to being a musician is an ethnomusicologist) stressed "the importance of these little clubs and these different places when there really was a music scene." Truly says that places like Jackson Station were "super important, in a lot of ways, to the development of a lot these bands. These [clubs] became little homes on the road when they were trying, struggling, to make it."[9] Music producer Scott Cable also says that Gerald Jackson "did a good thing for a lot of people. There are several of the older artists that probably wouldn't have had gigs otherwise, so to speak, out there, and that would help them connect to other cities."[10]

Gerald did most of all the booking of the acts himself, selecting the bands based on his own listening tastes and those of his friends.[11] Georgia bluesman Tinsley Ellis says that Gerald "didn't want to deal with any booking agencies, he only talked to bands themselves, which used to infuriate our agents, but he just had relations with us."[12] In the early days, bands would get between

$400 and $500 a night—decent money for the 1980s. By 1990, Gerald would be paying acts such as the Legendary Blues Band $750 for three, fifty-minute sets.[13] "Gerald didn't pay all that great, didn't pay all that bad . . . It was okay money,"[14] says the Reverend Billy Wirtz.

Gerald would put up the bands at Greenwood Motel, eight miles south of Hodges, and close to Lander College. Music producer Michael Rothschild had an interesting memory of staying at the Greenwood Motel with Tinsley Ellis after one of the latter's shows at Jackson Station: "We staggered in about five thirty or six o'clock," Rothschild remembers, "and about eight o'clock or so, somebody was chopping down trees with a chainsaw outside the hotel. We couldn't sleep, it was just deafening."[15] Despite the commotion, something good came from the experience. Tinsley wrote a song—"Greenwood Chainsaw Boogie"—that appeared on his 1986 album *Cool on It*.[16]

Once on site, musicians prepared for their performance in one of the old passenger waiting rooms, up in the loft, or down in the basement, wherever they felt most comfortable. Bob Margolin said that most of the time, his band would "hang out in the kitchen," where they could "eat as much as we wanted."[17] In addition to the money and the hotel room, other fringe benefits for playing Jackson Station included free food and drinks. In the spring of 1984, *Tottas Bluesband* from Sweden was on an American tour, playing forty gigs from Key West to New York City.[18] The band brought "wives, girlfriends, and children" with them, fourteen people in total. Normally the band was used to paying for everything for themselves on tour, even coffee and soft drinks. Of all the venue owners they experienced in the United States, they noted that Gerald Jackson was the only one to provide "hotel rooms, food, drink, and even free cigarettes" for every person in the group, all of the band's family and friends included.[19]

While Widespread Panic's Dave Schools has "many memories" of Jackson Station, "the overarching thing that [he] remember[s] the most—other than the décor of the place—was really, the Spur Burger, and the way that Gerald and Steve really looked after the musicians."[20] Schools said, "We'd come rolling in from God knows where after how long of a drive. And the first thing they wanted to see to was that we weren't going to collapse. So they fed us, with the food that they made lovingly themselves. That meant a lot in those days."[21]

Schools recalls an occasion where Gerald and Steve nursed a touring companion—a young percussionist named Dean from Richmond, Virginia— back to life. Schools remembers Dean "was really skinny and tall and had

stringy hair." He "looked incredibly unhealthy and drank way too much."
Schools says, "Gerald and Steve just took pity on him. They wanted to feed
him. They wanted to take care of him."

Schools was impressed to find such an ethos on the part of club owners.
"That felt good, because most people were like, you know, 'You guys aren't
going to do your second set because it's going to be cheaper for me to turn
off the heat or A/C and let you guys go than let you play another set.'"[22] On
the road, musicians are not only at the mercy of their audience—who may or
may not show up and pay the cover charge or buy the merchandise—but also
shady club owners with dubious business practices. Touring musicians worry
about club owners not treating them fairly, or in some cases, not paying them
at all. Dave Schools remembers "a bar owner in Raleigh [North Carolina]
that's taking his gun out of his desk and putting it on the desk in full view
of us so he can tell us we ain't getting paid." In other situations, Schools said
you have "the sob story and in the end he's taking the quarters out of the pool
tables to try to pay us." Jackson Station was nothing like that. "That stuff
never happened when we were dealing with Gerald," Schools said. "He was
stern but fair and he wanted everybody to be healthy and happy. Whether
he knew it or not, he had the Bill Graham[23] thing, which is take care of the
band and they'll play well."[24] At Jackson Station, musicians were treated like
honored guests. They focused on the basics: feeding people, treating them
kindly, and making them feel at home. "Gerald and Steve, they got it," Dave
Schools said. "And they really took care of us. It felt so nice to be taken care
of in that way."

Many of the musicians who played Jackson Station would have a notable
impact on the culture of their time. Some, such as Widespread Panic, would
go on to be highly successful. By and large, the performers at Jackson Station were highly talented men and women, career musicians used to playing
larger venues in bigger cities. By providing a venue for the production and
consumption of live music, Jackson Station was an important institutional
actor in its day.[25] The Reverend Billy Wirtz suggests that we should think of
Jackson Station as a "latter day version of the Chitlin' Circuit."[26] This was the
network of Black music clubs that existed across the country during the Jim
Crow era. Rhythm and blues singer Lou Rawls (1993–2006)—who is credited
with coining the term—explained in 1967: "These clubs were very small, very
tight, very crowded, and very loud. Everything was loud but the entertainment. The only way to establish communication was by telling a story that
would lead into the song, that would catch people's attention."[27]

Drink Small. Promotional photograph, ca. 1987.

While considerable research exists on the Chitlin' Circuit clubs in North Carolina,[28] little is known of the number and variety of music clubs that were on the South Carolina leg of tour. For example, Charleston and Columbia are the only South Carolina cities mentioned in Preston Lauterbach's 2011 work on the subject, and even then, only in passing. However, Frank Beacham's *Whitewash*, provides a very detailed portrait of one such venue, Charlie's Place in Myrtle Beach.[29] From the 1930s to the 1960s, this popular music club hosted some of the top names in Black music such as Ray Charles, Billie Holliday, and Little Richard.[30] The club's owner, Charlie Fitzgerald, welcomed Black and white patrons alike. Frank Beacham argues that the Shag—the state dance of the Carolinas—was actually invented at Charlie's Place in the late 1940s.

Like Charlie's Place, Jackson Station offered a safe haven for difference. It provided regular bookings for Black musicians, including artists like Nappy Brown, Drink Small, and Fats Jackson.

When people saw bands perform at Jackson Station, they were witnessing a part of history, watching the skills and techniques of musicians who learned to play from people who had been taught by some of the original blues performers in the Mississippi Delta.[31] As Tinsley Ellis explains, as a blues noviate, "you had to find some people that were older than you and they would teach you how to do it." Bob Margolin, for example, "learned from Muddy Waters who in turn learned from people like Son House and Robert Johnson. Music "gets passed down," Tinsley says. "The apprenticeship thing is really important."[32]

Blues guitarist "Steady Rollin'" Bob Margolin (1949–present) is arguably one of the most celebrated blues musicians to play Jackson Station, and he did so many times. Margolin is best known for his role as lead guitarist for Muddy Waters from 1973 to 1980. He can be seen standing to the left of Muddy during the performance of "I'm a Man" in Martin Scorsese's 1978 rock documentary *The Last Waltz*.[33] Margolin counts luminaries such as "Johnny Winter, Stevie Ray Vaughan, the Fabulous Thunderbirds, The Nighthawks, John Hammond, Etta James, Taj Mahal, and James Cotton" as "old friends."[34] Margolin played Jackson Station about three times a year beginning in the early 1980s and continuing until the club closed down. He fondly recalls his gigs there. Margolin said the band would normally play three sets,[35] "usually more than an hour each."[36] The music consisted of "Chicago Blues, Rock 'n Roll, Rockabilly and Funky Music."[37] He says, "We'd start about 11:30 and play 'til 4 or 5 in the morning. In the summer, the sun was always up when we quit."

Margolin said he always looked forward to playing shows at Jackson Station. On most occasions, he made the two-hour drive down from Charlotte, North Carolina, after playing another blues club, the Double Door, the night before. "I enjoyed the ride from I-85 down Route 25 to Hodges and Greenwood, where we stayed," Margolin said. "The ride through the country was like a tranquilizer. Playing there was a long night, but it was a pleasure to hang out with everyone, and often there were other musicians on the show. Gerald brought sax player Fats Jackson from Atlanta to play with us, and Fats brought singer Sweet Betty."[38] Margolin said, "Jackson Station was familiar like going home."[39] Gerald "loved to see people enjoying themselves at his roadhouse. He treated the bands well."[40]

At Jackson Station, patrons saw genuine musicians practicing their craft. That the club could attract such exceptional talent was one reason why it was such a special place. This made Jackson Station an attractive place not simply

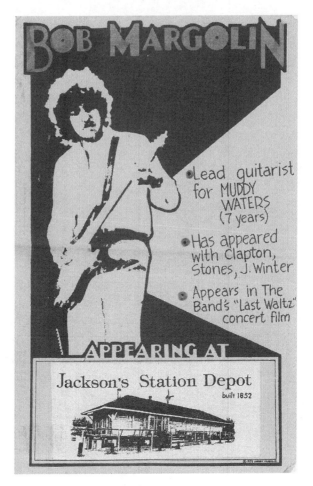

Bob Margolin Jackson Station flyer, ca. 1986.

for college students, "good old country guys, redneck guys,"[41] gays, lesbians, motorcyclists, and so on, but also for "blues aficionados" and "guitar players."[42]

"It was like the master class [of musicians]," said Greenwood musician Russ Fitzgerald, who attended Lander College from 1981 to 1983 and worked as a bartender at Jackson Station from 1985 to 1986. "That was what drew me to it . . . It was the hip place to go for the cognoscenti."[43] Fitzgerald went to Jackson Station and just "stare[d] at Bob Margolin's hands."[44] He learned everything "about how to be a Keith Richards clone from Max Drake of Arhooly."[45] Seeing these acts live and in the flesh helped him on his own musical journey.[46] It was at times a highly technical education. Fitzgerald says, "If you wanted to know the real specific differences, of say, when Fender changed such and such aspect of their construction, you had to talk to people who actually handled the instruments. You saw more of those guitars [at Jackson Station] than anywhere else."[47]

Beginning in the spring of 1982, a great many musical acts would perform at Jackson Station. When it first opened, the cover charge for shows was three dollars. The first band to play Jackson Station[48] appears to have been an act called Ex-Calibur on April 29 and April 30, 1982. Blues guitarist Drink Small made his inaugural appearance at the club on July 16, 1982. The Reverend Billy Wirtz played Jackson Station for the first time on September 17, 1982. He estimates he played close to fifty shows at Jackson Station, including gigs with Bob Margolin and Nappy Brown. Most of his shows there were between 1982 and 1984. Wirtz had learned many of his chops apprenticing with Chicago blues pianist Sunnyland Slim and said he considers Nappy Brown to be "one of [his] heroes."[49] Wirtz says he did a "wild piano act at the time," satirizing Southern gospel preachers. "Right around that time was when the PTL scandals were going on," Wirtz said. From his perspective, Jackson Station in the early 1980s was "fueled by a lot of alcohol and a fair amount of Bolivian marching powder."[50]

In an odd coincidence, Greenwood's very own gospel preacher, Leroy Jenkins[51] (1934–2017), the notorious faith healer and convicted felon had himself spent some time at Jackson Station just a few years before. Indeed, the club got a mention at Leroy Jenkins's 1979 trial where he was found guilty of conspiring to burn down the home of South Carolina patrolman C. R. Keasler, who had arrested Jenkins's daughter. During the trial, the solicitor, William T. Jones III,[52] mentioned Jenkins time as Jackson Station as an example of how the preacher presented "one front as minister during the daytime and another image when he was out at night." Reporter Leslie Brooks captured the moment in the courtroom: "At one point when Jones was portraying Jenkins as a hypocrite for his patronizing of Jackson Station, a bar in Hodges. Jenkins retorted that the second time he visited Jackson Station he met the solicitor's son Townes. After Jenkins' response, a group of spectators burst into applause."[53]

After getting some initial success with acts such as Drink Small and the Reverend Billy Wirtz, Gerald began booking bigger bands, especially those with a regional appeal. Athens-based band Love Tractor played Jackson Station three times between 1982 and 1984.[54] Love Tractor was another branch in the expansive family tree of innovative Georgia bands in the 1980s. As bassist

Armistead Wellford says, "I think of us as [Widespread] Panic's Uncles, and R.E.M.'s siblings."[55]

"The B-52s opened up the doors for us," Wellford comments. "The idea was to be able to play New York and be a worldly band." However, outside of Athens and Atlanta, there were not many places for New Wave bands to play in the area. Jackson Station provided an opportunity. "We wanted to get out there, so we gave it a shot."[56] Hearing about the club from their booking manager Paul Nelson (who had booked the B-52s' first gig at the Last Resort in Athens in 1978), Love Tractor made the eighty mile journey on two-lane country roads from Athens to Hodges.

"It seemed like an old blues club from Mississippi or something," says Wellford. "A juke-joint feeling."[57]

Love Tractor guitarist Mark Cline joked that, after arriving at Jackson Station, "my first impression was [whether] this [was] one of those places where there is a cage in front of the stage so you are not pelted with beer bottles."[58] He was was pleasantly surprised this was not the case. Cline found it memorable that Jackson Station "was this outpost for locals, for frat boys, girls, for gay people." He said, "There was an inclusiveness about the place that was very interesting."

Wellford said that playing at Jackson Station was a humbling experience. During the band's first gig there, he was puzzled to see people playing pool instead of listening to their music. "When we would finish one our songs, you'd hear the pool ball go CRACK! Because no one was really clapping. Not that they didn't like us. But they were coming to the club anyway. They weren't coming to see us. Nobody knew who we were to begin with." Wellford said, "You always want people to think, 'Oh, you guys were great,' and all of that. But we didn't get that feedback from the people playing pool."

The cool reception at Jackson Station was different from how audiences reacted to Love Tractor in other places. Wellford comments: "It was an important little learning process for us. Because the whole thing was new. We had played New York, [and had] got written up in the *New York Rocker*. We had played DC. But we still couldn't get too cocky because we had Jackson Station to conquer." Wellford said, "I didn't feel like we were hated. I just felt like we didn't destroy them with our power. And we did have a power, but it was a different kind."

Wellford remembers, "The crack of pool balls sounded after several of our songs the first night. On our return trips I think we earned some applause."[59]

Jeff Calder and J. E. Garnett of the Swimming Pool Qs, ca. 1983.

The Greenville, South Carolina, band Moon Pie (later named the Accelerators after a change of membership and a move to Raleigh, North Carolina) also played Jackson Station in the fall of 1982.[60] Another band that played Jackson Station early and often was the Atlanta-based Indy band Swimming Pool Qs, who at the time were just hitting their stride. By the time they played Jackson Station, the Swimming Pool Qs had already shared the stage with Devo, the B-52s, and the Police. They had played CBGB in New York. Creatively, they were considered on a par with other Southern rock groups like R.E.M. By 1984, they were opening for Lou Reed. In 1987, the *Washington Post* referred to them as "the best of the Southeast's new-wave bands."[61]

The Swimming Pool Qs were very popular in the Columbia, South Carolina, area, and before long, word spread to Hodges. Lead singer Jeff Calder said he received a phone call from Gerald Jackson one day, asking them to play there. Gerald told Calder he had heard of the band and "wanted to do something different" at the depot. Calder said, "He was pitching Jackson Station to us, and it sounded so unusual that we said, 'What the hell?'"[62]

Like other musicians, Jeff Calder was awestruck by the club. Jackson Station "was an adventure," Calder said. It was a "very peculiar, eccentric place."[63] Jack McConnell, Erskine College alumnus and former Jackson Station bartender, suggests that the Swimming Pool Qs song "Stick in My Hand" is particularly apropos to Jackson Station. He suggests the song is an allegory about the identity of the club as a whole.

The song is about a Moses-type figure commanded by God to travel from Cincinnati, Ohio, to Jackson, Mississippi, to interrupt a football game. The key lyric in the song—which was devoured by patrons at Jackson Station—was: "Goin' back to Jackson's with a stick in my hand . . . !" According to Calder, who wrote the song "Stick in my Hand," was an "elaborate song that had [quasi-melodic] aspects to it." Like the band's breakout single, "Rat Bait," Calder said, "[P]eople remembered it."[64]

Calder said, "One of my fondest recollections of going to Jackson Station, [was when] they put us in a back room. So we're in the dressing room and under the cot, one of the first things we noticed was a copy of a gay pulp paperback called *Dockboy* [*laughing*]. And we knew, when we saw that, we knew were in the right place. This is our kind of joint!"[65]

Unlike bands that played Jackson Station out of necessity when they were on the road traveling to somewhere else, the Swimming Pool Qs were deliberate in seeking out music venues. Calder said, "One of the things that didn't frighten us about Jackson Station before we got there . . . was that we were used to confronting and having to charm audiences that would normally have been hostile to the kind of band we were." He continued, "We were a brave little band at that point. We kind of knew how to do it. To disarm hostility. Not that there was at Jackson Station. There certainly wasn't. But when you walked in the door in the afternoon, you didn't really know what was going to be in front of you. You didn't really know what it was going to be. That audience was an all embracing audience."

The Swimming Pool Qs would be followed by jam band Widespread Panic, who played nine shows at Jackson Station between 1987 and 1989 (and are still very popular today). David Truly speaks of the connectivity of musicians on the road. He says they are constantly swapping information about gigs, saying: "'Hey this is a cool place to go,' or 'This is a great club for this,' or 'bad for that.'"[66] In such a manner, word spread about Jackson Station through the networks of the musicians who played there. Widespread Panic had first learned about the club from Tinsley Ellis, who himself had been clued in by the Georgia Satellites. "Gerald was very appreciative that I brought [Widespread Panic] there," Tinsley Ellis muses. "It was kind of a feather in my cap."[67]

For those readers who may not know much about them, Widespread Panic (1986–) is one of the most successful "jam bands" of all time. They have a status in musical circles today that was occupied by the Grateful Dead a generation (or more) ago. From their relatively humble beginning in Athens, Georgia, the band has since morphed into a global phenomenon with a gigantic fan base. Fascinatingly, Jackson Station played a small, yet decisive, role in their career. Without a doubt, Widespread Panic is the most famous band to ever take the stage at Jackson Station.

As Dave Schools recounts, "Tinsley put us in touch with a lot of people that meant a lot to us back in those days. And Gerald is definitely one of them. Michael Rothschild from Landslide Records is one of them. Colonel Bruce Hampton is one of them. But yeah, Tinsley, he's a big part of our humble beginnings. He really helped us out a lot."[68]

Widespread Panic can be seen as a reaction to the New Wave, or progressive rock, movement of the early 1980s (with drum machines, synthesizers, and so on). Founded in Athens, Georgia, Widespread Panic followed in the wake of acts such as the Allman Brothers and Lynyrd Skynyrd. Their jamming style—involving two drum sets, rhythm and lead guitars, keyboards, and throbbing bass—first got the attention of fraternity brothers at parties at the University of Georgia before spilling beyond Athens and taking the South (and then the rest of the country) by storm.[69] Widespread Panic, together now for thirty-five years, has become a band with world historical significance. The band has "huge, superstardom fame," notes Tinsley Ellis. They have played "Philips Arena, Madison Square Garden, [and] Red Rocks." It is somewhat amazing to discover that Jackson Station was integral to their development.

Music producer Michael Rothschild, who released Widespread Panic's first studio album *Space Wrangler* in 1988 on Landslide Records, was first introduced to the group through Tinsley Ellis. In February 1987—two months before Widespread Panic played their first gig at Jackson Station—Rothschild accompanied Ellis to see the band play at the Harvest Moon Saloon in northeast Atlanta. It was one of their first gigs outside of Athens. "I'll never forget just how crowded it was, because it had never been that way before," Rothschild remembers. "It was a whole different audience. I really got a kick out of the show and we became good friends."[70]

Widespread Panic (often referred to simply as 'Panic') is known for their dark, energetic shows and funky covers of classic rock tunes. Dave Schools said the band's early music comprised "the song book of the Seventies FM radio thing. We could do your 'Brown Eyed Girl,' Grateful Dead, Steve Winwood, Traffic . . . Stuff we all liked when we were learning how to play."[71]

Rothschild says Panic was interesting musically in that "they had a real knack for adding their own thing to versions of songs by the Grateful Dead and other sixties and seventies rock acts." Rothschild, impressed by "the way they delivered their songs," also thought that "lead singer John Bell was very charismatic." Rothschild says, "I loved the way all of them played, especially Dave Schools. It was just really fun seeing them."[72]

Widespread Panic music fans—known as "Spreadheads"—are made up of men and women across the social spectrum. As a subculture, there are family resemblances to fans of the Grateful Dead (i.e., Deadheads), but with perhaps an even more libertarian, or individualistic streak to them. Think Metallica meets Phish. Widespread Panic fan clothing is more monochromatic than it is psychedelic, and the meaning of Widespread Panic songs are often morally ambiguous. The grooving bass lines, kicking drum sections, and electric guitar pyrotechnics (which was initially the province of lead guitarist Michael Houser but are now subbed out to a rotating cast of lead guitar virtuosos) makes Widespread Panic a sonic tour de force. According to Widespread Panic's website: "Widespread Panic has broken attendance records across the country, including a staggering 60 consecutive sell-outs at legendary Red Rocks Amphitheatre, 18 sell outs at State Farm Arena in Atlanta, additional records in the UNO Lakefront Arena in New Orleans, Birmingham's Oak Mountain Amphitheater, New Orleans Jazzfest and The Fox Theatre in Atlanta. Panic has headlined most of the major U.S. festivals including Bonnaroo (eight times), Lollapalooza, ACL Festival, LOCKN', Outside Lands, Forecastle to name just a few."[73]

As with other jam bands such as the Grateful Dead and Phish, there is an important emphasis on community within the Widespread Panic subculture. It is not uncommon for fans to try go to as many shows as possible (the number of which is taken as a measure of dedication to the band), especially the so-called "pilgrimage shows"—where fans come from all over the world to gather—which creates bonds with the band and the music (as well as other fans) that can endure for decades. Such values are encouraged by the band itself. Dave Schools refers to the "communal ritual thing going on" for Widespread Panic fans. He said this involves "possible travel, the whole wanderlust thing, the whole *On the Road* thing, and the whole group celebration thing." Another notable characteristic of Widespread Panic is that they never play

Widespread Panic, ca. 1988.

the same show twice (i.e., the set lists are never the same), which makes their concerts much more interesting for the listener, because the audience never knows what to expect.

"They were definitely a throwback," says Michael Rothschild. "And their audience was dressed in tie-dyes and dancing and twirling and so forth." To him, it was reminiscent of being in New York in the 1960s and 1970s and seeing shows in Central Park or at the Fillmore East.

Though history has ultimately been kind to Widespread Panic, it was not easy for the band to initially find traction in the music scene. Dave Schools remarks that the band's connection with Athens, Georgia, often tainted audience perceptions of them.[74] The main kind of music in Athens at the time was "very closely linked to the B-52s and R.E.M., modern college rock," Schools said. "We weren't really doing that, but people expected it when they heard where we came from." Schools also said that in the beginning, audiences would be confused by the band's name. "'Widespread Panic' "sounded a little, almost punky, sort of violent or disruptive or something. And while some of our improv sessions could become that way, we weren't doing straight edge or hardcore or anything. So there was somewhat of an identity crisis until we grew into our name."

"We were kids; we were having fun," Schools reflects, referring to their nine shows at Jackson Station. "What a great place to have fun." Schools said that playing Jackson Station helped create the essence for what Widespread Panic shows would later be known. In a way, he said, Jackson Station was to Widespread Panic what the Cavern Club (in Liverpool, England) was to the Beatles. It was where each band found themselves.

"Definitely," Schools says, referring to the comparison. "We found ourselves because it was a really, sort of schizophrenic vibe there. And by schizophrenic I mean that, if we are going to use the Cavern Club Beatles analogy, [the Beatles] were honing their chops because [the Beatles] were playing to people who really didn't give a shit. So they had to, like, keep the attention of those people, and [the Beatles] learned a lot about being entertainers and performing in the Cavern Club."[75] Similarly, Schools said, at Jackson Station, most of the people they played for late night at Jackson Station were just "there for the drinks."

Jackson Station was a mesmerizing experience for Widespread Panic. Schools said, "We'd play to our fans, who'd show up first, and we could get away with anything, and the place was relatively empty. And then all the other clubs would stop serving at around one thirty or two in the morning. Jackson Station would become packed to the gills with people from all walks of life, who were there because they could keep the party rolling. And so at that point, our job became to keep the party rolling." Unlike other gigs where the band might play more conventional songs during their first set and then could "cut loose a little bit" later in the show, at Jackson Station it was the reverse. Widespread Panic had "a lot freedom early in the show before that milieu would roll in." As the night wore on, they faced more "constrictions" because they were playing to a crowd that did not know their material. This forced the band to work harder. "We learned a whole lot," said Schools. "We were learning how to be a band. We were writing a lot of original music. We were concentrating at that point most strongly on writing what became our batch of classic material, which was pretty angular and bizarre and unique to us."

While there are no direct references to Jackson Station in any Widespread Panic song, the club indirectly influenced the content of their music. "There were things that were present in Jackson Station in spades that were staples in certain bars we played," Schools said. "And pinball machines are one of them." He remembers that Jackson Station "had a stunning array of pinball machines." Schools notes the reference to pinball in the Widespread Panic song "'Dreamers and Barstools,' which, while not specifically about Jackson Station . . . epitomized what John Bell was writing about. Which is the kind of place where you know people, and you can play games, and you can have conversations, you can watch people forget that they are being watched on the dance floor and really cut loose. There's a lot that kind of imagery, because that was our life at the time. And [John Bell] liked to write from experience. And our experience was logging a lot of gigs on the road. A lot."[76]

"What was always interesting about Widespread Panic," recalled Greenwood local Reggie Massey, "was their followers from Athens. They would follow them up here. All these real young kids. All dressed like hippies, like we used to dress. But they would be driving up in BMWs and sports cars and stuff. Everyone was welcome."[77] When Panic would play the depot, Tinsley Ellis said, "They brought hundreds of people over from Athens and took over the place with tie-dyed T-shirts."[78] Dave Schools said, "It didn't take too long for our fans from Atlanta, and Greenville, and Athens to catch wind that there was something special happening at this joint. And so they came. It was like a road trip for them."[79] Dirk Armstrong remembers that the Widespread Panic fans would "show up and unplug the clock to plug in their hot pot to make hot apple cider." Camping tents would be set up around the property. Armstrong says the whole experience, "was just very interesting."[80]

While Dave Schools has very fond memories playing Jackson Station, the shows could also be quite stochastic. For example, Schools says, "people would stumble in" to the club and start yelling obnoxious song requests. "'Play some R.E.M.! You're from Athens ain't ya?!'" they would shout. "Or 'Rock Lobster'!! Or "What's this hippy music I hear?! Play some blues goddammit!'"[81] Invariably at some point during the night, someone in the crowd would want to get up onstage and play along with the band.[82] This would lead to some hilarious encounters. As Schools remembers: "What inevitably would happen was: someone would hear us play a 'Brown-Eyed Girl,' type cover, and then they'd want to sit in on harmonica . . . And it was never the person who wanted to sit in doing the asking, it was more like someone from this person's band." Schools recalled a particular story about:

> a woman who was a blues singer and had just gotten off of her gig at the Holiday Inn shag carpet lounge in the next county over. And her harmonica player would be the guy going, *"You need to let her sing. She sings blues real good."* And we'd be like, *"Uh . . . You know . . . We don't understand. We don't do that."* The guy would, he'd be relentless. He'd be like, *"No man, she sings Stormy Monday great!"* And we're like, *"We don't know it. We don't know Stormy Monday."* He's like, *"What*

kind of Southern band doesn't know Stormy Monday?!" Blah, blah, blah. I'm like, *"We don't know it! What more can I tell you?"* And so then, having forgotten about stumping for his singer, he's like, *"Just play anything. What key you got?"* So we let him sit in on a Grateful Dead song called "Sugaree," and embarrassingly for him (or maybe us) he could not navigate the chord changes on his harmonica.[83]

Schools says this sort of thing used to happen with uncanny regularity at Jackson Station. People would just "come out of the audience and want to join the band. I mean, we like a welcoming atmosphere as much as anybody, but sometimes they were pushy and they just didn't get that we might not know these (standard blues band) type tunes."[84]

Greenwood musician Clayton Sprouse claims that the set list for a particular Widespread Panic show—4/1/88—at Jackson Station is legendary in band aficionado circles. Here is what Widespread Panic played at the depot that night:

SET 1: "Don't Be Denied," "And It Stoned Me," "Fire on the Mountain > She Caught The Katy," "Ophelia," "Space Wrangler," "Dirty Business," "Walk On," "I Know You Rider"

SET 2: "Pigeons," "Me and My Uncle > Travelin' Light," "The Last Straw," "Dear Mr. Fantasy," "Holden Oversoul > Stop-Go > Let It Rock > Sugaree"

SET 3: "Feelin' Alright," "C. Brown," "Good Morning Little Schoolgirl," "Astronomy Domine," "Jam > Chilly Water," "L.A.," "Wish You Were Here," "Down On The Farm," "Barstools and Dreamers," "Werewolves of London"

SET 4: "Genesis," "Cryptical Envelopment > The Other One > Cryptical Envelopment > Contentment Blues > Sympathy for the Devil > Knockin' On Heaven's Door," "Knocking 'Round The Zoo"

"Are you aware of the show that they did on April 1, 1988, and, like, the mystique behind that?" Sprouse asked the author. Sprouse is a huge Widespread Panic fan and has seen the band play over eighty times. An amateur musician, in 2014 he formed a band, Jackson Station, named after the Hodges nightclub.

Sprouse argues that "4/1/88, Widespread Panic at Hodges, is considered by many Panic fans to be the greatest show on paper. Ever." However, he said, "There is no recording. It's like the one show that . . . there's nothing. Nothing. There's Panic fans that are like, *'Did this show even happen? Is it real?'*"[85]

Sprouse explained, "What makes it crazy is that it's four sets. And so, you have to think, they were there for . . . they played, like, a six-hour show, or something? I don't know." Sprouse said the 4/1/88 show is the "Holy Grail" of Panic bootlegs. "Where is this recording?" he demanded. "Nobody has it."

Sprouse is not the only Widespread Panic fan enamored by this particular concert. In January 2020, at the request of the author, Sprouse asked members of the "Widespread Panic Family" page on Facebook to chime in with thoughts about the show. One member, DP Swint, comments: "There have been many discussions about this show over the years. No recording has ever surfaced and I do not believe one ever will. If you look at the other shows played at this venue then you will see more four set shows as well. This was not an April fool's joke. Just another early show with no recording."

Another fan, Adam Smith, chimed in: "Damn, that was a monster! Four full sets? . . . Hmmm . . . Highly unusual. And why there?? Very interesting. Would love to have a listen to that one." David Wilson exclaims, "That's insane?!? Four set dream show. WOW." Another listener, Hayes Brown, said he once asked Dave Schools about Jackson Station when he saw him play at the 2011 Tunes for Tots fundraiser on the rooftop at Georgia Theatre. "Tell me about Jackson Station and why was it the only place that y'all ever played five sets?"[86] Brown said he asked Schools. Brown said Schools told him Jackson Station "was a roadhouse that was open all night long. He said the owner asked them to keep playing until he told them to stop, which only happened when the sun was coming up and the place was mostly cleared out."[87]

While Widespread Panic was arguably the most famous band to play Jackson Station, they were just one of many hugely talented musical acts to perform at the club over the years (see Appendix). Another band that was also highly popular at Jackson Station was the Sensible Pumps.[88] This all-female blues band was a staple at the club in the mid-to-late eighties. Formed in Charleston, South Carolina, by guitarist Mattie Phifer in 1985, members of the band tried to make a go of it as professional musicians. They quit their jobs, bought a motor home, and moved to Whitmire, South Carolina, about fifty miles east of Jackson Station.

"The rent was a lot cheaper up here,"[89] joked Phifer. She said the Pumps' first show at Jackson Station was in early 1986. The band played the club about "once a month or once every six weeks" over the next four years. Phifer says, "It was a regular place for us."

"We were somewhat of a novelty," noted Pumps keyboardist Catherine Brickley. "But people got to see that we weren't just a novelty. That we really could play."[90] In some ways, the Sensible Pumps took blues music back to its roots. After all, music listeners have female blues artists such as Mamie Smith (1891–1946), Bessie Smith (1894–1837), Clara Smith (1894–1935), and Elizabeth Cotton (1895–1987) to thank for bringing blues music into the collective consciousness.[91] Phifer and her band "were taking mostly old classic blues and putting our spin on them. We had the big hair, and Lycra tights, and too much make-up. It was quite a sight to see."[92]

Brickley said touring was often difficult for the band because "[w]e always had to prove ourselves. There weren't any other women out there doing that. There weren't any women groups and they certainly weren't playing R & B."[93] The Pumps festooned their gigs with various shoe motifs. "We kind of did a take on shoes," said Phifer. "Our bass player always had on high heels with fishnet stockings and did the Nancy Wilson[94] kicks. I wore high-top tennis shoes. We'd put a little décor on the stage, shoes and things, just to jazz it up a bit."[95]

Jackson Station was "a good place to be" says fellow South Carolinian Freddie Vanderford, a blues harmonica player from Union County, South Carolina. With his band The Shades, Vanderford was another frequent act at Jackson Station. As a teenager, Vanderford had honed his harmonica skills from famed harpist Peg Leg Sam (1911–1977). Vanderford was 16 when he met the blues player. Peg Leg "let me hang out with him," Vanderford says. "He had one leg, and I had access to a car sometimes. It worked out for us. We became friends." Freddie took Peg Leg to "liquor houses, card games, [and] moonshine places." Hanging out with Peg Leg Sam made Vanderford grow up real fast. "I'm a teenager and these guys are in their sixties," he recalls, "and they were passing that bottle around." He and Peg Leg would alternate playing songs for the group. "He'd play a little bit, and then ask me to play." Vanderford thought he knew something about playing harmonica before he met Peg. In fact, he "didn't know nothing. I learned a lot from him, I can tell you that."[96]

Another prominent musician who played regularly at Jackson Station was Atlanta-based guitarist Glenn Phillips. He said Jackson Station was "a grueling gig" and one that was "unlike any other place I played."[97] Phillips said Jackson Station was tough because "you didn't start playing until really late."[98] Phillips normally played two sets at Jackson Station. The first set started about 11:30 p.m. or midnight, and the second set began at 2:00 or 3:00 a.m. Like many other musicians, he would often still be playing music at sunrise.

Jackson Station bartender Dirk Armstrong recalls how, on one occasion, Widespread Panic's manager "was freaking out because they were still playing at six in the morning and they had a gig in Myrtle Beach that night."[99] In a memory of what may be the same incident, Schools said, "I literally remember one morning, there was only one guy left, and they were still serving him. The sun was up, and we were loading out. We put the last piece of gear in the van and closed the door. And that's when they decided it was time for this fellow to quit drinking because the band packed up."[100]

Glenn Phillips says packing up the band gear at the end of the night could be especially onerous. "Loading out of that place was intense," he said. Jackson Station was often still jammed with people at 4:00 in the morning. "People were packed in there like sardines." Phillips would wonder, "Where are all these people coming from?"[101] Invariably, instrument cases, speaker cabinets, and other band equipment would have to be "pushed into people" just so the musicians could leave the premises. Phillips said, "If you got out of there by 5:00 in the morning, you'd be doing pretty good."

"Everybody was really plastered, one way or the other, by that time of the morning," remembers Susan Cree, bass player for the Sensible Pumps. "So you had to fend them off, as well as load."[102] Catherine Brickley still has vivid memories of, "driving out of Jackson Station at six o'clock in the morning. The sun is up and your head is buzzing from the music all night long."[103]

Some bands, such as Widespread Panic, that played Jackson Station would go on to be highly successful. Independent music fans might appreciate knowing that Athens-based musician Andrew Rieger of the band Elf Power (1994–present) played his first real gig (outside of high school parties) at Jackson Station. At the time Rieger was performing with his grunge band Grubworm (1988–1990). In the spring of 1990, Grubworm opened for the Killbillys, a punk/bluegrass outfit from Athens, Georgia. Rieger says the gig at Jackson Station was "exciting for us" since it was the "first time playing in a real club." He says the venue had a "homey kind of feel to it," like you were "just hanging out."[104] As Dave Schools—a friend and admirer of Rieger and Elf Power—comments: "See. That's how you get a musical genius like Andrew. You throw [']em to the wolves at Jackson Station right off that bat. Sink or swim kid. Or find the rainbow."

Jeff Calder of the Swimming Pool Qs has seen a tremendous array of music venues in his forty years as a musician. Some of his most memorable experiences were playing at Jackson Station. "We played in some weird fucking places," said Calder. However, Jackson Station was "the most unique place. No question about it." He said that Gerald "knew about us. They knew about all the groups then emerging in the South." As was the case with many other bands, Jackson Station would play an important role in their career. "For us, that is how we found ourselves as a group," Calder said. "We'd go to all these places nobody in their right mind would go. Hodges, South Carolina? What the fuck?"[105]

SEVEN

LIVING THE GOOD LIFE

I was having a high time, living the good life, well I know
The wheels are muddy, got a ton of hay,
Now listen here, Baby, 'cause I mean what I say.
    —The Grateful Dead[1]

Jackson Station was in the middle of nowhere but on the way to everywhere. Like other rural parts of the Palmetto State, Hodges, South Carolina, is a hardscrabble place of "farm country, clapboard houses, trailer homes, hulks of cars lifted on cement blocks surrounded by high weeds, and tiny churches."[2] Yet from Hodges, you could be in Asheville, North Carolina; Augusta, Georgia; Athens, Georgia; Greenville, South Carolina; Columbia, South Carolina; or Charlotte, North Carolina, all in two hours or less and vice versa.

Greenwood County has always had proud people, in all stations of life, where extreme wealth stands side by side with abject poverty. Whether one is native to the area matters deeply. Outsiders rarely enjoy full acceptance. Even those who have lived in the area for thirty or forty years will not be fully embraced by the locals. South Carolina is still paying the price for the Civil War. Centuries of bleak poverty and institutional racism have hardened the collective conscience for many of its people. Greenwood embodies a culture where religion has historically been not so much a choice, but a necessity. Churches became people's second homes because their original family lives were often filled with so much heartbreak and tragedy. Until recently, South Carolina's Blue Laws dictated the rhythms of the community. Before the laws were changed just a few years back, the Greenwood Wal-Mart actually had a long yellow rope across the store on Sunday mornings. This was to stop customers from purchasing ostensibly inessential goods until after they had gone church. Yet the proscribed items were totally arbitrary with dubious religious justification. For example, cigarettes, diet soda, and fireworks were permitted.

Light bulbs, frying pans, and underwear were not. Thankfully, such sanctimonious absurdity (which was phased out when local leaders finally realized the policy was decidedly anti-business in orientation) no longer exists. However, liquor sales still end at 7:00 p.m. six days a week. Schoolchildren are off for more than a week during Easter Break. People are not embarrassed to ask what church you belong to, and if you say that you do not attend any church, they will happily invite you to theirs. Certainly, there are vibrant pockets of progressive liberalism in Greenwood, just as there are in places like Athens and Asheville. Nevertheless, much of social life in Greenwood—historically at least—has been dictated (directly or indirectly) by tribal, churchly relationships. Ironically, these relations are also quite splintered, as the sheer quantity of different churches in Greenwood attests.

The community also splits in relation to allegiance to college (and to a lesser extent professional) football teams. Greenwood County is roughly equidistant between the state's two flagship institutions, both with nationally recognized football programs: Clemson University and the University of South Carolina. Locals take whether you are a Gamecock, a Tiger, a Bulldog, a Seminole, a Gator, and so on quite seriously. College football games dominate the lives of many on Saturday and Sunday afternoons in the fall. People celebrate such events with plenty of food and beer. Despite whatever ideological differences that may exist, most Southerners still agree on the importance of eating and drinking.

The greater Greenwood area has considerably history to it. John C. Calhoun, seventh vice president of the United States, was born fifteen miles to the east of Jackson Station, in Abbeville, South Carolina. Benjamin E. Mays (1894–1984), mentor to Martin Luther King Jr.,[3] perhaps Greenwood County's most distinguished son (though he would despise Greenwood for most of his life), was born at the Southern end of the county, in Epworth. The institutionalized discrimination that Mays experienced as a boy propelled him to flee Greenwood County for the North, first to Bates College in Maine and then the University of Chicago. Later Benjamin Mays would become advisor to three U.S. presidents: John Kennedy, Lyndon Johnson, and Jimmy Carter. Serving for twenty-seven years as the president of Morehouse College in Atlanta, Mays would spend his life decrying the sort racism found in the place of his birth. He was especially critical of segregationist Christianity, which Mays argued could not be found in any Gospel.

Civil rights were slow to come to South Carolina, but as Jim Crow segregation slowly faded away, a more insidious, hidden racism arose. While the textile mills of South Carolina once provided decent employment for people of all races, the globalized world and the shift to a postindustrial, service-based economy made it harder for African Americans to find decent work. There was a Great Migration to the north in the early decades of the twentieth century, as many Black folks abandoned the South for the promise of a better life up north. The ones who remained had to face a persistent culture of latent white supremacy.

Today, injustices of race intertwine and reverberate with gender and class inequalities, which continue to be evident, particularly in area schools, which are among the worst in the nation.[4] Despite the presence of a state-supported liberal arts college (Lander University) and a thriving community college (Piedmont Technical), deep pockets of a know-nothing nativism and xenophobia in Greenwood County that would be considered repugnant elsewhere remain. Such an unashamedly ethnocentric ethos can make life particularly difficult for members of minority groups, not just racial or ethnic minorities, but also gays and lesbians, whose very existence still seems to offend many in the area. Even today, for example, some residents (oddly enough, members of the local clergy) in the greater Greenwood area are fretting about the social impact that drag shows might have on the community.[5]

Historically, gays and lesbians have not been recognized by the conservative, patriarchal culture of the South. It was not so much that Southern folk expressed direct antagonism toward gays and lesbians—though surely, there was plenty of that, too—it was more a matter of simply pretending that they did not exist. As long as sexual minorities did not do anything to proclaim their identity—by "coming out of the closet" or expressing romantic affection publicly—then everything would seem to be fine. The Southern penchant for "keeping up appearances" applies to norms of compulsory heterosexuality as much as, say, apparent financial status. For example, Steve Bryant's mother, Hazel Bryant, said her son "never said" he was gay. She says Steve told her that "he was either/or." Most of the time, though, her son's sexuality was "never mentioned"[6] in the family. "Nobody much knew about that," she said. People just "didn't talk about it."[7] The various historical, geographical, and cultural realities of the greater Greenwood area make for the emergence of a place like Jackson Station in Hodges, South Carolina, rather anomalous. Part of the job of a sociologist is to explain why things happen. Just how did Jackson Station become such an integral part of the Greenwood community?

Jackson Station satisfied at least four significant—and overlapping— social needs for the Greenwood community. First, it offered revelry (with music, food, and libations) and celebration for an incredibly diverse group of people. Second, it provided a safe space for women, gays, lesbians, and supportive (and/or "questioning") others. Third—and despite the owners' best intentions—it was a site for the experimentation of proscribed substances. Finally, Jackson Station facilitated the creation of romantic, and even occasionally sexual, relationships.

Let us consider the celebratory aspect of Jackson Station first. Jackson Station filled a niche as the area's only blues venue and late-night music club. Jackson Station "wasn't a listening room," said Sensible Pumps guitarist Mattie Phifer. "It was a party room. It was dancing and getting down." Part of the attraction of the club lay in its operating hours. Jackson Station was the only late-night place around. It was open from 5:00 p.m. to 5:00 a.m., Mondays through Thursdays.[8] On Friday, it was open from "7 pm until you are ready to go home."[9] On Saturday, due to state Blue Laws that prohibited the sale of alcohol on Sundays, Jackson Station shut down at midnight.

Jackson Station was arguably at its best at about 3:00 or 4:00 on a Saturday morning. The early hours of the day take on a surreal hue. The mood gets wild and funky in the predawn light. Some people look more attractive; others become quite grotesque. In eschewing sleep for the sake of the party, Jackson Station exemplified the core of rock 'n' roll sensibility. Staying up all night as a form of youthful rebellion has been a theme in rock music songs going back at least as far as "Rock Around the Clock" by Bill Haley & His Comets in 1954. More than twenty years later in "Anything That's Rock-n-Roll" (1976), Tom Petty told the story of staying up with his friends "all through the night":

> Some friends of mine and me stayed up all through the night
> Rockin' pretty steady 'til the sky went light
> And didn't go to bed
> Didn't go to work
> I picked up the telephone
> Told the boss he was a jerk

Another example (among many others one might choose from) might be the Grateful Dead's "Friend of the Devil" (1970):

> I set out running but I'll take my time
> A friend of the Devil is a friend of mine
> If I get home before daylight
> I just might get some sleep tonight.

It is likely Jackson Station regulars could identify with such sentiments. People in the place celebrated life that was up and awake in the early hours of the morning, and they happily flipped the bird at straight society, most of whom were fast asleep.

During the week, Jackson Station was a lowkey watering hole, the kind of place to take out-of-town guests to appreciate the indigenous culture of the South Carolina countryside. One might find local musicians like Buzzy Boles, Bruce Cobb, and Jimmy Campbell picking bluegrass on the back deck.[10] Children of close friends to Gerald and Steve, like the Masseys and the Colemans,[11] would tag along to Jackson Station with their parents. Gerald and Steve treated the children as their own, letting them hang out in the kitchen or outside with the cows.[12]

Seemingly parochial yet in fact quite cosmopolitan, Jackson Station was the closest thing to civilization one could get in Greenwood. Bartender Will Holloway said, "Jackson Station was where I learned all my manners."[13] Happy Hour would last a solid four hours (from 5:00 to 9:00, on weekdays). Jackson Station advertised a large and impressive selection of beer and wine, and later on, mixed drinks. Gerald "introduced imported beers to Greenwood at a time when Heineken was about the only one anyone knew about," says David Goldman.[14] Guinness Draught was available by the pint.[15] Landslide Records president Michael Rothschild remembers that Jackson Station "had one of the greatest beer lists that I had ever seen."[16] The liquor came later, and with it the hamburgers. "We had to fortify our menu" to comply with state law, said Dirk Armstrong. "When we got liquor, that's when we started doing hamburgers. We'd also do steak night occasionally."[17]

People came to Jackson Station during the week to enjoy a drink, shoot pool, or play a game of pinball. Here is a snapshot of life inside Jackson Station from 1983: "Two young men shoot a game of bumper pool sipping beer from goose-neck bottles. Their spirits are high. Another trips over a log stool sitting in the middle of the floor, laughs, says something jokingly to [Gerald] Jackson."[18]

"There was an old nickel-a-play pinball machine," recalls Lee Rush. "It was so old it didn't even have flippers on it. You just pulled back the spring and watched where the ball went."[19]

Dave Schools of Widespread Panic also remembers the pinball machines. He said, "We liked to play pinball, we liked to play pool. And I remember they had that, just horribly named machine, I think it was called, 'Space Shuttle' pinball machine, and of course this was a year or two right after the

Challenger disaster. It was just so creepy to play the pinball machine and your ball goes down the tubes and you hear this astronaut voice go 'Aggh!' It was like 'Oh my God, this is so weird!'"[20]

All successful parties must—at some level—be catered affairs, and Jackson Station was no exception. Alcohol without food is a deadly combination, and if there is one thing Southerners have in common is that they like to eat. Jackson Station was renowned for its late-night cuisine, offering some of the area's best chili hot dogs, grilled cheese sandwiches, and cheeseburgers. The chili for the hot dogs was made by Gerald himself, using a carefully guarded recipe. Gerald's chili was the stuff of legend. Dirk Armstrong said, "After enough times watching him make the chili I finally learned the secret, which I will not reveal."[21] Tommy Kidd said Jackson Station had "really great hot dogs,"[22] with "some of the best chili around." He says the key ingredient to the taste was "they put sausage in the chili."[23] The grilled cheese sandwiches were also a popular item. These were made on Roman Meal bread with local Hoop Cheese bought from Godfrey's Market. Duke's mayonnaise was spread on the inside.[24] Bartender Dirk Armstrong says he made "anywhere between four to six loaves of grilled cheese sandwiches," ahead of time "to get us set up for a Friday night." Bob Margolin was especially fond of the Jackson Station cheeseburgers, which were also a favorite of Grady "Fats" Jackson, the saxophonist from Atlanta. Brand Stille recalls that Fats Jackson would always take two cheeseburgers to go as he was heading out the door.[25]

On Friday nights, the scene at Jackson Station was appreciably different that it was during the week. Nationally recognized bands and musical artists took the stage at about 11:00 p.m. and would often still be jamming out until 4:00 a.m. or later on Saturday morning. "Everybody was there,"[26] says Will Holloway.

Partygoers would begin the evening at places like the Holiday Inn bar in Greenwood. They would then go to Starnes out near the Greenwood Civic Center,[27] before ending the night at up at Jackson Station.[28] "I never went until ten or eleven o'clock at night, because I'd always go somewhere else and beer up real good before I got there," said Bruce Cobb.[29] Gay Coleman said it was a given "the last place you ended up was Jackson Station."[30] Tommy Kidd agreed: "Everybody wound up at Jackson Station and it would be absolutely packed."

"It was amazing to me, given where it was," muses Michael Rothschild. There was "nothing around there, people seemed to be coming from all over, especially college-aged people. They would drive a couple of hours to get there, best I could tell."[31] On the big band nights, Jackson Station did indeed become quite a different place. Gerald joked that his clientele was made up of "hunters, doctors, lawyers [and] crooks."[32] He said, "People come here from all over—Atlanta, Columbia, Laurens, Abbeville. When other places start closing down, folks jump in their cars and drive over here. Things usually start hopping here around 2:30 or three in the morning."[33]

In 1988, *Southern Magazine* interviewed well-known musicians about the best music venues in the South.[34] Bluesman Tinsley Ellis nominated Jackson Station as among his favorites, calling it "the ultimate Southeast roadhouse."[35] Thirty years later, Ellis stands by this designation. "It really was," he said in a telephone interview. "To this day, I'm sure that every region of the country or state has got one that would claim that, but that was the one in our area."[36] Ellis liked Jackson Station so much that he would often go there to party after he finished his own gigs (e.g., in Athens, Georgia; or Greenville, South Carolina). "My show would get over at midnight or one," Ellis said. And "we'd go over there and just hang out with whoever was playing." He says Jackson Station "was such a hoot. We'd end up doing it over and over again."[37] On February 10, 1984, Ellis says he "did two shows in two states." At the first gig, earlier in the evening, he opened for Stevie Ray Vaughan at Tate Hall at the University of Georgia. Ellis said, "We played the show, got in the van, and drove to Jackson Station, and played from 11:00 to 4:00. It was an amazingly long night of music."[38]

People in places well beyond Greenwood County started to hear about Jackson Station and would drive miles and miles just to go there. Roland Tranter was one such pilgrim. A divorced dentist in Charleston by day, Tranter spent many Friday nights at Jackson Station throughout the 1980s. He made the three-hour drive to Hodges in his VW Rabbit. He says he would "get there around 11:00," right "when it started getting cranked up." Tranter would often party all night, "sleep an hour or two in the car, and then drive back to Charleston."[39] Tranter says he went to Jackson Station because there "was no bar like that in Charleston. There was no bar like that anywhere."[40]

Some merrymakers even brought their recreational vehicles to Jackson Station. Ware Shoals native Bruce Cobb, who once worked in the Information Technology Department at Lander College, went to Jackson Station regularly in the 1980s. He would often drive his custom-made motorhome to the bar. This was the famed "Weinerbago"—a tiny, somewhat bizarre, almost post-apocalyptic camper that looks to have been made in shop class. The Weinerbago has a storied history as a de facto party barge and mobile crash pad.

The Weinerbago, McCormick, South Carolina, September 2018.

"The way I used to advertise it, it will sleep four, fuck eight," Cobb jokes. He had a handwritten sign on the back window that read: "Don't come knocking when the Weinerbago's rocking."

Cobb bought the vehicle, which had been originally built from the wreckage of a 1966 Chevrolet Van, from a friend in Shoals Junction, South Carolina. "A mobile home manufacturer down in south Georgia just built that square body to set on top of it. It's got beds and a table and all this kind of stuff." Cobb said, "Just about every weekend, back in my bluegrass days, I was loading that thing up going to bluegrass festivals all the way from Galax, Virginia, to local ones in South Carolina, North Carolina, and Georgia. I also took it to a lot of Georgia football games."

Cobb would often fill up the Weinerbago with friends and drive it to Jackson Station.

"Go up there, stay all night,"[41] said Tommy Kidd, who worked with Cobb at Lander. "We would take the Weinerbago up to Jackson Station, park it in the parking lot. We'd get drunk and at the end of the night or morning, we'd go sleep in the trailer."[42] The Weinerbago attracted a lot of attention. "A lot of people would stop in and see what in the hell that thing was, because it's very odd," Cobb said. "Especially when you're traveling."[43]

What made Jackson Station so exceptional was the diversity of the people who went there. The crowd "was just eclectic," said Roland Tranter. "Of course, most were southern white rednecks, but there were a lot of other kind of people. There were doctors, lawyers, Indian Chiefs, I mean, gay people, straight people. It was wide open. And there were Blacks, whites, never any trouble."[44]

It is interesting to reflect on the question of race at Jackson Station. "Race was not an issue there," suggests Anita Clinton.[45] Roland Tranter said, "There weren't a lot of Blacks, but there were Blacks, especially on Fridays for the music, because of the blues." Harris Bailey offers a slightly different take. He said that often "Friday nights were rough" for Black people. "Lots of drinking, party girls, rednecks. If you were Black and did not want to get in trouble you stayed away or you were cool enough to blend in."[46] Tommy Kidd remembered there being "not many," Black folks who went to Jackson Station—unless there was a Black band playing—but the Blacks who did go "were very welcome." According to Tinsley Ellis, Jackson Station was "very unique because it was an integrated place in a part of the country and in an era where that sort of thing didn't happen out in the country much like that."[47]

The most famous African American artist to be associated with Jackson Station was rhythm and blues legend Napoleon Brown Goodson Culp—also known as Nappy Brown (1929–2008). Whereas some musical acts, such as the Swimming Pool Qs and Widespread Panic, were still developing their identity when they played at Jackson Station, Nappy Brown experienced the club late in his career. A contemporary of, and influence upon, Elvis Presley, Brown was one of the most talented R&B singers in mid-century America. Some of his hits included, "Don't Be Angry" (1955), "Night Time is the Right Time" (1957), and "Down in the Alley" (1960), all released on the acclaimed Savoy record label. "Night Time" also became a hit song for Ray Charles in 1958.

"Nappy was a huge star," says the Reverend Billy Wirtz. "He played the Apollo; he was on all the Alan Freed shows. He was huge. He was a major, major star."[48] Brown was so famous that even Elvis went to see him perform in Memphis, Tennessee. "Elvis would come and kind of check out [Nappy's] moves and stuff," says Scott Cable,[49] a blues guitarist and Nappy Brown's former producer. Music legend Little Richard once told Michael Rothschild that "back in the day of shows with multiple acts, he hated to follow Nappy because he was such a great performer."[50] Brown was an incredible vocalist,

Nappy Brown, ca. 1985.

and his singing was supported by accomplished studio musicians. Scott Cable claims, "His Savoy sides had the best bands at that time on the planet. Even today, those bands were insanely great. You know, King Curtis, you name it. The people on his sides were the cream of the crop."[51] In 1962, Nappy Brown shared the stage with a band named Billy Cox and the King Kasuals. The lineup featured a young guitarist named Jimi Hendrix.[52]

In addition to his singing, Nappy Brown was also known for his tremendous personality. According to Cable, Brown got his start in entertainment "crownin' and clownin'"[53] at family picnics in Charlotte, North Carolina. He would entertain everyone by playing his nose as a musical instrument. "Nappy was the funniest guy in the world," said Freddie Vanderford, who played with Nappy Brown at Jackson Station and went on tour with him. After experiencing tremendous popularity (though not much financial success) in the 1950s, Nappy Brown's career went dormant in the mid-1960s. Like most early R&B artists, the contractual terms under which Nappy Brown worked were tilted decidedly against the artist. Despite his relative fame, he could not make a living from his music. By the 1970s, Nappy Brown was singing gospel music and working as a janitor in a North Carolina high school. Then, in the early

1980s, his career experienced a surprising resurgence. Nappy Brown's career revival was due, in large part, to Gerald Jackson.

"He was singing gospel, all over," remembers Cora Garmany, Brown's longtime companion and *de facto* wife. Garmany was in a relationship with Nappy Brown for 33 years. She recalls meeting him for the first time [this would have been around 1975]. Garmany said, "Nappy come to my church, home church and he was singing. I fed him that day. He said[,] '*Are you married?*' I said '*No.*' He said, '*Gimme your number.*' And I met that bus in Winnsboro [SC] many nights [*laughing*]." Garmany said she met him on the bus for "six or seven months and then he moved on in," with her in Pomaria, South Carolina, a small town about an hour east of Jackson Station. Brown would spend a good chunk of the rest of his life in Pomaria. However, at the same time, Brown also had a *de jure* wife, who lived in Charlotte, North Carolina. As Scott Cable comments: "Believe it or not, Nappy had two families, two relationships going on, with Cora and with a lady named Ann in Charlotte."[54]

The actual social mechanisms responsible for resurrecting Nappy Brown's musical career in the early 1980s have been obscured until now. Vague references to Nappy Brown being "rediscovered"[55] after renewed "interest in the roots of R&B and rock ['n'] roll,"[56] pervade accounts of how Nappy Brown started performing again. In 1969, having been eclipsed by the music industry for most of the decade, Nappy Brown had released his swan song album, *Thanks for Nothing* (Elephant). In the 1970s, under the name Brother Napoleon Brown, he recorded two mesmerizing gospel albums, *Yes I Know the Man* (Jewel) and *When I Get Inside* (Savoy Jazz), where he was accompanied by four glorious backup singers known as the Southern Sisters.

Cora Garmany argues that the two individuals most responsible for Nappy Brown's pivot away from gospel music and back toward the blues were men from up north: "Teddy" and "Bobby." She says, "Teddy, come down here and got on [Nappy Brown] about going back into the blues. So when he got out there he never would come back in. He just stayed out there."[57] Garmany is referring to Teddy Roberts, a former blues guitarist, harmonica player (and later in life, an apartment Superintendent) from Norwalk, Connecticut. In the late 1970s and 1980s, Roberts was an aspiring musician, performing in a band with his partner Bobby, called Bobby White & the Cougars. Roberts says the band used to play clubs in Connecticut, New York City and Chicago. Before their act self-destructed, Roberts says the band was almost on the verge of making it.

According to Roberts, lead guitarist and bandleader Bobby White "loved Nappy"[58] Brown. Sometime in 1982 (or thereabouts), Roberts says that Bobby White reached out to the singer. He says White found contact information for a North Carolina church on the liner notes of one of Nappy Brown's gospel albums. Roberts says, "[Brown] was a hero to us. We just wanted to meet him." Bobby wrote to the church in Charlotte. When the pastor saw Nappy, he gave him the "letter that Bobby sent."[59]

In the letter, Bobby White included the phone number of Teddy Roberts's record store in Norwalk, Connecticut. One day, Teddy picked up the phone and Nappy Brown was on the line. He said Nappy "invited us to come down [to Pomaria, SC]. So me and Bobby went down. Hopped in my car and I drove down. When we got there, they treated us so good. I fell in love with the family, especially the kids." Roberts said they arrived at "five o'clock in the morning and we immediately started to play." He says they stayed in Pomaria for about a week. They played music and "recorded a shit load of songs. They were Nappy songs. Bobby played guitar, and I played harmonica."[60] On Sunday, Roberts says, "they took us to the church where they had a gospel concert. And that just blew my mind." Nappy was the soloist. "He got up and sang a couple of songs by himself, *a Capella.*"[61]

Teddy Roberts would later negotiate Nappy Brown's comeback album with Landslide Records. "I made all the phone calls, I did all the talking," Roberts said. "I set up the deal." He met with Michael Rothschild and "brought the recordings" they had made in Pomaria. "And they were good. Nappy sang really good and our playing was right on the money."[62] Yet Roberts says he "didn't get a dime," from the deal. "I didn't make any money with him."[63]

Michael Rothschild remembers listening to the tape Teddy Roberts sent him. He says Nappy's "voice was really strong." Rothschild said the recording "sparked some interest," and he reached out to his friend Fred Mendelsohn, who had produced Nappy's recordings with Savoy Records in the 1950s. "Knowing that Nappy had not had a release in several years, Fred recommended that I record him," Rothschild says.[64] "Nappy came over to Atlanta with Cora to discuss." Rothschild says he "met with Teddy in New York around that time, and we worked out a recording deal. We offered a fairly basic contract with minimal front money, and Teddy said any payments should go directly to Nappy. They were happy about the opportunity."[65]

Landslide Records had just released a live album of Tinsley Ellis and the Heartbreakers featuring Chicago Bob Nelson on vocals and harmonica.

However, Chicago Bob had recently left the band. Rothschild said, "While in Atlanta, Nappy sat in with the Heartfixers for a set, and it turned out to be a good musical fit. So we all felt we could make a successful blues album that would promote both acts and lead to some touring together."[66]

The resultant album, Nappy Brown and Heartfixers' *Tore Up* (1984), was produced and engineered by Eddy Offord at his studio in Atlanta. A veteran of the music business, Offord had extensive production experience with artists including Procol Harum, Billy Squier, and Yes. In 1970, he had engineered John Lennon's album *Imagine*. Michael Rothschild says Offord was able to get a "crisp, modern sound for the album." He said, "The record generated some excellent reviews. We then set up club and festival bookings for Nappy and the Heartfixers around the South, and into the Northeast, including dates in DC and New York (at the Lone Star), and eventually booked a European tour."[67]

It was around this time that Nappy Brown started touring with Bob Margolin, who he met through Gerald Jackson at Jackson Station.[68] "I'd heard of Nappy from Muddy Waters in the [']70s," said Margolin. "Muddy loved his singing and Muddy's standards were high!"[69] Margolin said that Muddy Waters had "befriended the younger singer. Muddy's musical tastes were as elite as you might imagine, so Muddy's respect and friendship are a high compliment." Bob Margolin was playing Jackson Station in 1985 when Gerald Jackson mentioned to him "that Nappy lived nearby in the tiny town of Pomaria and asked if I thought he could do some songs with my band next time I played. What an opportunity! I didn't know what had become of Nappy and never even hoped to meet him, let alone play guitar behind that voice."[70] According to Margolin, "it was fateful when [Gerald] told me that Nappy Brown lived nearby, in Pomaria . . . and asked if my band could work with him when we played there. It began a musical and social friendship that lasted until 2008, when Nappy passed."[71]

"It was a thrill to back him up on guitar, to learn from his stage presence and stories, and to present him to the audiences that he always devastated," Margolin said. "Singing harmonies with him on a few songs is an experience that is otherworldly and one of the delights of my life."[72]

"[Margolin and Brown] had never played together before they played at Jackson Station," emphasizes Reggie Massey. Margolin dismisses the idea that he "brought him out of obscurity." He says, "Nappy had been working with Gospel groups again and he was already on his way back to our Blues World when I met him."[73] However, it was through his relationship with Bob

Margolin that Nappy Brown started playing more shows and touring more widely.

Nappy Brown's most well-known song was "Lemon Squeezing Daddy," a perennial favorite at Jackson Station, as it was elsewhere. The performance involved the singer, clad in his signature white suit,[74] rolling around on the floor[75] simulating various sexual maneuvers, including cunnilingus. "That was his act," said Cora Garmany. "Get on that floor."[76] Brown's wild stage presence was matched by his extraordinary vocal skills.[77] "He had a double voice," explains Billy Wirtz. "And he sounded like, completely two different people. He had this very deep-throated *la, la, la, la, la* and a high, almost, like tenor type thing. So you would think it was like two different guys singing but it wasn't, it was just Nappy." Wirtz says Nappy was a "terrifically talented guy."[78]

"Nappy was on most of our gigs [at Jackson Station] from 1985 to 1990," Margolin said. "Nappy had seen and done everything as an entertainer. He was very at home in a roadhouse in the country."[79] In a similar way that Widespread Panic fans should appreciate Jackson Station for the role the club played in their career, R&B fans who appreciate Nappy Brown (especially his later work) have Gerald Jackson to thank, in part, for his role in the process. Nappy Brown was happy to credit Bob Margolin for the comeback of his career. "Bob Margolin got me back into it," Nappy Brown told the *State* newspaper in 2002. "He used to play for a good friend of mine, Muddy Waters. You've heard of him. We were playing at a place called Jackson Station, and he asked me why don't I come back. And that's why I did. It didn't take much."[80]

"I think the first place Nappy sung at was the Jackson Station," suggests Cora Garmany. "When he first started back out. That was the first one. He started out right there at Jackson Station."[81] During the three decades they were together, Cora would use the vacation days from her job at the lumber company in Pomaria to travel to gigs with Nappy. She went "everywhere but flying." Along the way, they met all the high priests of blues and R&B, such as Buddy Guy, B. B. King, Bobby "Blue" Bland, James Brown, and Little Richard. Cora went to all the shows at Jackson Station, making the trip with her sister and other members of her family. "I would go over every time Nappy played," she says.

Every time Nappy Brown played at Jackson Station, "the place was packed,"[82] remembers Reggie Massey. Cora would arrive "with all the food, a big batch of food . . . Cook up a big meal, sit around and eat."[83] Michael Rothschild also has fond memories of these events. Cora was "a wonderful cook," he says, and was "especially good at making cakes and pies." He recalls

being at Jackson Station one night watching Nappy Brown and Tinsley Ellis perform. Cora was there with "all these cakes and pies." He said they "set
them up on the amplifiers and around the room. And then Nappy auctioned
them off during the break."[84]

"We got real close with Gerald and them," remembers Cora Garmany.
Not only would she travel to Jackson Station with Nappy but "Gerald and
them" would also visit her and Nappy in Pomaria. "I fixed them a big dinner,"
Cora said. "Many times."[85]

"Nappy could sing anything," says Scott Cable. "The best singer I've ever
worked with. Easy."[86] After regaining his sea legs at Jackson Station, Nappy
Brown once again became something of a celebrity. In the United States and
abroad, he resurrected his classic tunes at blues and jazz festivals. He made
the mainstream in 2007 when he appeared on the (then quite popular) *Prairie Home Companion* show with Garrison Keillor. It had been a long journey
from Jackson Station.

"Nappy loved it there," says Cable. "He really liked the people. The
crowds were good. It was a great club."[87] Jackson Station "became like his
second home."[88] Nappy "loved to just go and sit in the crowd and if he sat in
he did, if he didn't, he didn't." Cable says that "Gerald was so kind to him and
good to him." At Jackson Station Nappy Brown was treated "like royalty."[89]

Sensible Pumps keyboardist Catherine Brickley also remembers the welcoming crowds at Jackson Station. "They were the nicest people that were
there," she says, laughing. "Who goes out at 11:00 at night until 4:00 in morning?"[90] Her bandmate, bassist Susan Cree, says that playing Jackson Station
was a pleasant relief from other biker bars and blues clubs where the all-female
band often "took it on the chin." She said Jackson Station was "very receiv-
ing to everybody, very welcoming to everybody. It was really a great place to
play."[91]

"I think that's what gave the place character," says Joseph Cabri, former
Lander University tennis coach.[92] "There'd be liberals. There'd be conserva-
tives. It was harmonious once you got in there. There were lawyers, there were
doctors, there were farmers. It was just crazy how, in that one place, it erased
all the bias and bigotry that was more general in the surrounding areas."[93]
Somehow, despite the diversity of its clientele, Jackson Station managed to
treat each customer as an individual. "Nobody had any sort of elevated status," said Jack McConnell. "Everybody was on an equal playing field."[94] For
this reason, Jackson Station was a "safe place to go," for a "mix of people who
stayed up late at night for whatever reason," according Glenn Phillips. There

Sensible Pumps were among a number of all-female
bands to play at Jackson Station.

were "all these misfits." It was a "freak show. You could be part of the act. It
was fun to be in the middle of it."[95]

Jackson Station was a particularly welcoming space for gay, lesbian, bi-
sexual, or otherwise gender nonconformists. Thursday nights were known as
gay nights.[96] Sunday nights, when the depot was officially closed, were known
as the "guy nights."[97] This is when most of Gerald and Steve's gay male friends
would congregate in a more intimate setting, out of the public eye. It must
be stressed, however, that although Jackson Station had a reputation of being
a "gay bar," the moniker is somewhat misleading. Though Gerald and Steve
were clearly gay themselves, of all the people who would frequent the club,
gay men were in the minority.[98] Billy Wirtz remembered early 1980s Jackson
Station as a "combination of real, heavy, diesel, butch lesbians and not too
many gay men." Wirtz said, "I'm sure women were dancing together quite a
bit in the place. I never recall seeing guy-guy dancing. The dancing was always pretty much always heterosexual, with the exception of lesbian couples."
Wirtz remembers a live and let live philosophy at Jackson Station. He says,
"Gerald's great quote was, '*Our motto here is: We don't fuck nobody any way they
don't want to be fucked.*'"[99]

David Goldman says while it is true a group of "gay friends formed the
center" of the people who frequented Jackson Station the most, "it was never a
gay bar."[100] Gays were never the predominant demographic at Jackson Station
and there is little indication that Jackson Station was a place where gays—
more so than anyone else—sought out intimate relationships. "Now, get this

straight," says Hazel Bryant, Steve Bryant's eighty-eight-year-old mother. "That was not a gay bar. No way, no way. That was family. They brought children in there all the time. A lot them brought their family with them."[101]

"If anybody was gay, it'd probably be five percent," suggests Tommy Kidd, Steve's childhood friend from Liberty. He thinks it "was by no means," a place where gay people would go. "In fact, it might be one of the *last* places they would go,"[102] Kidd says, ironically. Nevertheless, at Jackson Station, "people were just accepted for whoever they were," says Deborah Milling,[103] who went Jackson Station while attending Lander University in the late 1970s. Milling is now a psychiatrist in Charleston. She said Gerald and Steve's club was particularly hospitable to women, in a way that many establishments today are not.[104] "I always felt safe and welcomed there," she says.[105]

However, occasionally Gerald Jackson would have to intervene to protect the club's patrons from threats posed by the drunken horde. Tersh Harley, Gerald and Steve's close friend and Erskine College alumnus, tells one such story. He remembers one evening during a Halloween party, when a young couple, friends of Gerald, arrived from the Low Country. They were dressed up like aliens with David Bowie–esque body suits and crazy wigs. They had ingested LSD as soon as they arrived at the depot. Things quickly got strange and they were having a great experience until it was time for the Costume Contest. The couple was in the contest. They marched across the stage in their costumes, camping it up mightily as they went. This caused affront to some of less urbane members of the crowd, who started jeering. Harley remembers that Gerald immediately jumped on the stage to defend his tripped-out, genderbending patrons. He scolded the hecklers: "This is Jackson Station, damn it! And anything goes at Jackson Station!"[106]

Brand Stille recalls Gerald Jackson breaking up several fights at Jackson Station. "There were some rough people who hung out at Jackson's," said Stille. Gerald would get right in the thick of the altercation and split the troublemakers apart. This was the no-nonsense side to Gerald Jackson that had been forged during his service in Vietnam. Gerald "was not intimidated by people," says Stille. People who might have caused trouble in other settings were put in their place at Jackson Station. "Come up to Jackson's and they weren't tough," states Roland Tranter. "Gerald didn't put up with it."[107] Gerald was "very empathetic of others no matter what their position was," says Jack McConnell. He was a "wise, mature guy."[108] Even troublemakers were not permanently banned from Jackson Station. Gerald would simply say, "Y'all come back some other time."[109]

"In general, there wasn't a whole lot of judging going on," remembers David Truly of the Truly Dangerous Swamp Band.[110] Jack McConnell agrees, saying that "Jackson's was completely non-judgmental about everything. That's one of the things that I really remember and liked about [Gerald] Jackson's. I think he was sort ahead of his time in a lot ways in terms of social acceptance and stuff like that."[111]

Perhaps partly because of its reputation for being such an inclusive and tolerant place, Jackson Station also provided an unsanctioned site for the intake of and experimentation with proscribed substances. There are differing accounts of the drug culture at Jackson Station. While the number of illegal drugs at the depot would have ebbed and flowed over the years, in one form or another, drugs were a constant presence at the club. Once the clock hit 11:00 p.m., it was customary to find people smoking marijuana—what bluesman Mississippi John Hurt once referred to as "poor man's whiskey"[112]—openly out on the back deck.[113]

People might take a whiff of more serious drugs such as cocaine during a quick visit to the restroom. Sheila Carlisle, leader and cofounder of the band Arhooly, said, "Someone always had some crank (methamphetamine) at Jackson Station." She said, "We toured so much, a little help from our friends was always welcome."[114]

"There was a lot of drugs there," remembers Tommy Kidd. "There was a lot of meth, crystal meth, and MDMA, stuff like that. Drug dealers would go there and just be available to sell whatever."[115] Kids says, "There was a lot of Quaaludes around, too. That was very popular back then. That was really prevalent, probably more than, or as much as the cocaine. For sure. It would just make you really screwed up like you smoked twenty joints or something. You'd get tore up. I would imagine that half the people at Jackson Station were doing Quaaludes."[116]

Jackson Station had operated during the so-called "Jackpot" era, the time in the late 1970s and early 1980s when large quantities of marijuana and cocaine were being smuggled into states like South Carolina from the Caribbean.[117] "There was a lot going on, a lot of money being thrown around. There was a lot of people involved with cocaine and meth and stuff like that," says Kidd.[118] While Jackson Station was never a front for a drug-selling operation, drugs would follow patrons into the club and many people would use drugs while they were there.

"There was always a little bit of cocaine around, enough to get you through the night,"[119] said the Reverend Billy C. Wirtz. "It was just one of those things that everybody did a little bit of." He remembers cocaine being doled out to bands in small quantities free of charge. If people wanted more than that, he says, ten dollars could buy "a couple of lines."[120]

The "adrenaline-inducing and ego-enhancing powers of cocaine"[121] have long been recognized by professional musicians and their fans. As case in point, take the song "Take a Whiff on Me," the well-known American folk-song that has been recorded by artists such as Lead Belly (1888–1949) and Woody Guthrie (1912–1967). Cocaine could be useful to touring musicians, numbing the pain of the road. It offered a speedy alternative to the spaciness of psychedelic drugs and the tranquilizing effects of heroin. With cocaine, a musician felt omnipotent. They could get things done. In the 1970s and early 1980s, cocaine became "appealing to middle class users"[122] in the United States. It was a party drug often used as a complement to other substances, such as alcohol and marijuana. The drug "didn't make your teeth fall out." Cocaine got people to "shake their booty on the dance floor and get high all night long."[123]

References to cocaine pervade the popular culture of the post-Vietnam era. The Grateful Dead sang of "riding that train, high on cocaine" in their cautionary railway song "Casey Jones." JJ Cale (and later, Eric Clapton) explored the ambivalence of cocaine in a song with the name of the drug as a title. Cocaine allowed people to stay up late, drink copious amounts of alcohol, and dance feverishly. People with cocaine were instantly more interesting and attractive to those around them. The drug also had its dark side. As David J. Haskins of the band Bauhaus (1979–1983) tells it, cocaine is "a nasty, mean-spirited drug that brings out the egotistical worst in people, and results in awful depression and psychosis."[124] In the 1980s, cocaine was not only available in the bigger cities and among the wealthy classes in America, but also found its way into relatively impoverished towns such as Hodges, South Carolina.

Roland Tranter said that on many visits to Jackson Station, he and his friend Tommy Kidd would have a "big sack of cocaine" in their pocket. "It was just the way it was," Tranter said. "It was the eighties, you know? And people in there, especially the ladies, they knew we had it. So we had an entourage." Kidd said that the "girls would love to run into somebody who had a sack of cocaine."[125]

"Even the bands knew we had it," Tranter comments. He says, "We would go back to the back, with Gerald and Steve, the bands, all of us, just have a big time." Sometimes Tranter said they would still be partying "[']til two or three o'clock, on Saturday afternoon. We had some wild, wild times in there."[126]

Often Tranter gave the bands one more toot on their way out of town in the morning. We "got [']em ready for the road," Tranter said. "They didn't have to worry about falling asleep."

Such tolerance was extended to other drugs. Gerald and Steve would let you "do what you want," said Dave Schools of Widespread Panic. He says on one occasion the band "took some psychedelics and we got too high and we wound up playing a really convoluted version of something like 'Low Spark of High-heeled Boys'[127] for half an hour." After a while, the band could not take it any longer. "We'd be like, 'Argh! We gotta' take break!' you know." [*laughing*] "We'd take a break and get our act back together and everything would be fine and they were cool with that." Schools says Gerald and Steve were cool with it. There "wasn't ever anyone sitting there with a stopwatch going, '*Take a break, so we can sell more beer!*'"[128]

Widespread Panic would not be first band to perform on psychedelics while performing at Jackson Station. Mark Cline of Love Tractor had taken some as a lark when he played there a few years before. He had traveled to the show (this would have been late 1983 or early 1984) with his friend, fellow Athens musician Nicky Giannaris of the Tone Tones. Cline took the LSD soon after getting to the club. "What the fuck?" Cline thought to himself. "We're playing in the middle of nowhere to people who don't know who we are. [I] might as well have some fun and see what this is like."[129]

In some respects, Jackson Station operated as a kind of autonomous zone. It was in the backwoods of South Carolina, with authorities at least fifteen minutes away.[130] It is a testament to the easygoing nature of the proprietors that Jackson Station largely policed itself. There was no need for external authority. "Anything went, as long as you didn't bother anybody," said the Reverend Billy Wirtz.[131] Gerald and Steve tried to handle everything in house. However, law enforcement was not unaware of what was going on at Jackson Station.[132] John Sanders remembers both plain clothes and uniformed police officers unsuccessfully trying to bust a group of musicians for smoking pot during a set break early one morning (the culprit ate the evidence). Tersh Harley says that Steve would not hesitate to call 911 if a fight inside the club spilled out into the parking lot.[133] But this was rare.

"I never saw police in there," said Roland Tranter. "Not inside." Occasionally he said a Greenwood County Sheriff Deputy might "just come through the parking lot, just cruise through," but Tranter said he never saw the police inside. "I think I would remember that. I mean, when something happened up there, they didn't call anybody. Which is smart. You see, you don't want that reputation. When law enforcement starts coming to your place, you're not going to have a place long."[134] David Truly thinks the political influence of some of the patrons at Jackson Station also worked to keep the police away: "There were a lot of congressmen or political people who came there to let their hair down. Nobody wanted to rock that boat."[135]

While the drugs may have attracted some people to Jackson Station, it kept others away. Gerald Jackson's old friend Linn Johnson says that as the years passed, some residents of Greenwood County became less tolerant of Jackson Station and the people who went there: "As it got on closer to the eighties and that culture, Jackson Station was no longer accepted." Johnson says, "It really was drugs, and cocaine, and they equated that with everything at Jackson Station."[136]

Johnson had a wedding reception at Jackson Station after her second marriage. Given the club's reputation, she said not a single doctor she worked with at Self Memorial Hospital responded to her invitation. As it turned out, on the day of the event, one doctor did attend, and he was on call. Johnson said she "happened to be out front on the front deck" when the doctor drove up. The doctor "parked under a light, full [streetlight], closest he could get to that ramp to get in there." Johnson says, "He was petrified," [laughing]. "He told me he was. He thought a queer was going to kill him!"[137]

Gerald and Steve tried best to keep a lid on all the mischief. Tommy Kidd said Gerald did not condone people smoking pot on the back deck. "He would make you leave if he caught you smoking pot. Bitch about it. And then let you back in."[138] However, Tersh Harley said that if it was a really slow night and no one was around, Gerald might go "out there and take a hit real quick, too, and then run back in."[139]

It should also be noted that, despite the evidence of illegal substances that were sometimes present at Jackson Station, many observers do not associate Jackson Station with any drug activity. "Anybody not seen nothing," remarks Gerald Jackson's security guard, John Sanders, curtly, in response to the idea that Jackson Station might have been a drug den. "Gerald did not want to see it. You had to go. He'd smell it. He'd bird dog it."[140]

"Anybody who said there were any drugs at Jackson Station, they didn't really understand there really weren't," explains Tersh Harley. "It wasn't like any drug deals were going on and it wasn't like there were any major drugs."[141] Harley says there was "a very big coke problem" in Greenwood in the 1980s, which had spillover effects into places like Jackson Station. "Gerald didn't like it," Harley said. "But he kind of had to put up with it, especially on those weekend nights."[142] Billy Wirtz said that, in comparison to other clubs, especially those in Columbia's Five Points area,[143] Jackson Station was "a pretty clean operation." He says that he "didn't notice amyl-nitrate, or anything like that. People weren't doing poppers on the dance floor."[144]

Gerald and Steve knew they had to be careful regarding how they managed the use of illegal substances among their clientele. If they were too heavy-handed, they risked alienating their customers. If they were too lax, the police could come in and shut the club down in a heartbeat. Gerald tried to keep his patrons in line. He posted warnings on the Jackson Station flyers:

"THREE REMINDERS FROM JACKSON STATION"[145]
No pot smokin' on the porches (or in the building)
No coke snortin' in the bathrooms
A good party is a <u>safe</u> <u>trip</u> <u>home</u>!

Dave Schools of Widespread Panic remembers "going out to the van for an attitude adjustment." He says such activity "certainly wasn't frowned upon, it just wasn't done inside the venue. And having to pass the scrutiny of Gerald's mom, as the door person. You know, she'd give you that, sort of, 'Uh huh, right,' look. But we weren't doing anything worse than anyone else, I can guarantee you that."[146]

Jeff Calder of the Swimming Pool Qs says that Jackson Station "didn't seem like a druggy place. Gerald's mom wouldn't have tolerated that shit."[147] Tinsley Ellis reminds us that both Gerald and Elizabeth Jackson were "tough" people. "They didn't want any problems there. They didn't want anything to cause them to be shut down."[148] Tersh Harley agrees. He says, "No way in hell, would they let that kind of crap in there. They had their stern rules, however lenient."[149] Gerald's dear friend Anita Clinton said he was "was very concerned about underage drinking and drug use."[150]

Gerald walked a fine line between going with the flow and cracking down. Jack McConnell observes, "Gerald was really under a microscope there because he was different than everybody else. His sexual orientation was different. And his general sort of laissez-faire sort of social philosophy was different."[151] He simply asked his patrons to behave. People were asked not sit on the porch railings nor walk around the club in bare feet.[152] Gerald told them: "It is not necessary to destroy the building when you come. No fights, no drugs, no minors, no liquor (or any other beverage brought in). Please be courteous of your friends at Jackson's. If you have grievances with someone please go to a private place and settle it as no one here wants to be involved in your personal affairs."[153] Gerald reminded people that "[a]nyone causing a disturbance, vandalism, or threatening bodily harm will be prosecuted to the full extent of the law. All personal and private arguments are to be kept to the outside of the building (people come here to escape all that)."[154] For well over a decade, Jackson Station was remarkably successful at providing a place "to escape all that." As David Truly comments, "It's just fascinating to me how this place" could operate. "When you walked in, it was kind of like, all bets were off, and all kinds of bullshit went out the window."[155]

As noted above, band members and those in Gerald and Steve's inner circle could gather in the more private spaces of the club such as the loft, in the basement, and in the old segregated waiting rooms. The private spaces in the club were strictly off limits to the public. Here, one might encounter a more intimate smoking session, a snort of blow, an amorous rendezvous, or a place to crash out for a spell. Gerald would generally adopt a hands-off attitude with musicians and his friends as long as people were discreet about what they were doing. In the fall of 1988, one of the waiting rooms was repurposed and made available to patrons seeking a more subdued Jackson Station experience. On a concert calendar for November/December 1988, it was announced: "NOW OPEN. The Old WHITE Waiting Room . . . *T.V. *Magazines *Solitude (away from the buzz of the main bar)."

Roland Tranter recounts a story of being in a back room at Jackson Station one night. He says, "Gerald got me one night. The place was closing, pretty much closed, might have been ten people in there, and I had met this girl. And we were over in that room, you know, [and] one thing led to another." Tranter and the woman forgot the door was ajar. He says the woman "was up there in my lap, and we was getting down." Then "Gerald . . . [laughing] . . . Gerald . . . [laughing] . . . Gerald came walking by. He had been outside. And he just kind of looked. [Laughing] And he looked back again, and he said, 'Oh, my goodness!'" [Laughing]. "I just said, 'Gerald!' [Laughing], and he just walked away, didn't say anything else about it."[156]

Such shenanigans were possible, of course, only when Mrs. Jackson was away. When she was working the club, an even stricter moral code was enforced. Mrs. Jackson had zero tolerance for drugs and sexual misconduct. "She would totally NOT allow that stuff," states Anita Clinton, emphatically. When Mrs. Elizabeth was working, her watchful eye was everywhere. It would have been inconceivable for Mrs. Jackson to be unaware of any hijinks at the club since her station at the door was in such proximity to both the back rooms and the restrooms. Clinton said that Mrs. Jackson "did not let a person dilly

Tinsley Ellis, ca. 1985.

dally" in the restroom. "After two or three minutes, [Mrs. Jackson] would know." There was "no fixing make-up or hair, etc. and taking a lot of extra time." If people took too long, "you can bet she would be banging on the door for them to get out."[157]

Blues guitarist Tinsley Ellis corroborates this. He says one night "my bass player took one of our female fans into, um, the sort of dressing room area of Jackson Station and was having his way with her." The romantic interlude was swiftly interrupted, however, when Elizabeth Jackson "got wind of it." She started banging on the door, demanding they come out. Mrs. Jackson "was furious with us," Ellis chuckles. "She got so mad. Gerald had to have a talk with us. Gerald was saying, '*Now it's OK with me, but my mother, she doesn't want anything like that going on here.*'"[158]

Intimate encounters would also take place out on the porch, and in the parking lot in people's cars. "I first kissed my wife on the back porch of Jackson's,"[159] admits Greenwood musician (and former Jackson Station bartender) Russ Fitzgerald. More brazen souls "would have sex out there [on the back porch]," states Tommy Kidd. "Not out in front of everybody," but surreptitiously, after most people had gone home. A couple might sneak into the shadows along the bench on the back deck to get better acquainted.

Bruce Cobb said Jackson Station was "not necessarily" a pickup bar, "but it happened. Sure it happened. But it seems like there were always more men there than women."[160] Jack McConnell remembers "a very open-minded culture," at Jackson Station. "It was probably a great gay pickup bar. It was definitely a pickup bar for heterosexuals. It was kind of like the last call to try to get laid on a Friday night." He says many people "were sniffing around desperate for action or whatever you want to call it." McConnell remembered some folks who were clearly "on the prowl," "flirtatious college girls" (who "were just teasers"), as well as more obviously promiscuous types.[161] Tersh Harley says if Jackson Station resembled "a little bit" of a meat market, "it was from both sides, trust me."[162] Gerald's good buddy David Goldman says that "[i]n my mind, Jackson's will always be synonymous with the sexual freedom that flourished at the end of the pre-AIDS era."[163] Tommy Kidd says, "Everybody was up there looking to get hooked up. After two or three hours of being there, you found someone to take home and you went home. It was before anyone knew about AIDS."[164]

It deserves pointing out that the idea that Jackson Station was a place for sex is not shared by all Jackson Station patrons and is vehemently denied by some. Anita Clinton, for example, is adamant that Jackson Station was "NOT a hook up bar. No one I knew, male or female, thought that." Clinton is "not saying that drunk people in bars don't hook up, but they did NOT go there for that reason." She declares that Jackson Station "was about the MUSIC. Seriously. If you wanted to hook up you would leave other bars and go do it. Not wait and drive to Jackson's to drink more and stay up ['til] 4 or 5." Without a doubt, the gender balance at Jackson Station became considerably more lopsided as the night progressed.[165] Ben Hawthorne says that by 3:00 a.m., most of the women had gone and all you had left were "just a bunch of drunk rednecks."[166] Whatever the case, any carefree sexual encounters that did occur at Jackson Station would be significantly curtailed by the end of the 1980s. "AIDS did start coming around, being known, around that time," says Tommy Kidd.

EIGHT

APRIL 7, 1990

And in just one moment, you know, he ruined a lot of things.
—Roland Tranter[1]

By early 1990, Jackson Station had developed a reputation throughout the South as a funky, off-the-wall juke joint in the backwoods of South Carolina. It was a place to get some good food[2] and drink, see some awesome music, and even stay up all night if you wanted. The acoustics and the playbills pleased the music aficionados.[3] "The sound in there had a beautiful echo," said Teddy Roberts. "It was just a great sounding club."[4]

Gerald continued to bring impressive bands to the Station on Friday nights.[5] Dirk Armstrong said Gerald was booking "bands from Norway and Sweden to come over there. I mean, far reaching, you know? And I don't think anybody really ever appreciated it. It was just, kind of, background noise for them. We had some amazing performances."[6]

Yet these large concerts were often hectic affairs for everybody. David Goldman says that over the years, the big band night Jackson's Shows had become a "giant scene" with "hundreds of cars" in the parking lot.[7] The masses had discovered Jackson Station. The number of people going to Jackson Station had grown exponentially. Multitudes of eager customers were now showing up to the club, paying cover charges and consuming tremendous amounts of beer, hot dogs, and grilled cheese sandwiches. Gerald, Steve and Elizabeth, and Jackson Station employees were all doing well, making some decent money, getting a piece of the action. While many locals were enthusiastic about Jackson Station's popularity, others missed the downhome, low-key version of the club from a few years earlier. Deborah Milling was amazed at "how crowded and popular," Jackson Station was at its peak. "It got to be wild, sometimes."[8] Tersh Harley, who went to Erskine from 1980 to 1984 and later lived in Greenwood fixing and flipping houses, said he preferred the

Gerald Jackson at Jackson Station, ca. 1983.

quiet times at Jackson Station, not the nights when it was "crazy and nuts." Ben Hawthorne notes that Jackson Station "made money on Friday nights, not the other nights." However, he adds," Friday nights were the only trouble-some nights."

In Jack McConnell's view, when it first started out as a club, Jackson Station was "a little more fresh, and a little more innocent. And then in later years it sort of degenerated into a little more redneckish sort of atmosphere."[9] Because Jackson Station was crawling with so many patrons on the big band nights, "they had to really limit the people that came in. There was just so many people trying to get in there. Long lines. People would be frustrated because they couldn't get in."[10]

Despite such inconveniences, Gerald was proud of what he and Steve had accomplished. He had successfully carried on the family tradition. Jackson Station, he said, "is like what you found in my daddy's general store, the basics."[11] After about a decade in business, Jackson Station had a regional (perhaps even quasi-national) reputation as a phenomenal blues club. It was a unique musical venue and gathering spot. Bands were keen to play there and fans faithfully sought out shows there. Dave Schools of Widespread Panic, who has played shows at literally thousands of different music venues, captures well Jackson Station's inimitable quality. As he puts it, "There's a family vibe,[12] there's a safe vibe, and there's an anything can happen vibe."[13] Schools continues: "They were just like home, like your old home folks. We were all like family. That was the feeling of that place. They ran a great club that we loved to go and play." Schools says that Jackson Station, overall, "was different, and it was weird, but it was welcoming, and there was a bit of adventure and exploration involved, going out of one's own comfort zone. But going to a place where the people around the venue cared."[14]

Gerald basked in the success of the depot in an interview with the *Greenville News*. "The whole experience has been a pleasure," he said. "I've never enjoyed anything more."[15] Gerald and Steve, now forty-four and thirty-eight years of age, respectively, were approaching the middle of their lives together. They lived as two openly gay men in a tiny conservative Bible belt town. As is common knowledge, the vast majority of small businesses fail. Considering how far they had come since 1975, on balance Gerald and Steve had done very well for themselves. "He did some serious business," notes Billy Wirtz. "That place was fucking packed on any weekend night. Packed."[16] As David Goldman says, "Gerald accomplished what he had set out to do."[17]

In the "PROPAGANDA" section of the May 1989 band calendar, Gerald publicized the club's achievements. "EXTRA-EXTRA-EXTRA," he wrote. "In the past Jackson Station has been featured in articles published by *Showtime Magazine* (from Sweden), *Southern Magazine*, the *State*, the *Atlanta Journal and Constitution*, the *Greenville News*, and the *Stockholm Daily News*. The Station has recently been contacted by *Rolling Stone*, who will be featuring Jackson's later this summer in an article on clubs nationwide."[18] Gerald and Steve had finally gotten to the point in the growth of the business where the club was starting to develop its own momentum.

Musicians such as Andrew Rieger of Elf Power were amazed this could happen. How could two gay guys successfully run a blues club in Hodges, South Carolina, while still managing to maintain cordial interactions with the "local redneck population"?[19] In a location where one might think, "They would be likely to be judged negatively and possibly run out of business and out of town,"[20] as Deborah Milling puts it, no one seemed to bother them. Of course, this is not to say that Jackson Station was financially sustainable. Anita Clinton, Gerald's and Steve's close friend and bookkeeper, said that

Jackson Station barely broke even over the years. Terry Pierce, Steve Bryant's brother-in-law, agrees. He says, "My impression was that it was not a profitable enterprise and that Gerald ran it on a shoe-string."[21] Nevertheless, business was solid enough for Gerald and Steve to buy a Craftsman style house in the middle of Hodges right next to the Presbyterian Church. The plan was to fix it up after Gerald had finished the renovating his mother's place. In the meantime, they planted some shrubbery and maintained the yard.[22] "It was just like the station," said Reggie Massey. "A labor of love. He was going to do it until he got it right. And he was going to do most of it himself."[23] Unfortunately, Gerald and Steve would never move into that Craftsman home. Their visions of domestic tranquility would be smashed to pieces.

Gerald had spent his entire life turning his dreams "into something positive not only for himself, but for those whose lives he touched."[24] Then one day, everything came crashing down on top of him. In the early morning on April 7, 1990, the life of Gerald Jackson, the fate of Jackson Station Rhythm & Blues Club, and the nature of Hodges, South Carolina, would change forever. Gerald let his guard down. In violation of his own security protocol, he followed an intoxicated customer into the parking lot.

Friday, April 6, 1990, was blues night at Jackson Station. The Legendary Blues Band—formerly known as the Muddy Waters Back-up Band—was in town. The show would exemplify Jackson Station at its best. "It was a big night for us," recalls Dirk Armstrong, who was working that night. The Legendary Blues Band was indeed legendary. In addition to backing up Muddy Waters, band members had also toured with Bob Dylan, the Rolling Stones, and Eric Clapton.[25] They had a brief appearance in the hit movie *The Blues Brothers* (1980). Other acts onstage at Jackson Station that night included Drink Small, The Blues Doctor (out of Columbia, South Carolina), as well as Grady "Fats" Jackson (1927–1994)—a tremendous musician renowned for playing two saxophones at the same time—and gospel singer Sweet Betty, both from Atlanta. Ticket prices were $10.

Like usual, the club opened at 5:00 p.m. People started trickling in about 6:00. By 8:00, there was a sizable crowd at Jackson Station.[26] People were drinking beer, smoking cigarettes, milling about, playing pool and pinball, eating hot dogs, cheeseburgers, and grilled cheese sandwiches. Dirk Armstrong and Steve Bryant were on bar. Terry Tinsley and Alan Wagoner were in the kitchen. John Sanders was working security. Gerald was hosting. For the first time in a long time, Elizabeth Jackson was on the door, collecting cover charges. As the years had passed and Mrs. Jackson (now sixty-eight) had aged, Gerald's mother had not been around the club as much.[27] It is not clear why she was working that night.

Meanwhile, nine miles down the road in Greenwood, Terry Daniel Stogner and Tommy Craig Douglas were starting a night on the town. It was about 10:00 p.m. and they were drinking at Legends, a dive bar in the center of Greenwood. The two men worked together at the Paul Wash Surveying Company. They had met while Douglas had been working his old job at Legends. Stogner had come in for a drink. Stogner told Douglas he could hire him on with the surveying company. Taking Stogner up on his offer, Douglas had been working as Stogner's assistant on Paul Wash's crew for the past three months.[28] Craig Douglas had walked to Legends from his apartment on Elliot Street. Stogner was already at the bar when he arrived. Douglas got a drink and the two men "generally just talked about work." Stogner and Douglas stayed at Legends until about 1:20 a.m.[29]

There was more drinking to be done. Stogner and Douglas left Legends and got in the Paul Wash company work truck—a White 1985 Dodge pickup—that Stogner had borrowed for the evening. Stogner drove them a short distance over to Sports Break—a private club in Greenwood that had just opened up.[30] They drank more alcohol at Sports Break and chatted with people they knew.[31] At about 1:45 a.m., Sports Break turned on the house lights and announced last call for alcohol. People started heading for the doors. Stogner and Douglas were still not ready to call it quits for the night. They decided to continue to party up at Jackson Station.

Stogner and Douglas left Sports Break and drove to Hodges. It would be a fateful trip that would forever change the course of many lives, particularly their own. While some details of the events that would subsequently unfold early that morning remain opaque, there are basic facts that are beyond dispute. Stogner and Douglas did go to Jackson Station together. They arrived at around 2:00 a.m. in Paul Wash's White pickup truck.[32] They had been drinking beers and hard liquor at least for the last four hours. The men got out of their truck and made their way to the entrance of the club.

A waxing gibbous moon peered down from the western sky. It was early spring in South Carolina, with the air crisp and cool. The music was still playing. Elizabeth Jackson was working the door, looking to collect $10 from each entrant as a cover charge. She was known to refuse entry to anyone of whom she did not approve. It is not known what she thought of Stogner and Douglas that night. Mrs. Jackson must have had some sort some sort of communicative exchange with these men as they were coming in the door. We do not know the nature of this exchange—how each party greeted each other and what transpired next. We do not know whether Mrs. Jackson collected $10 from each of the men and allowed them to go into the club, or if she rebuked them at the door and told them to go away.

John Sanders, a church going, self-professed Christian, lives in Hodges, just a few miles south of Jackson Station. Sanders had grown up with Gerald and been friends with him throughout his life. Trained as an electrician, Sanders became a long-haul trucker and then later developed a good business fixing golf carts. Now retired, Sanders experienced a freak accident a few years back when he lost the use of his right arm after a doctor's injection severed a nerve in his back. That has slowed his stride and made him bitter, but there is little he can do. He says his lawyers screwed him over. Back in the day, Sanders liked to ride Harley-Davidson motorcycles. Sanders cannot ride motorcycles anymore because of his disabled arm.

Back in the day, Gerald would occasionally ask Sanders to work security for him on Friday nights. "I was like a bouncer," Sanders says. "I just helped maintain and watched for problems brewing so we that could get ahead of it. I was everywhere."[33] Sanders claims he was at the door of the club in the morning of April 7, 1990, when Mrs. Jackson turned Stogner and Douglas away. According to Sanders,[34] Douglas "had a bit of a bar tab" that "he had owed from the time he had been there before." He said, "The guy [Douglas] owed Gerald some money.[35] Mrs. Jackson knew it. She wouldn't let him in. Mrs. Jackson made him leave." Sanders said Stogner and Douglas started to argue a little bit with Mrs. Jackson, who "had to call Gerald up there." Sanders went up to the front of the house with Gerald.[36] After more quarrelling with Gerald and his mother, Sanders says Douglas and Stogner backed away from the entrance of the club and seemed to leave the premises. However, Sanders said Stogner and Douglas did not go away. "After she turned them away, they go around back and climb up over the railing . . . They helped each other get in. One boosted the other one up. He got in, reached down, pulled the other one up."[37] Sanders says Douglas and Stogner went inside the club and ordered some beers. About half an hour later, Mrs. Jackson spotted the two at the bar. She said something to Gerald. Sanders is adamant that Douglas and Stogner did not pay a cover charge to get into the club that night. "No," asserts Sanders. "No. I know this to be a fact. That was part of my job."[38]

"Those SOBs came in without paying,"[39] Mrs. Elizabeth told her son. Gerald said he would take care of it. Sanders said he was puzzled that "after she and Gerald told them to leave," Douglas and Stogner "are walking around in there." He said, on their next trip up to the bar, Steve also pointed them out to Gerald. Gerald called Sanders over. They escorted Douglas and Stogner to the door. At no time, Sanders says, did Gerald put his hands on either man.

On the way out of the club, Sander says Stogner started exchanging words with Gerald. "They were arguing back and forth." He said that Stogner "was argumentative, the other guy [Douglas] was gullible, I mean he did good. He didn't say a word." They accompanied the men to where the wheelchair ramp meets the dirt parking lot. They stopped. Stogner and Douglas kept on walking. After they got about twenty feet away, Sanders says Stogner "turned around and started hollering back at Gerald, one thing or another." Sanders says Gerald turned to him and said: "'*I'm going to go talk to him, calm this down. I don't want any hard feelings, anything like that.*'" Sanders says he told Gerald not to go and talk to Stogner. "Gerald," he said, "I wouldn't do it. Just let him go. He's on the way. Let him go."

"*Well, if I call the law,*" he said Gerald told him, "*They're going to give him [a] DUI. I don't want that. That's revenge down the road. I'm just going to try talk to him tell him to chill, give him water, a Pepsi, let him to sober up.*" With that, Sanders says Gerald went out into the parking lot to talk to the men. Sanders turned, walked up the ramp and went back inside the club. He assisted Mrs. Jackson with another customer.

For reasons that are not entirely clear, the situation in the parking lot escalated very quickly. After Stogner had started arguing with him, Sanders claims Gerald went out to the parking lot to try to defuse the situation.[40] This did not happen. Sanders said Gerald "gets out there" and tries to make amends with Craig Douglas. "He was just asking . . . '*Did I not do . . . ? Was I not nice about . . . ?*' You know. And [Douglas] said, '*Hey, I got no problem with it . . .*' And about the time the guy [Douglas] said, "*Watch it!*" [Stogner] done snatched a bush axe out of the back of the truck. When Gerald turned around, *Bam!* It hit him."[41]

With considerable force, the sharp end of a bush axe made direct contact with the right side of Gerald Jackson's head. The blade stuck there, four inches deep inside Gerald's skull.[42] Gerald made no sound. He crumpled to the ground. Standing over Gerald, Stogner tried to remove the bush axe.[43] He could not get it out. It was stuck in Gerald Jackson's head. Stogner stepped on Gerald's head with his boot. He pulled the axe free. Nic Massey says, "That's one thing I remember about overhearing parents talking about it was that he had to step on Gerald's head to pull it out. It was in so deep he just couldn't get it out like that, so he actually like stepped on him."[44] In John Sanders's words, "The boy literally put his foot in Gerald's face and worked the bush axe out of his head."[45] After he pulled it loose, Stogner threw the bloody axe in the bed of the truck. He got in the passenger seat of the truck. Douglas was behind the wheel. He started the truck and peeled out of the parking lot. They drove south toward Greenwood.

Inside Jackson Station, people had no idea what was going on in the parking lot. They were having a good time at a hot blues show on a Friday night. Sweet Betty was still singing on stage accompanied by saxophonist Fats Jackson. Dirk Armstrong and Steve Bryant were in the bar area. Alan Wagoner came in behind the bar from the kitchen. Mrs. Jackson had told him "Gerald was in an argument out in the parking out and somebody needed to go out there."[46] Dirk said, "Steve, I'm going to go see what's going on."[47] Alan was right behind him.

Mattie Phifer, guitar player with the Sensible Pumps, was in the audience at Jackson Station that night. "We were all standing up down near the stage," she said, cheering on Sweet Betty. Suddenly, Phifer says, "I just heard a voice. Somebody ran into the bar and said, 'Gerald's been hurt!'" She hightailed it to the door.

When Dirk Armstrong "got out to the parking lot," he found Gerald "laying there with blood pumping out of his head."[48] Alan Wagoner said, "We could not tell where he was bleeding from." Wagoner went back into the club "to get towels to bring back so we could try to stop the bleeding."[49] Mattie Phifer, who was also quickly on the scene, said Gerald's "head was just bashed in. There was blood gurgling out of his face." Phifer "was afraid, because of the gurgling sound, he was not going to be able to breathe because the blood was going back down his throat."[50]

It was 3:33 a.m., when Greenwood County Sheriff Officer Randy Miles received word of an assault at Jackson Station. An eleven-year veteran on the force, Deputy Miles was in the Creason Hill subdivision of Ware Shoals, about ten miles north of Jackson Station, when the call came in. Miles raced down US 25 in his patrol car arriving at the depot at 3:47 a.m., a few moments before the ambulance arrived.

Deputy Miles encountered a chaotic situation. It would have been a terrible, confusing scene for the 150 or 175 people[51] still left at the club, about a dozen of whom gathered around Gerald in the parking lot, not knowing what was going on or what to do. Miles tried to determine what had happened to the bleeding man on the ground and who was responsible for the attack. "It was late at night," said Miles, "and there was a lot of people, and a lot of people were excited, and we just tried to keep people back and keep people calm."[52]

Armstrong, Wagoner, and Phifer all provided medical assistance to Gerald while waiting for the ambulance to arrive. Dirk Armstrong said Gerald was in a "semi-conscious" state. Dirk removed the long-sleeved shirt he was wearing over his T-shirt and put "it up against [Gerald's] head trying to stop the flow of blood."[53]

"It was pretty grim," said Armstrong. "Thankfully, I'd had some First Aid" (first in the Boy Scouts and later in an ROTC class at Erskine College).

Maxine Syrkett, a Jackson Station regular and former employee, came outside to find people "on the ground helping Gerald." She remembered, "They were holding a tourniquet to his head, you know, towels and stuff to stop the bleeding . . . I had taken CPR and stuff so I just jumped in and helped them."[54] Syrkett sent someone to her car to get a pillow to put under Gerald's head.[55] Gerald was sputtering. They put him on his side to help him breathe.[56] Mattie Phifer "just held Gerald's head in a position to keep it elevated a little bit, but turned to the side so the blood would drain out so he wouldn't choke. It was obvious it was bad. I didn't know if he would live or die."[57]

"It was ugly," recalled John Sanders.[58] The blow from the bush axe had "parted his hair."[59]

It seemed to take the EMS crew an eternity to get to Jackson Station. Eventually the ambulance did arrive, and technicians started attending to Gerald. They seemed to be working at a snail's pace to the people watching them. Tersh Harley suggests there was a delay in the medical crew treating Gerald due to an argument among the first responders "over who would touch his body in case one of them may catch AIDS by helping him."[60]

"I know we were outside out of town, and it took a while to get them out there," Dirk Armstrong admits. Nevertheless, he was "beside [himself] because they were sitting there working on him in the parking lot, when I felt they should have been going to the hospital. They sat there and I guess tried to stabilize him or something. I just remember beating on the back of the ambulance saying '*TAKE-HIM-TO-THE-HOSPITAL!*' I am sure a few expletives were dropped, which probably didn't help the situation."[61]

After the ambulance left the depot, a number of friends followed along to Self Memorial Hospital in Greenwood. They held a vigil for Gerald, awaiting any news about his condition. Maxine Syrkett went back inside Jackson Station. She consoled Steve and helped him close up the bar for the night.[62] She went back to the parking lot and noticed the pile of blood-drenched towels.

She picked up the towels and threw them in the garbage. On the ground, she saw a small pocketknife. It was closed and had a penny wedged in it. She picked up the knife and gave it to Alan Wagoner, who later turned it in to the Greenwood County Sheriff's office.[63]

Steve Bryant called his parents in Liberty, South Carolina, to tell them the horrible news. It was impossible for him to verbalize what had happened to Gerald. "Steve called me that night," says his mother, Hazel Bryant. "In the middle of the night, he called and we couldn't even understand what he was saying. I finally realized Steve was expecting [Gerald] to be dead any minute."[64] Steve called her back three other times before sunrise, keeping her updated on the situation.

As all of this was unfolding, Craig Douglas and Terry Stogner were exchanging goodbyes at Stogner's apartment on East Cambridge Avenue in Greenwood. They had left Jackson Station in a hurry after Stogner had struck Gerald in the head with a bush axe. Patrons had started coming out of the club and into the parking lot. They had decided not to stick around. It must have been a fraught drive back to Greenwood. Douglas told police that Stogner "scared me so bad."[65] As they rode in the pickup heading south on US 25, Douglas said to Stogner:

"Terry, you have killed that man. You have fucked up. You have killed that man."[66]

"He said, '*Craig, I don't give a damn; he cut me three times.*'
I said, 'Terry, you do give a damn.'
He said, '*You right I do. But you know I fucked up a long time ago.*'
What he meant by that, I didn't ask. I was wanting to get home."[67]

They arrived at Stogner's apartment on East Cambridge Avenue. The old Southern house, across from the First Presbyterian Church, had recently been converted into rental units. Stogner's apartment was at the back of the building, the first door on the left.[68] When they got to the apartment, according to the police transcript, Douglas said he and Stogner cleaned themselves up: "I said get that bush axe and let's go in the house and wash the blood off ['cause] it scared me so bad. Got in the house, and he said look on your tennis shoes. I had blood all over my left tennis shoe. I took my left tennis shoe out, put in his sink. He washed the bush axe off."[69]

Douglas took the shoelaces from his tennis shoes and rinsed them off. He told Stogner he needed to go home. He left Stogner's place, got in the pick-up truck, and drove to his apartment on Elliot Street, near the old

American Legion Hall. Douglas called "the authorities about an hour later, while Stogner went to sleep."[70]

Now back in Greenwood, responding officer Deputy Randy Miles stopped by Stogner's apartment at 4:45 in the morning. Stogner did not answer the door.[71] Miles said he "went to his door and tried to—I knocked on the door, and I could get no one to the door."[72]

Over on Elliot Street, Douglas had been hesitant at first to call the police, but his girlfriend urged him to do so. "She said, you need to call the law and tell them now. I said, no. I ain't going do it. I'm scared. I told her to get out of my way." Douglas then called his brother. Craig told him he was "freaked out" and "real upset." He said, "I ain't never seen nothing like it in my life."[73] Just before 7:00 am, Randy Miles went to Elliott Street to bring Douglas to the Greenwood County Detention Center for a deposition. Douglas told his version of what had happened the night before.

Douglas said he and Stogner had been drinking at Legends and then they went to Sports Break. At 2:00 a.m., they "went to Jackson Station. We paid a ten-dollar cover charge. I drank one beer, two beers. At approximately 4:00, to my knowledge, I told my boss man Terry Stogner let's go home. The band was boring. Let's go home. He said all right I'm following you. I said, I'm following you. So, I followed him. We went out to our truck to go home."[74] Douglas said he and Stogner "walked out to our truck alone. All of a sudden Gerald Jackson pops up out of the blue. He says, looking at me, Craig Douglas, don't you owe me something, he said. That was his exact words. *Don't you want to give me something?* I said, Gerald I had a slack week last week because it rained. I didn't get a big check, and I owe rent."[75]

Douglas explained why Gerald was asking him for the money. "I owed Gerald twenty dollars. Well, he was going to charge me interest on that, and I had already given him seventeen dollars. Well, I said, hey. I'll still owe him twenty dollars. Regardless of the seven dollars. That will be the interest."[76] Douglas told him, "I don't have it Gerald. He said, '*Well.*' He got to mumbling something." Then Terry Stogner "mumbled something back to him."[77] Douglas then said Gerald "swung back and was swinging at Terry." Douglas said Gerald Jackson attacked Terry Stogner. He said, "Gerald was swinging at Terry. He kept saying, '*I'll cut you son-of-a-bitch.*'" He said, "Gerald cut him three times."[78] Despite the allegation of being "cut," Douglas's memory was fuzzy on whether Gerald actually had a knife in his hand. "I don't know how he cut him. I'm not saying he had a knife. I'm not saying he did, and I'm not saying he didn't. I couldn't see."[79]

While Gerald was attacking Stogner, Douglas said, "Terry stood there," and "never put his hands on Gerald." Rather, "Jackson swung at Stogner. Stogner ducked the first time. Stogner got up there close to him with his glasses; had glasses on. Swung again, knocked his glasses off, and cut him some kind of way. . . . Swung at him four times; made contact three. Then, Stogner took three steps back to our truck where we were getting in; had our door still open. He grabbed a bush axe, swung it one time and missed, hit our truck. The second time he hit Gerald Jackson in the head. I said, he's dead. I said, Man I can't believe you did this."[80]

After finishing the interview with Douglas, at 8:30 a.m., Randy Miles and three other police officers went to Terry Stogner's apartment with a search warrant. They were looking for three objects in particular: a bush axe, a pair of snakeskin boots, and a pair of shoelaces.[81]

Deputy Miles provided the legal justification for the search. He wrote:

> At approximately 3:30 a.m. on April 7th 1990, an altercation oc-
> curred between Gerald Jackson and Terry Stogner at Jackson Station
> in Greenwood, SC. During the altercation Terry Stogner did take a
> bush axe from a pickup truck in the parking lot of Jackson Station
> and strike Gerald Jackson in the head causing a severe head injury
> that required treatment at Self Memorial Hospital. After striking
> Jackson with the bush axe Stogner did get into the pickup truck and
> head towards Greenwood. The investigation has revealed that Stogner
> lives at 115-C East Cambridge Ave. in Greenwood and that the items
> listed above are there at his residence.[82]

This time the police knocked, Stogner came to the door. "I told him what we had," Miles said. Stogner was "very uncooperative. He didn't help us a bit."[83] After executing the search warrant, police confiscated a burgundy shirt found in the bathtub, a pink towel on the towel rack, a pair of leather skin boots and a pair of shoestrings in the kitchen sink.[84] Miles said that "these things, you know, appeared to have had blood on them, and they were wet, like they had been washed."[85] The officers looked for a bush axe, but could not find one. They searched outside the apartment, under the porch, and in the surround-ing areas. "We could not find a bush axe."[86]

Miles said that during the search of his apartment Stogner "was very hostile towards us." In response to "anything we would say, he would cuss."[87] Miles "smelled alcohol about his person," and observed that Stogner had "several little—they appeared to me to be scratches on his face."[88] The officers arrested Terry Stogner and transported him to the Greenwood County Detention Center. The confiscated items were delivered to Major Tony Davis.[89]

Twenty-nine-year-old Terry Daniel Stogner stood about 6'1". He had brown hair and brown eyes.[90] Originally from Simpsonville, South Carolina, at the time of the incident he was living in Greenwood and working for the Paul Wash Surveying Company. He had a leadership position and enjoyed a close relationship with the owner. Wash appreciated Stogner's technical and computer skills, which were then becoming a vital part of surveying work. Craig Douglas said Terry Stogner "drew up most of the plats on computer. After we go out and take shots with this gun from point to point, locating stuff, he can draw it up on the computer and make it come out on a plat."[91] Stogner also acted as a supervisor for Wash, managing other workers on the surveying crew, including Craig Douglas.

While he may have been a good employee, Stogner was no stranger to the police. According to his FBI report,[92] Stogner had been arrested numerous times in Greenville County for driving under the influence. Stogner was arrested (and then later charged and convicted) for his first DUI on January 7, 1979. He was eighteen at the time.[93] He was arrested for a second DUI in April of the same year. In December 1981, he was arrested, charged, and convicted of a third DUI offense. He was arrested for yet another DUI in July 1985.[94]

In March 1981, Stogner had been arrested by the Greenville County Sheriff's Office and charged with housebreaking and grand larceny. In September 1983, he was arrested, charged, and convicted for possession with intent to distribute Quaaludes. In April 1987, Stogner was arrested by the Mauldin, South Carolina,[95] Police Department and charged with "damage to city property; resisting arrest; simple possession; and drunk and disorderly."[96] In June 1988, in Greenwood County, Stogner was arrested, charged, and convicted of littering, resisting arrest, and disorderly conduct. In August of that year, he was arrested and charged (but not convicted) of assault and battery of a high and aggravated nature.[97] In May 1989, he was again charged with assault and battery of a high and aggravated nature as well as malicious injury to private property. In that case, Stogner was convicted of simple assault and battery, fined, and sentenced to thirty days in jail.[98] Less than six months later, on October 30, 1989, Stogner was again arrested for assault and battery. Those charges would be dropped.[99]

In a letter to Gerald's mother from a man named Eddie Blakely, which was sent to her soon after the attack on her son, Stogner was described as "nothing but trouble." Blakeley told Mrs. Jackson that "[t]his very Terry Stogner (the one who hit Gerald) was involved in two previous incidents. He hit David Flowers in the face with a beer bottle (requiring more than 100 stitches) at the Embers Club (where Montague's is now). He also hit a convenience store clerk in the head with a credit card machine awhile back."[100]

For the alleged attack on Gerald Jackson, Stogner was arrested, charged with assault and battery with intent to kill, and received a $50,000 bond. A little after 8:00 in the morning, Deputy Tony Roberts escorted Craig Douglas back from the Greenwood County Detention Center to his apartment on Elliot Street.[101] Roberts retrieved a blood-splattered pair of Reebok tennis shoes from the residence. He took photographs of bloodstains in the back of the pickup truck. He also found the bush axe.[102] Roberts returned to the Greenwood County Sheriff's Office and gave the items to Tony Davis.[103]

About an hour later, Deputy Sherry Scott of the Greenwood Sheriff's Department interviewed Terry Tinsley at the Greenwood Detention Center. Another Jackson Station employee who had been working the night before, the 24 year-old Tinsley had been out in the parking lot right before Gerald had been struck. Like a number of Gerald's friends, he had been at the hospital all night, waiting on news about Jackson's condition. The police had called him shortly after he got back to Hodges.[104] Tinsley told the police his version of events from the night before.

Tinsley said he had been working when "Gerald's mother came into the kitchen and told me they were fighting with Gerald in the parking lot. She wanted to see if I knew what was going on and for me to try to help him." Tinsley went outside and saw Gerald arguing with two men. He said he "tried to talk to Gerald and tell him to come back inside. I heard him tell those two guys that he would have them arrested in the morning. I don't know what for."[105]

"They were standing toward the back of the truck," Tinsley said to Deputy Scott. "The shorter of the two guys [Douglas] was trying to tell the other guy [Stogner] to get in the truck so they could leave." Tinsley said that, "Gerald was angry. He wasn't yelling, but he had an angry tone. The other guy, the taller of the two [Stogner], he was just staring he wasn't really saying anything. The shorter of the two [Douglas], the only thing I heard him say was let's get out of here. Come on get in the truck and let's go."[106] Tinsley said Douglas was at the driver's door and Stogner was standing on the passenger side. Stogner "picked up something up out of the back of the truck. I didn't see what it was. He picked something up and went toward Gerald."[107]

Terry Tinsley said he ran inside Jackson Station.[108] He grabbed the first person he saw and told them he needed help. He reemerged from the club just as Douglas and Stogner were "pulling out of the parking lot . . . Gerald was laying on the ground bleeding." Tinsley told the police, "From what I could tell it looked like he had a cut on the side of his face. He sounded like he was choking. He was gurgling. He wasn't moving."[109] Tinsley said he then called 911. "I ran and called them . . . I don't know if anyone called them before or not. But I did call them."[110]

NINE

PICKING UP THE PIECES

I get by with a little help from my friends.
—The Beatles[1]

Gerald Jackson was not the first person to be attacked by someone with an axe in Hodges, South Carolina. On October 12, 1865, the front page of the *Abbeville Press and Banner* announced news of a "brutal murder" to the community. On October 6, Major James Adams, one of the area's "most respectable citizens," was found dead. Adams had lived near Hodges Depot, and had gone turkey shooting the day before. As reported by the *Press and Banner*, "On Friday morning his dead body was found near Hodges Depot, very much mutilated. Upon his side were the marks of a wound inflicted by an axe. There was a deep gash on the back of his head, and his whole face was beaten in, so as not to be recognized." The paper stated that "Major Adams was one of our most peaceful and orderly citizens and sustained the character of a kind and indulgent master."[2]

Unlike Major Adams, Gerald Jackson somehow survived his attack. Dr. Harold Schmidt was the first medical specialist to examine Gerald when he was brought to the Emergency Room at Greenwood's Self Memorial Hospital in the morning of April 7, 1990. The doctor found the patient "lying on a table with a dressing placed over his head." The doctor said Jackson "could not move his left side, could not move his right side, and appeared to be awake." There was a three-and-a-half-inch laceration across Gerald Jackson's "right cheek, angling back towards the temporal portion of his head."[3] The injury was "massive . . . It was [an] extensive injury."[4] Schmidt said, "You could see that there was brain tissue coming through the laceration, associated with a dark blood and red blood."[5] He also noted, "There was a fair amount of swelling over the laceration, around the area of the laceration itself."[6]

Dr. Schmidt and other Emergency Room staff provided immediate medical care to Gerald at around 4:30 in the morning. They tried to "remove bone fragments of a fractured skull, remove the damaged brain as much as we could, and stop the bleeding." There was an unsuccessful attempt to "close the hole of the bone covering the brain." They "sutured the laceration on his face," before realizing Gerald had a broken cheekbone.[7] They administered an ethanol alcohol test to see if he had been drinking.

Gerald Jackson's high school friend Linn Johnson was working as a Surgical Technician at Self Hospital when Gerald was admitted. "I was in the operating room," she said. "Gerald came in. Between cases, I went up to intensive care. The girls on the floor knew me, so they let me go back there." Johnson says Steve Bryant and Elizabeth Jackson were already in the room with Gerald, who by then was unconscious. He had slipped into a coma. "I'm glad he was in a coma," Johnson said, reflecting on the trauma that Gerald had gone through. "And his face was just . . . Oh, his eyes."[8]

A group of Gerald's friends and loved ones spent the early hours of the day at the hospital "waiting to see what was going on,"[9] hoping and praying Gerald would survive. Gerald was in a coma, but in the moments and hours after the surgery, his condition gradually stabilized. People began to breathe again. They slowly turned back to their everyday routines. Mattie Phifer remembers leaving the hospital "in a daze and blown away that this all had happened."[10]

Among those who were standing watch, Dirk Armstrong eventually left the hospital, got in his car, and went back to Hodges. He was surprised to find saxophonist Fats Jackson outside the depot waiting for him. "Fats Jackson was there wanting to get paid," Armstrong said. "He hadn't gotten paid." Armstrong was irked by the apparent callousness of the request. "Coming back from the hospital and there he is wanting money. It's like, are you serious?"[11]

Later that morning, Major Tony Davis of the Greenwood County Sheriff's Department drove up to Jackson Station. He surveyed the scene looking for evidence. He took some photographs of a large bloody stain in the parking lot. He recovered a pair of wire frame spectacles near the scene of the crime. They were found facedown in the dirt. The left arm of the glasses stood perpendicular to the ground. The right arm was closed. One of the lenses had been broken out.[12]

Jackson Station opened for business as usual in the evening of April 7, 1990. "It was a Saturday night," Dirk Armstrong said. "It was a short night for us. We didn't usually book music or anything because we had to close by midnight. But the phone was ringing off the hook with people calling and wanting to know what was going on. And the rumor mill was starting about this, and that, and the other. It just got kind of ugly."[13]

Linn Johnson said she "went over there every day" to visit Gerald while he was at Self Memorial Hospital. Steve, Elizabeth, and Elizabeth's sister (Gerald's aunt) were all there in the hospital room, watching over Gerald, sitting next to his bed. At times, everyone got along amicably enough, at other times, less so. "That became somewhat of issue," said Johnson, referring to the creeping antipathy in the situation. "Mama or Steve? Who's taking care of Gerald?"[14]

"Steve stayed with him," said John Sanders, the Hodges electrician and Jackson Station security guard. Sanders also visited Gerald while he was at the hospital in Greenwood. He said Mrs. Jackson "didn't want Steve around him."[15]

After about ten days, Gerald awoke from his coma. For a man who had recently experienced a bush axe nearly four inches deep inside his skull, his consciousness was amazingly intact. Gerald was as "vibrant minded as you and I are," recalled close friend Bonnie Capps. His "mind was clear and bright. He knew everything you were saying."[16] However, Jackson could not walk or sit up, had lost the ability to speak, and could not use his hands. Francesco Clark, who, at twenty-four years of age, suffered a life-changing spinal cord injury after diving into the shallow end of a swimming pool, describes something of what Gerald Jackson might have been feeling at the time. As Clark writes: "I cannot feel or move most of my body. Lying in my bed, it's as if there is a giant invisible weight pressing down on me. If I am thirsty and want to drink from the glass of water on the nightstand, I can't reach for it. If I want to get into my wheelchair and leave the room, I have to ask someone to move me. If no one's available to help, I wait."[17] Though paralyzed, Gerald Jackson was extremely lucky to be alive. The odds of anyone surviving such a blow to the head must be infinitely small. Gerald Jackson might be considered a case study in resurrection. However, he would no longer be the person he was before. He would not be able to take care of others. Gerald Jackson would himself require medical attention and round-the-clock assistance for the next twenty years. Such care would mainly be provided by Steve Bryant.

News of the grisly attack shocked the greater Greenwood community. While some locals, including Gerald himself, often relished the rough history of Hodges, with its stories of "frequent shootings and cuttings,"[18] they were dismissed as old tales of yore. No one thought they were applicable to the here-and-now. While there were a few scuffles now and then, and despite its somewhat nefarious reputation, no one really thought of Jackson Station as being a dangerous place. That was the beauty of the club. Most of the time, everyone got along very peaceably. Even former Greenwood County Sheriff Tony Davis would tell you the Jackson Station was known as a "good place, with good people."[19] Generally, the people who went there were remarkably tolerant and respectful of each other. Locals were also stunned, not only by the very fact of the crime, but also by its apparent viciousness. People were horrified that Gerald Jackson had been assaulted and they could also not bring themselves to terms with fact that Terry Stogner was responsible. Stogner was generally regarded as a decent-enough fellow about town. As a surveyor for Paul Wash, he was known professionally in Greenwood for the good quality of his surveying work, and he was known socially in the bar scene. Reggie Massey had a friend who worked at the Greenwood Clerk of Court's office. He says she was flabbergasted when she heard about what had happened. "She couldn't believe it," Massey said, "She did not believe that guy had done that."[20] Stogner "wasn't no thuggish guy or nothing," concurs arresting officer Randy Miles.[21]

Weighty feelings of sadness and remorse descended upon Jackson Station. "Gerald's attack was truly the day the music died, for Greenwood, anyway," said Reggie Massey, somberly.[22]

"When Gerald got hurt, it was just devastating," said Bonnie Capps.[23] "We just couldn't believe it." She could not understand how someone could be "that mean, that drunk, that cruel."[24]

"The whole thing was just so completely unnecessary," says Dave Schools of Widespread Panic, philosophically. "But that's what happens."

"It was just unreal," notes Nic Massey. "It's always the best people that kind of thing happens to."[25]

"They should have shot him," states one unnamed Jackson Station regular, bluntly, referring to Gerald's assailant. Other people report that a hit by a local motorcycle gang was in fact very nearly placed on Terry Stogner, but that Gerald Jackson called it off. Nic Massey says he "heard from so many different people, that there was . . . I guess there's tougher people that loved Jackson's that actually reached out to Gerald and said '*When he gets out*' . . . some type of retaliation and Gerald said he didn't want that at all . . . I've heard several different stories . . . And Gerald was always like '*No. Never.*'"[26]

With Gerald incapacitated and unable to assist, decisions had to be made about what to do with the club. Bills do not stop arriving during emergencies. Despite the tragic nature of the situation, Jackson Station was still a thriving music venue, bar, and restaurant. It had a clientele that expected to be served. While Jackson Station regulars would soon find out what had happened to Gerald in the parking lot that night, word did not travel so fast to oblivious out of town patrons, still eager to show up and party until dawn. From an economic standpoint, despite the difficulty of the circumstances, it would be beneficial to keep the depot up and running. Yet this would be hard to accomplish, both socially and psychologically. The two other main principals at Jackson Station—Steve Bryant and Elizabeth Jackson—were also essentially out of commission since they were spending most of their time with Gerald at the hospital. Friends like Reggie Massey and Tersh Harley stepped up and helped where they could, for example, by running the door and marketing the shows. Dirk Armstrong now became the "point of contact for booking bands."[27]

The difficulty of the situation was compounded by the fact that Elizabeth Jackson's house across the street (the family home at 4113 Moorefield St.) from the depot was in a state of complete disrepair. Gerald had been in the middle of renovating it when he was injured. The house was like a war zone. "It was a torn up mess," said Linn Johnson, "a real torn up mess."[28] Someone else would have to finish the work.

The news eventually spread to the musicians who were such a focal point of the club. Nappy Brown, Drink Small, Fats Jackson, Sweet Betty, and other blues musicians organized a benefit concert—"Keep the Station on Track"—for Gerald Jackson on June 8, 1990.[29] A benefit show by the Sensible Pumps—"Sing the Blues for Gerald Jackson"—was held the following week. All proceeds went "directly to Gerald Jackson to use as needed."[30] For a moment, it seemed like the club might pull through. On a visit to Jackson Station in July 1990, David Goldman noted that Steve was "taking this all like an absolute champ and determined to keep everything going."[31] Steve was optimistic about Gerald's results on a recent psychological test. Gerald had been asked questions "about how he got there, who everybody was, etc., and he had only missed one question."[32]

Elizabeth Jackson was understandably shattered by the attack on her son. Eddie Blakely said Gerald's mother spent "day and night with him since it happened."[33] For reasons that remain unclear, she felt partially responsible for the tragedy. According to Bonnie Capps, she "had a really hard time" after the attack. She says Elizabeth Jackson "always blamed herself" and that night "changed who she was."[34] It became difficult for Mrs. Jackson (then sixty-eight years old) to cope. She soon started developing health issues of her own.

In an August 24, 1994, letter to the South Carolina Department of Probation, Parole, and Pardon Services, Reggie Massey shared his thoughts on how the attack had affected Gerald's mother, who he referred to as "the other victim of Mr. Stogner's attack." Massey wrote,

> Her own health problems severely limit Mrs. Jackson's ability to visit Gerald, and she has had to watch him suffer unimaginably as a result of the well-documented violent behavior exhibited by Mr. Stogner in his attack on her son. I sat with her for hours on end for the first few days and weeks following Gerald's injury and watched as he fought for his life against all odds. I've seen her despair since then and can only imagine the emptiness she is forced to endure daily.[35]

Despite feeling awful about what had happened to him, some people suggested that perhaps if Gerald had done something differently, the tragedy might have been avoided. "The lesson in that situation is to let them keep the money, it's not worth it," mused Dr. Larry Jackson (1925–2017), former president of Lander University, who visited Jackson Station from time to time.[36] Jeff Calder of the Swimming Pool Qs notes that Gerald was "very funny, a great raconteur. But he wouldn't take any shit. If somebody was like, not doing right, in the club, he was not meek. He would straighten it out right away. And his mother was the same way."[37]

Otis Harvley, who runs the "Waterhole" bar adjacent to Jackson Station, has heard some locals question, at times, Gerald's occasional practice of physically ejecting patrons from the club. The implication was that Gerald might have occasionally been a little too hands-on.[38] Harvley also says that Gerald himself knew he made a mistake by following Douglas and Stogner into the parking lot that morning. "I fucked up going out there," Otis said Gerald told him one day years after the attack.[39]

It is true that parking lots are dangerous places. Under the right circumstances, they can become miniature gladiator rings. According to the National Crime Victimization Survey, approximately 7.3 percent of all violent victimizations occur in parking lots.[40] "Saw a lot of fights in the parking lot," says Tommy Kidd, referring to Jackson Station. He estimates there were fights during about 20 percent of his visits to Jackson Station.[41] Kidd said the fights would "start inside" the club, and "continue outside," after Gerald booted the troublemakers out. The axe attack on Gerald was "horrible," admits blues guitarist Tinsley Ellis. However, he also said "when you go that late at night, and when there's hard liquor involved,"[42] there are going to be problems.

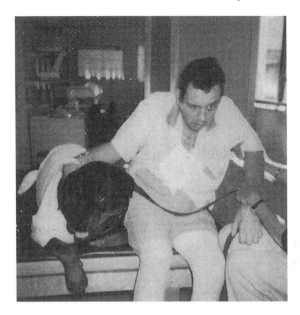

Gerald Jackson, November 6, 1990.

"Anything can happen."[43] Dave Schools of Widespread Panic agrees: "Stuff did get weird," he says, pensively. "But that's what the game was." He said, "I know that there was terrifying shit that went on in the parking lot. Any time there's late night and alcohol and people from different walks of life get all mixed up together some terrible shit can go down. And obviously what happened to Gerald was some terrible, terrible shit."[44]

"Unfortunately," as the Reverend Billy Wirtz reflects, "barroom violence is of that kind that when it goes bad, it goes bad quick, and it's over quick, usually, but the damage is done by the time you can really do much of anything."[45] In a case of tragic irony, the attack would have been averted had Gerald simply adhered to his own security rules about not going out into the parking lot. "Gerald's rule was do not leave that ramp and go into the yard," says John Sanders. "Inside the building only. Don't go out in that parking lot with anybody. That's a no-no."[46] Gerald "knew he had limited control of things that happened beyond his doors,"[47] says Jack McConnell. However, for some reason, at that particular moment, Gerald did not heed his own advice.

It could also be that one of Gerald Jackson's most laudable character traits contributed to his downfall.

"Gerald was not someone who would be bullied," said David Goldman.[48] Roland Tranter agrees: "Gerald was a strong person," he says.[49] "Everybody thought, well Gerald was gay, and everybody thinks gay people are weak, and that wasn't the situation with Gerald. I've seen him separate several [fights], you know, by himself. And just, get [']em up, shake [']em. Tell 'em, you know, *'Straighten up! Go outside! You get calmed down. Then we'll see. Maybe then you can come back in.'*[50] "Gerald . . . he was pretty tough there," agrees Tinsley Ellis. "If someone acted up, they bounced them out."[51] "Gerald just tried to keep people from fighting," recalls Tommy Kidd. "Tried to keep people from falling into the pot-bellied stove. Kept order."[52] John Sanders says, "He was good at it. And Gerald was strong. He amazed me at some of the things he would do. He wasn't hurting for strength."[53]

Guitarist Glenn Phillips said that hearing about the attack on Gerald surprised him. He said performing artists and club owners often develop a "kind of radar to anticipate situations." Phillips says Gerald was "so good at spotting things before they happened."[54] Jack McConnell also says that if Gerald noticed trouble, he was usually "very good at running to the situation and sort of diffusing the situation."[55] He said, "When some crazy stuff started happening on the floor, Gerald would be right over and straighten it out very quickly."[56] In Maxine Syrkett's recollection, Gerald would simply treat the malcontents as family. He would "just run in there and separate them, and tell them to sit down, you know, and talk to them like they were more or less their brothers or something, and they'd go on, and they'd either break it up or some of them I'd saw, they'd apologize to each other, and went on, but chances are they came together. So he'd just break them up and tell them to go about their business."[57]

Catherine Brickley of the Sensible Pumps remembers very few problems at Jackson Station. However, she said, "if there was trouble there, I remember Gerald opening that side door and just throwing somebody out and then closing the door back. It wasn't like he punched him or anything. He just opened the door and he pushed the guy out and they shut the door."[58] For her part, Brickley's bandmate, Mattie Phifer, describes the attack on Gerald as "an anomaly of the culture of the club." She says, "It was not a violent, fighting, type place. I don't remember there ever being a fight at Jackson Station or anybody not getting along."[59]

The attack on Gerald Jackson on April 7, 1990, marked the beginning of the end of Jackson Station. Gerald was almost completely paralyzed, could hardly speak, and would spend the rest of his life bedridden or in a wheelchair. He was, according to his doctor, "totally disabled."[60] He would survive the next twenty years only because of the time, care, and attention that Gerald was given by his best friend and loving partner, Steve Bryant.

Steve tried to hold on to the club as best he could. Linn Johnson remembers Steve being in a state of shock "for several months."[61] On October 7, 1990, David Goldman visited Jackson Station and was informed that things were not going well. "Gerald's mind is great, but his body is totally fucked," Steve said to his friend.[62] According to Goldman, Steve had "lost even more hair." He was "drinking more than usual." Goldman said, "Heavy smoking was taking its toll, and he often disguised real emotion with a rasping, nervous laugh." He said that "Steve explained the dire financial situation to me." Without Gerald, Steve said Jackson Station "was just a big building." The club was "losing lots of money" and "was likely to close soon."[63]

Even worse, it sounded like Gerald and Steve might be splitting up. As Goldman put it in a journal entry, "Gerald had decided that, when he is released from the rehab center, he wants to come home to his mother." Because of this, Steve was "preparing to leave" and "return to his mother's house."[64] Goldman said, "Steve fought as long as he could to keep his and Gerald's club open." While some might suggest that Steve "just freaked out and threw up his hands" after the attack on Gerald, Goldman said this was incorrect. Such a view would imply Steve was "weak, hysterical and a quitter, and he was none of those things."[65]

However, according to Jackson Station regular Tersh Harley, it soon became obvious that "Steve was just not able to run the place as well by himself. The drinking age was 21 so that really knocked off a lot business. It just got overwhelming for Steve." To make matters worse, Gerald would soon be moving from Self Hospital in Greenwood to the William Jennings Bryan Dorn Veteran's Administration Hospital in Columbia, South Carolina. Steve was unsure how to proceed.

"I've got to figure out what to do," Steve told Tersh about a week before Jackson Station would shut down. "I can't have [Gerald in Columbia at the VA Hospital], and me here trying to run this thing."[66] As it happened, Tersh Harley had recently bought a house in Columbia. For years, Harley had been one of Gerald and Steve's closest friends. On the quiet nights, he hung around the bar a lot. He was known for being a good tipper, often ran errands for the guys, and generally just helped them out when and where he could. Because of his loyalty, for about eight years Tersh had been drinking beer more or less on the house. He would often make valiant attempts to pay for his beer, but his bar tab would never materialize, even when Tersh asked to see it. The question of "Tersh's Tab" was a long-standing joke and source of mystery.

Given the circumstances, especially Gerald's medical status and the imminent closure of Jackson Station, Tersh felt it was time to settle accounts. Tersh said, "Look Steve, how about this tab? Any idea what we can do here? This tab is a little bit, to say the least, long overdue." Steve replied, "*Tersh, I have no idea what's going on with that. I don't even know. Gerald is the only one who knows anything about that.*" Tersh took $300 out of this wallet and stuffed it in the tip jar. He turned to Steve and told him: "Look, all right, this is the way this is going to happen: When you shut this place down you're going to move in with me down in Columbia . . . When you get yourself up and going, we'll talk about rent . . . When you find a job, when you start working on things, we'll talk about rent then. That's only when you start feeling comfortable."[67]

Steve Bryant took up Tersh on his offer. He closed Jackson Station and headed to Columbia. "We made it through October," recalls Dirk Armstrong, of the waning days at the depot. "People were talking trash . . . Work is work, but you could also have a little bit of fun. It just got to be a drag off of Steve and I to keep the place up and moving when the whole spirit of it was Gerald . . . That was Gerald's baby."[68] Dirk worked at Jackson Station until the day it shut down. Before he drove back home to Tampa, he amended the letters on the Jackson Station billboard. He took the letters that had once spelled "OPEN" and rearranged them to say "NOPE," instead.

Later in October 1990, Steve moved in with Tersh Harley at 3829 Capers Avenue in Columbia. "All he had to his name was a duffle bag full of clothes and an old Volkswagen Beetle," says Harley. "I mean that's it. That's all he had."[69] First Steve lived in the spare bedroom in the main house, and later in a small outbuilding in the back, which Tersh had converted into an apartment.

"I had plenty of room," Harley said, adding that his girlfriends "loved Steve." One day his girlfriend at the time asked him what the story was. "As strange as this sounds," he told her, "'I've had this tab with them for many, many, many years. And I kind of feel like this is going to be kind of like my tab for them'. . . . That's why I didn't even blink about it. I was like, 'Look, first of all, I'm real good friends with y'all, and for God's sake, y'all had this tab for me for years. The least I can do is pay you back this way.'"[70]

The Capers Avenue house was just two miles away from the William Jennings Bryan Dorn Veteran's Administration Hospital. The close proximity allowed Steve to keep a close eye on Gerald. At first, Steve worked various bartending jobs around Columbia. Then he was encouraged by staff to apply for a job at the VA since he was spending so much time there.

Steve Bryant lived in that apartment on Capers Avenue for the next twenty years, even after Tersh Harley sold the property and moved to Charleston.

TEN

THE TRIAL

The words in that indictment are never proof of the charges contained therein. The only proof is going to come to you from this witness stand.
—Judge Thomas Hughston Jr.[1]

The trial of the *State of South Carolina v. Terry Daniel Stogner* took place in Greenwood on February 11 and February 12, 1991. Proceedings began at 11:20 in the morning at Greenwood County Courthouse. The Honorable Thomas Hughston Jr., was the presiding judge. Townes Jones IV was the solicitor (prosecuting attorney) for Greenwood County. Marvin Watson, who had been working as an attorney in Greenwood since 1957,[2] was counsel for the defense. Terry Daniel Stogner, wearing a blue tie and gray coat,[3] sat next to his boss from the surveying company, Paul Wash. Gerald Jackson appeared in court in a wheelchair, wearing a red-striped shirt. He was seated behind Mr. Jones. Margaret F. Briggs was the Court Reporter for the trial.

Townes Jones's job was to prosecute Terry Stogner to the fullest extent of the law. His father, Townes Jones III (1922–1998), a famed Greenwood attorney,[4] had held the solicitor job now occupied by his son, who had taken the position in 1985. Jones called the attack on Gerald "one of the most tragic and vicious assault cases I've ever been associated with."[5] Witnesses for the prosecution included: Captain James Henderson, Sergeant Randy Miles, Sergeant Tony Roberts, and Major Tony Davis, all with the Greenwood Sheriff's Department. Other witnesses included Maxine Syrkett, Alan Wagoner, Terry Tinsley, and Craig Douglas. Dr. Harold W. Schmidt, a Greenwood neurosurgeon, and Dr. Robert E. Desach of the South Carolina Medical School appeared as expert medical witnesses. Elizabeth Jackson, Steve Bryant, and Reggie Massey were also in the courtroom and would be called as additional state witnesses if needed.[6]

The jury was selected (some potential members were excluded from serving) and sent to the Jury Room while the court took a brief recess. A few minutes later, Judge Hughston recommenced the proceeding. "All right," he said. "Anything else before we bring the jury out?"[7]

Moments earlier, Gerald Jackson had been wheeled out of the courtroom to the reception area to be given some medicine by his nurse. Townes Jones approached the Judge and asked for a two-minute delay to wait for Jackson's return. "All right," said the judge.

Marvin Watson objected to Jackson's presence in the courtroom. "Your Honor," he said. "I want to ask the court to require the solicitor to remove the victim from the courtroom because of his condition. It's very obvious, the way he's dressed, the way he's . . ."[8]

The judge stopped him. "I'm not going to make him not be in the courtroom. I think the solicitor has a right to have him here," Hughston said. "He is in a wheelchair and dressed in what appears to be some type of pajama clothes, with a lap cover and that kind of a thing, but I don't know of any reason why he can't be in the courtroom."[9]

The judge then called for the jury. He appointed Chester Ouzts as foreman. The jury was sworn in. Judge Hughston reminded the jury that "the oath that you just took was an oath whereby you swore you would decide this case based on the testimony and evidence presented here in court and my instructions to you on the law."[10] He said members of the jury were "finders of fact, or judges of the facts of the case." He said, "You're going to decide what facts are established by the testimony and evidence from this witness stand."[11] Judge Hughston continued: "The state has charged, claims, that this defendant, Terry Daniel Stogner, committed the crime known as an assault and battery with intent to kill on April 7th, 1990, against Gerald Jackson."[12] Stogner, the judge said, had "entered a plea of not-guilty." He reminded the jury that "A person charged with committing a criminal offense, no matter how serious that charge may be, is never required to prove himself innocent. The burden of proof is on the state to prove him guilty . . . beyond any reasonable doubt."[13]

The trial began with opening statements. In his remarks, Townes Jones said he would prove to the jury that, when Terry Stogner assaulted Gerald Jackson with a bush axe, he did so with an intent to kill him. Jones then told the jury about Jackson Station, where the crime took place. He said the place was "a club that offered live entertainment in the way of musical presentations. Bands would play there. In Hodges, South Carolina. Right up there Highway 25, about eight or nine miles from town . . . Just as you go up the hill there, as you go by. The old Jackson Station."[14] Jones said he would "attempt to prove that in an effort to collect moneys due to him, [Gerald Jackson] walked out into that parking lot." He said Jackson did so in "a civil, appropriate manner."[15] However, he claimed Terry Stogner "interrupted a conversation that Mr. Gerald Jackson was having with a Mr. Craig Douglas." Jones said Stogner did this is in an "opprobrious, obnoxious, and uncivil manner." Jones said Stogner had "initiated an argument" with Jackson. This lead to a "physical confrontation between those two" and that Gerald "Jackson did, did to some degree, involve himself in that physical confrontation."[16] This was due to what Jones called "a slap," after which "the defendant turned, and walked in a cool and deliberate fashion to the back end of the pick-up truck and armed himself with a bush ax."[17]

Jones went on to describe how Stogner then delivered "one horrid blow" to Jackson's head with the bush axe. He said "the defendant then walked over to Mr. Jackson, who was laying unconscious on the ground, unwedged the bush axe from his head, tossed the bush axe in the back of the truck, got in the truck, and drove off to his residence, where he proceeded to wash the bush axe and wash other clothes and retire for the evening. Go to sleep."[18] Concluding his opening remarks, Jones told the jury they needed to examine the facts of the case and decide for themselves "whether or not there was an intent to kill when a bush axe was used to hit somebody square in the head."[19]

In his opening statement, Marvin Watson—Stogner's lawyer—was more circumspect. He kept his remarks short and to the point. He told the jury to listen to the testimony of the witnesses, to pay attention to the evidence presented, and to remember the instructions from the judge. Watson then offered a very somber prediction. He said, "When this case is over, in all probability all of you will wish you hadn't served on the jury. It's going to be a technical case, it's going to be a serious case. It's going to be a case where there is conflict in testimony and you have to decide who to believe."

Four people who witnessed at least part of the altercation testified at Stogner's trial: Terry Tinsley, Craig Douglas, Gerald Jackson, and Terry Stogner. Terry Tinsley and Craig Douglas, who each had given their accounts of the attack to the police on the morning of April 7, 1990, also gave testimony at the trial. Gerald took the stand and spoke briefly in court but could not recall anything that had happened the night in question. Terry Stogner was the last to take the stand. His telling of the incident would differ from those of all the other witnesses, including Craig Douglas.

Terry Tinsley testified in the afternoon of February 11, 1991. He told the court that he had been working at Jackson Station the night of the attack. He said Gerald had "asked me come give him a hand in the kitchen and keeping the bottles and cans and things in the trash, off the floor."[20] Tinsley said he was in the kitchen making food when Gerald's mother, Elizabeth Jackson, came in. She was concerned because Gerald was out in the parking lot with a couple of customers. She asked him to see what was going on.[21] Tinsley went outside.

"Gerald was standing there talking with some other guy about something," Tinsley remembered. "I couldn't understand what they were talking about. I asked [Gerald]—told him his mother wanted to come back inside, she needed him inside."[22] He said Gerald spoke to him and said, "*No, you go back inside.*"[23] Tinsley said he could not make out the details of the conversation between Stogner and Jackson. He said he "didn't hear them fussing, really arguing. I just heard them like mumbling. I couldn't understand what they were saying. They weren't yelling when I was there, no."[24]

Tinsley did what Gerald told him to do. He "turned around and walked back towards the building."[25] Looking back at the men as he was leaving, he saw they had "moved in the parking lot down toward the truck."[26] At that point, Tinsley said Stogner "reached into the back of the truck and pulled something out." Tinsley thought it was perhaps "a stick or a club or handle."[27] He saw Stogner bring the object up, lift it behind his left shoulder, and "brought it forward toward Gerald."[28] Tinsley said he raced into Jackson Station, knocking over a girl on crutches in the process. He ran "straight into the bar area and started hollering and grabbing people."[29]

The next day, at 9:00 in the morning of February 12, 1991, Craig Douglas took the witness stand. He wore a blue jacket and a red tie.[30] He was no longer with Paul Wash Surveying Company but was now working for the Commission for Public Works (CPW), the local utility company. Douglas told the court that, on the night in question, he drove Stogner and himself to Jackson Station after they had finished drinking at Sports Break. He said that getting into Jackson Station had not been a problem. Douglas said, "I parked the truck and then we walked in and paid a cover charge, ten dollars. And then we went to the bar. We got a beer. We split times buying."

During their second round of drinks, Douglas said, "This guy bumped into Terry Stogner." However, he said that Stogner "didn't say, '*Excuse me,*' he said '*Excuse you.*'"[31] Douglas was worried that "there was going to be some trouble" between Stogner and the other man, and he suggested a hasty exit. Stogner agreed. Douglas said he finished his beer and said, 'Well, let's go. It's time to go.' So we walked out of Jackson Station, down the ramp." Douglas asked Stogner for the truck keys, which he said were handed to him. Douglas said, "We walked out to our truck alone."[32]

They got to the pickup truck. Douglas said, "I went to the driver's side of the truck, and [Stogner] went to the passenger's side of the truck. He opened the door of the truck."[33] Then, all of the sudden, "Mr. Jackson popped up. We never looked back or anything. He popped up, and he leaned against the bed of truck." Douglas said Gerald looked at him and asked, "'*Do you have something you want to give me?*' talking about a previous bar tab that I had with him that I had not thought anything about."

"No, I don't[,] Gerald," Douglas said to Jackson. "I had a slack week this week, only made $118 this week."[34] Douglas said Gerald replied, "'Well, you all just don't come back no more then,' and I accepted that." Douglas says it was at that point that Stogner inserted himself in the conversation. He said Stogner "started cussing at Gerald and said, *'Listen here, you goddamn son-of-a-bitch. Get the hell out of my way and leave me alone.*' And all this stuff."[35] Douglas said while Stogner was cussing at Gerald he "backed Mr. Jackson up approximately 27 feet, or nine steps" from the back of the truck. Douglas said that he "tried to get between them to stop them" from arguing. He told the court that he said to the men, "You all shut the hell up." To Stogner he said, "*Terry, get in the truck and let's go home.*"[36] However, "Stogner kept standing there cussing at Mr. Jackson."

Douglas claimed that "Jackson hit Stogner-slapped him three times in the face. The second and third time, his glasses came off, Mr. Stogner's glasses." Douglas said that "after he was slapped three times, Stogner was running back toward the truck and grabbed the bush axe out of the back of the truck." He says Stogner "swung it around, and I heard something go ting on the bumper." Douglas said Stogner swung the axe again. "The second time around, he come around with the bush axe on the left side. He hit Mr. Jackson in the head."[37] Douglas said, "I just saw him fall. I was waiting for him to scream."[38]

Douglas turned to Stogner and said, "You killed that man. You ignorant son-of-a-bitch. You have killed him."[39] He helped Stogner drag Jackson's body from out of the way of the back wheels of the truck so they could drive away. Douglas said he "grabbed the defendant by his right arm and pulled him over to the driver's side of the truck, away from Jackson Station."[40] Douglas then said he told Stogner, "Get your ass in this truck and let's go home."[41] He said Stogner "got the axe out of the man's head and put it back in the truck, and got in the truck and we proceeded to go home."[42]

On the drive back to Greenwood, Douglas said he asked Stogner "why he done it." He said Stogner responded by saying, "I don't give a damn. He cut me."[43] When they got to Stogner's apartment in Greenwood, Douglas said he "ran into the house and the bathroom." He said he was "hoping [Stogner] would come in right behind me so that I could look at the cuts he said he'd gotten."[44] Douglas saw a "slight cut over [Stogner's] eye," and a "fingernail mark on his ear."[45] Douglas himself "had blood all over my left tennis shoe."[46] Douglas said he cleaned the shoe while Stogner washed off the bush axe.[47] Douglas then got in the pickup truck and drove home to his apartment. He said, "I told him I had to go home, because I didn't feel like his statement was true about being cut."[48]

It is important to note that Craig Douglas's testimony in court differed markedly from the account he gave to the police in the morning of April 7, 1990, right after the attack. For example, then he had made no mention of Stogner forcing Gerald to back up twenty-seven feet in the parking lot. In his earlier statement, Douglas had described Gerald Jackson as being the instigator of the argument. In court, however, Douglas said that it was Stogner who was cussing at Gerald, forcing him to retreat. In his interview with the police, Douglas said Gerald had almost immediately started to threaten Terry Stogner, saying to him, "I'll cut you son-of-a-bitch."[49] He also claimed that Gerald actually cut Stogner three times, possibly with a knife, he was not sure. During the trial, Douglas did not mention any of this. He did not discuss Stogner being cut at all. Now he said that Stogner "backed up Mr. Jackson by cussing him out." Gerald was also described as being more reasonable than before. Douglas said, "Mr. Jackson was just wanting to get his money and talked to me. He didn't say nothing to Mr. Stogner."[50] Despite the differences in Douglas's two statements, there were also a couple of common threads. In both accounts, Douglas asserted that it had been Gerald who initiated physical contact with Stogner (first by cutting him, later by slapping him). At both the police station and during the trial, Douglas said Stogner swung the bush axe at Gerald not once but twice.

Stogner's counsel, Marvin Watson, identified the inconsistencies in Douglas's story. Asked why his recounting of the incident had changed over the past ten months, Douglas said, "at the time I gave my statement, I was scared, I was in shock, and I was going through a stage of denial."[51] Watson then had Douglas read aloud the statement he made to the police on April 7 and had Douglas essentially agree with him that, contrary to what he had just told the court, Gerald had indeed threatened to cut Stogner that night at Jackson Station.[52] Douglas admitted that he had not told the truth about Stogner because they socialized together "and he gave me a job." Douglas said, "I tended to lean a little his [Stogner's way] because I didn't want to see nobody get in trouble."[53] By the end of the cross examination, however, Watson managed to manipulate Douglas's testimony to make it sound as if Gerald and Douglas had been the best of friends all along. Watson asked him, "In fact, if you've got a good friend in this whole outfit, it's Gerald Jackson?" Douglas replied, "Yes, he's a friend of mine."[54] By the time Douglas stepped down from the stand, what had actually occurred in the parking lot that morning at Jackson Station was still incredibly murky. When he had given his first statement to the police, Douglas told them that Gerald Jackson had been the one cussing at Stogner. Now he said Stogner was the one cussing out Gerald. The swinging of Gerald's arms had turned into cuttings, then into slaps, and now back into cuttings.

Gerald Jackson would then make a brief appearance on the witness stand. While he had undoubtedly been a witness to the crime (as well as the victim)—and his presence less than a year after the attack certainly carried symbolic weight—Gerald's testimony did not help his case. Jackson said he did not remember anything about the night he was attacked. He had no idea who struck him. He did successfully answer questions about his service in Vietnam and his understanding of the legal processes associated with of the trial. Gerald denied that the pocketknife recovered by Maxine Syrkett at the scene of the crime was his.[55]

If the members of the jury were still unclear about what had exactly transpired at Jackson Station the morning of April 7, 1990, these doubts would only increase with the testimony of Terry Stogner. The defendant's characterization of the incident differed significantly from all the others presented at the trial. Stogner agreed that he and Douglas had been drinking together at Legends and then at Sports Break. Contrary to Douglas account, however, Stogner said he had driven the two men up to Jackson Station. Once there, he said they made their way to the entrance of the club. Stogner said that "an older woman, Gerald Jackson's mother," was working the door. He said that Douglas paid a cover charge for the both of them. They ordered a round of beers, and then a second round, after which Stogner said it was "time for me to go. There wasn't no point in staying up there any longer. If [Douglas] wanted to stay, feel free, but I was leaving, and he said no, he would leave with me, and we both left the bar."[56]

Stogner said he and Douglas walked out of the club into the parking lot toward the truck. "I was on the driver's side," he said. "I unlocked the driver's side and got in, reached across and unlocked the passenger door for Craig, who was standing outside the door there."[57] Waiting for Douglas to get into the vehicle, Stogner said he heard him talking to someone at the back of the truck. Stogner "turned and looked, and Gerald was standing behind the truck. They seemed to be arguing about some matter. Something was said about some money."

Stogner said he got out of the truck. Across from him was Douglas. Gerald was "right there at the back of the truck." Stogner said Douglas told Gerald that he "didn't have the money he owed him." He said Gerald responded by saying he was going to teach Douglas a lesson and "have us both arrested for trespassing." Stogner said he then spoke up, saying, "There's no reason to have either one of us arrested for anything. We've not done anything. We're just going to leave and Mr. Douglas can take up your financial matter later."[58] Stogner said Gerald "turned to me very angrily, as if I shouldn't have opened my mouth at all, and he told me he was going to teach me a lesson, too." He said Gerald "swung at me, took a swing at me."[59] Stogner said Gerald "seemed very upset, out of control," and "swung wild" at both of them. He says he and Douglas "tried to calm him. '*Hold it right there, Gerald. We're not going to fight you,*'" Stogner said they told him. However, Stogner claimed that Gerald was unstoppable. "He continued coming at me. I was backing up the whole time. He came at me swinging. I stepped out into the parking lot. He swung at me. I continued backing up. He swung at me again and hit my glasses, knocked my glasses off my face." According to Stogner, Gerald said, "'*I'll cut you, you son-of-a-bitch,*' not once but 'several times.'" Stogner said he "stumbled and kept backing away" from Gerald. Gerald then "reached into his pocket, and he pulled out a pocketknife. He continued coming toward me."[60] Stogner said Gerald "finally connected several times with the knife." Stogner said he sustained a "pretty good cut over my left ear. Where he hit me in the ear was almost a knot. It wasn't a slice. It was a chunk taken out. And then behind the left ear was a very slight cut."[61]

Stogner testified that after Gerald cut him a third time, he "ran towards the truck." He stated, "I reached into the back of the truck, and I grabbed for anything I could."[62] Stogner came out with a bush axe. He argued that his choice of this particular object as a defensive weapon was arbitrary. He told the court, "I never looked and specifically chose the bush axe . . . I knew if I reached into the back of the truck, then I might find a pipe, a shovel, there was a number of axes in the truck, wrenches, long wooden stakes. Just anything to hold him at bay while I got in the truck and left. And an axe is what I came out with. Mr. Jackson didn't seem the least bit afraid of the axe as I swung it and warned him, and I had no intentions of hitting Mr. Jackson with the axe. My full intention was to protect myself and hold him at bay while I got in the truck and left."[63]

Stogner said he "took the axe out of the truck. I held it with both hands. I swung it back and forth. I banged it up against the side of my truck." Stogner said Gerald "was at a distance, still coming at me."[64] He said he warned Gerald to leave him alone. "Don't come at me again," he says he called out to Jackson. "You're not going to cut me again. Don't come at me again. I'll hit you."[65] Stogner claimed, "Mr. Jackson never slowed his place. He continued straight towards me. I was still swinging the axe. He ran straight into it with his head."[66] As Gerald fell, Stogner said he let go of the axe. "When he fell, the axe was still in his head." Stogner said he "reached down, [and] removed the axe from his head."[67] Stogner said he took the bush axe and threw it in the back of the truck. He said he "was very much in just a daze. I was in shock or whatever. I think Craig was, too. He began screaming and said, '*You've killed the man. You've killed the man. Let's get the hell out of here.*'"[68]

Stogner said that patrons soon began to emerge from Jackson Station, spilling into the parking out. "There [were] quite a few people coming from the bar area then," Stogner said. He said Douglas's suggestion "sounded as reasonable to me as anything."[69] However, first Stogner said he had to stop Douglas from backing over Gerald's injured body. Stogner said he turned to Douglas and said, "But you can't . . . Craig you can't run over him." Stogner said he grabbed Gerald by the arms and that Douglas took him by the legs. Together they dragged him out of the path of their truck and left him in the middle of the parking lot, behind another car. Stogner said, "[We] moved him about three feet over closer to the rear of the car that was parked beside us and we left him there, got in the truck and left."[70]

Stogner insisted he was acting in self-defense when he struck Gerald Jackson with the bush axe. "I knew I was in danger," he told the court. "He had already cut me three times with his knife. However, when I got the axe out of the back of the truck, I felt like that would stop him." However, Stogner said Gerald did not stop attacking him until he hit him with the bush axe in the head.[71] Stogner said Douglas had driven the men home. He said when they got to Stogner's apartment, Douglas took care of him. "'*Come one, let's get you inside, get the blood stopped,*'" he claimed Douglas said to him. "*Let's get you inside the house. Get you cleaned up. Let's clean the bush axe up. Let's clean up this blood.*"[72] Stogner said he was "bleeding pretty good from my forehead," but "behind the ear wasn't bad."[73]

In fact, this was the first time Stogner reported he had been stabbed on the forehead. There was no mention of his forehead being injured when he discussed his injuries earlier in the trial[74] where he said he had been cut on, in, and behind his ears. During his first interview with the police, Craig Douglas never told police Stogner had been cut on the forehead. And as we have seen, during the trial Douglas never mentioned Stogner being cut at all.

Continuing with his testimony, Stogner said he went to the bathroom and put napkins on his head where he was bleeding.[75] Stogner denied washing off any bush axe. He "had blood on the front of my shirt from the wound on my head."[76] Stogner had blood on his boots and blood on his pants. He said Douglas washed his boots off for him before leaving Stogner's place and heading back to his own apartment.[77]

"If looks could kill, he would be dead," comments Mattie Phifer of the Sensible Pumps, pursuant to Terry Stogner's appearance on the witness stand. "Because I was in that courtroom and I know I was staring bullets through him I was so mad. I was just so mad. Like, 'How could you possibly do this to this human being'?"[78]

Terry Stogner was the final witness in the trial. It was then time for closing arguments. First, Townes Jones gave the jury a summary of the legal aspects of the case. He reminded them of the presumption of innocence on the part of the defendant and that the burden of proof to convict Stogner needed to be beyond that of a reasonable doubt. Jones told the jury, in making their determination of guilt or innocence: "You must judge the credibility of witnesses; you must judge their believability; you must determine who was telling you the truth."[79] Jones said he hoped "you do not leave your common sense and your sense of reality and your sense of the way humans interact outside here. Take it back there in the jury room with you."[80] Townes Jones also told the jury that their verdict must be unanimous. He reminded them of the three possible verdicts in the case: (a) guilty of assault and battery with intent to kill; (b) guilty of assault and battery of a high and aggravated nature; or (c) not guilty. He described how the charge of assault and battery with intent to kill hinged on the concept of "malice aforethought" and how such malice "can be expressed or implied."[81] He said that while there was no express malice on the part of Stogner, there was the presence of implied malice. Jones said, "Implied malice may arise from the use of a deadly weapon, such as a gun, or an ax."[82]

Jones stated that a conviction on the charge of assault and battery with intent to kill befitted an individual with a "depraved heart, a heart bent on ill will, a heart determined to do mischief, a heart determined to do wrong, a human being that's determined to do wrong. That's assault and battery with intent to kill."[83] Jones concluded his legal synopsis by discussing the evidence and lack of evidence needed for the two other possible verdicts, which would entail finding Stogner guilty of assault and battery of a high and aggravated nature (a verdict which does not presume malice aforethought), or finding Stogner not guilty of either crime.

Marvin Watson begun his concluding remarks by calling attention to the discrepant statements offered by Jackson Station employee Terry Tinsley and Craig Douglas. He said that although neither men had bothered to officially change the statements they had made to the police on the morning of the attack, when they spoke in court, they had indeed changed them. "All of the statements were changed to in an effort to try and help their friend, Mr. Jackson," Watson argued. "Nothing was changed in favor of the defendant."[84]

"We're all sorry for Mr. Jackson," Watson told the jury. "It's a terrible situation." However, the defense attorney argued that Gerald Jackson was largely to blame for the fate that had befallen him. Watson said, "The facts are the facts, and the statements that were given to the police officers shortly after this incident occurred, I submit to you, should be the most believable statements given."[85]

Watson claimed that some facts in this case were clear on all sides. "The first thing that's undisputed is that everyone involved had been drinking. Have you thought of that? Everyone had been drinking, including Gerald."

Watson said the second indisputable fact was that there had been some sort of an argument between Gerald Jackson and Terry Stogner.

"The third thing that's undisputed—and remember this—Jackson passed the first licks." Marvin Watson is not being truthful here. While Townes Jones did refer to a "slap"[86] in his opening statement, in fact, only Douglas and Stogner's testimony supports this assertion. Tinsley never said Gerald attacked Stogner, neither in the statement he gave at the police station, nor in his testimony on the stand.

Watson said the fourth undisputed fact was "that there was a knife involved somehow in the dispute."[87] Again, it would be a stretch to say this was undisputed. There were literally hundreds of people at Jackson Station that night. Any one of them could have lost the pocketknife that was found closed in the parking lot with a penny in it. No one who knew Gerald said he owned a pocketknife. Gerald denied it was his. Nonetheless, Watson emphasized to the jury Douglas's initial comments about Gerald trying to cut Stogner, as well as Stogner's own testimony about Gerald cutting him. Watson boldly asserted it simply must have been Gerald's knife since it was found at the site of the altercation. Watson questioned Gerald's ability to remember whether the knife was his. He said, "Whether that's his knife or whether he got it the night before or somebody gave it to him that night or he took it off somebody there that night of the dance, I can't say. And I don't think Gerald can say that it wasn't his knife."[88]

A fifth undisputed fact, according to Watson, was that a pair of glasses had been found in the parking lot near the highway, some distance from where Gerald had been lying on the ground bleeding to death. Stogner claimed that Gerald had knocked them off his head. "So what does that tell you?" Watson asked the jury. "If the argument started up near the truck, then certainly it proceeded a great deal away from the truck."[89] Watson said Stogner was "true and correct" when he stated that he and Gerald "went down and came back" to the road "arguing and striking and pushing and shoving."[90]

As he wrapped up his closing statement, Watson gave a relentless final defense of his client. He argued, "If you believe, which is undisputed, that Gerald Jackson brought on all of this problem, that he was the first one to strike the licks, that he had a knife, that most of the undisputed things I've told you are true and correct, then you shouldn't have very much trouble eliminating assault and battery with intent to kill."[91] Watson said he hoped the jury would "write a verdict of not guilty."[92]

Townes Jones then gave his closing statement on the facts of the case. He responded to the implication that Stogner's choice of the bush axe was an arbitrary one. He said to the jury, "Mr. Watson said it could have been a gun. He said it could have been a knife. He said it could have been a pipe and it could have been an ax. It was an ax. It was not a pipe. It was not a gun. Not a gun that's easily used. Not a knife that's brandished. It was an ax. Labelled as evidence in this case. This is the weapon used."[93] Jones then attacked the credibility of the defendant, Terry Stogner. He asked the jury:

Were you impressed by his coolness? Were you impressed by him? Were you impressed by the fact that his version of what he told you, that his version of what he told you happened out there not only re- moved him from any guilt in assault and battery with intent to kill? Why, he didn't swing at Gerald, did he? His testimony was that Ger- ald ran into this bush axe. Ran into it. Not only absolves him of any guilt of assault and battery of a high and aggravated nature, his testimony puts him right in the self-defense realm. Right in self-defense. Couldn't do anything else. Had to do this. No other alternative.[94]

Clearly, Townes Jones was not convinced by Stogner's story, and he did not think the jury should be, either. He declared Stogner to be one of the "coolest, coldest human beings you will ever lay your eyes on."[95] Jones had members of the jury contemplate the amount of force Stogner must have used to wedge the bush axe "three and a half to four inches . . . in to the right side of Gerald Jackson's head and brain."[96] Jones declared:

> Nobody is going to walk into three and a half to four inches of this blade. It's going to take some force to get that blade three and a half to four inches in. And I suggest to you that not only does it take force, but it takes knowledge in the use of this weapon, it takes ability to handle this weapon and use it, and it takes accuracy to place this blade, not against a man's legs, not into the midsection, not a blow here, not a blow to the upper body, but to the head. Intent to kill?[97]

Jones also questioned Stogner's actions after he struck Gerald in the head. He said Stogner "went around and pulled it out of his head, having to twist it and get it out. But he didn't pull it out to administer first aid. He didn't pull it out to help this man that had accidentally walked—that had intentionally walked into his bush [axe]."[98]

Jones rebutted claims on the part of the defense that Gerald Jackson had been acting irrationally the night that he was attacked. He questioned the "neat package" the defense team provided that painted "Gerald Jackson as an animal. He wasn't acting normal." Jones asked the jury to consider, why Gerald Jackson, a beloved member of the community and successful business owner for fifteen years, would suddenly be scrapping in the parking lot with a customer over a twenty-dollar bar tab. Jones stated:

> And this man had hundreds of people in there at a ten-dollar cover charge that night. Did you hear that testimony? Hundreds of people in there. Four different bands playing from Atlanta and Columbia. Over twenty dollars. This man wants to tell you that he beat him around in the parking lot and that once he had him down on the ground, he reached in and pulled out a pocketknife and flipped it open and decided he was going to cut his face up.[99]

Jones asked the jury to consider if Stogner's story "makes sense . . . if [it's] believable . . . if [it's] credible."[100]

Townes Jones argued that the testimony of Terry Tinsley most accurately captured the actual interaction between Terry Stogner and Gerald Jackson directly prior to the attack. Jones said, "You can believe Terry Tinsley when he says that [Gerald] wasn't chasing that man around the parking lot with a knife. He was not chasing him around that parking lot with a knife. They were standing there arguing. Terry Tinsley has said that from the beginning, and nobody has disputed his saying of that."[101]

When it came to the testimony of Gerald Jackson, Townes Jones said, "You can believe him or not believe him. That's your business. That's your job."[102]

Regarding Craig Douglas, Jones said, "[There's] no question but there were areas where he admitted that his testimony was inconsistent with a prior statement that he's given." Jones contrasted Douglas's personality to that of Stogner. "He, in his nature as a human being, is very different from the defendant. Very different. You have different human beings there. You have different needs emotionally. You have different human being responses to situations. The defendant did not need to call the police. He did not need to stay there with Gerald Jackson. He did not need to explain, Craig Douglas did."[103]

Jones briefly addressed the question of the pocketknife. Assuming for a moment that it might have been Gerald's knife after all, Jones reminded the jury it was nonetheless found closed with a penny in it. He asked the jury, "Do you think Gerald could close a knife he had after he got hit in the head with this thing? I suggest to you he didn't."[104] Jones said Maxine Syrkett's statement about the knife "expressed as much truth in this court room as could be expressed."[105] As we have seen, she had found the knife with a penny in it when she was cleaning up the parking lot on the night of the attack. The knife was turned over to the police the next day. In Jones's view, the pocketknife had had no bearing on the case whatsoever.

Townes Jones also questioned the significance of the eyeglasses found at the scene of the crime: "Ladies and gentlemen, as far as the glasses are concerned, Mr. [Tony] Davis said they were found somewhere in this area [i.e. away from the parking lot, where the attack occurred]. It doesn't make sense. Doesn't gee-haw." Jones asked, "How did they get over here?" He argued, "Contrary to what Mr. Watson said to you on the stand—I mean up here— the defendant never said these were his glasses."

Jones also asked the jury to reflect upon the relatively trivial nature of Stogner's alleged injuries. "Did you see a gash in his ear?" he asked them. "Did you see a cut on his face that required medical attention? That could have been caused by someone slashing a knife at him? If you did, you did. I didn't."[106]

Jones doubted Stogner's claim that it was Douglas who was the controlling partner in the relationship. "Who was this man?" asked Jones. He's Craig's boss." If members of the jury thought that Terry Stogner was deferential to Craig Douglas, "then you have believed something he wants you to believe."[107] Jones reminded the jury that Douglas and Stogner "left [Gerald Jackson] there bleeding to death." He said, "You run when you know you're wrong. You run when you know you have done wrong, when you have not acted appropriately."

Townes Jones told the jury they could not allow a man who sliced "open Gerald Jackson's head . . . [to] walk out of this court room." He said, "Your verdict is a very, very crucial one." Jones forcefully rejected the view that Gerald had initiated the conflict with Stogner. Rather, he said, "[Gerald] was the one who was a peacemaker. A peacemaker. Not a troublemaker, a peace maker."[108] Jones said, however, that even if there had been a physical confrontation between the two men, Stogner's self-defense argument would still be spurious because he "could have walked away from it."[109] Jones apologized for the length of his closing remarks. "I would much rather overdo my work," he told the jury, "to run it in the ground when I am trying to do my job, than not to do enough." The solicitor rested his case. He said Terry Stogner was "as guilty as the day is long."[110] He asked the jury to convict the man of assault and battery with intent to kill.

The court took a brief recess, after which Judge Hughston addressed the jury. He reminded them of the charges that had been made against Stogner as well as the defendant's not guilty plea. He restated his earlier remark that "a person charged with having committed a criminal offense in South Carolina is never required to prove himself innocent. The burden of proof is on the State." He went on to say that such a burden of proof must be "beyond a reasonable doubt." The judge continued: "I tell you that a reasonable doubt is not a fanciful or an imaginary doubt; rather it is a doubt which those words imply, a doubt for which in your own mind you can give a reason. If you have such a doubt for which you can give a reason as to the guilt of this defendant, Terry Daniel Stogner, then he's entitled under the law to a verdict of not guilty."[111]

The judge explained to the jury the exact nature of the charges. He told them, "An assault may be defined as an attempt to do violence to the person of another in a rude, angry, and resentful manner. A battery is defined as the carrying into effect an assault by using or applying force, however slight, in a rude, angry, and resentful manner."[112] The judge clarified that the charge of assault and battery with intent to kill hinged on the presence of malice. He said "malice is any formed or planned decision to do mischief, whether it arises from hatred, ill-will or otherwise."[113] In other words, to be found guilty of committing this crime, Jones would have had to prove that Stogner made a conscious decision to attack Gerald Jackson and in doing so, knew that his actions may have killed him.

Hughston then discussed the lesser charge of assault and battery of a high and aggravated nature. The jury had been informed at the beginning of the trial that they were free to reach a guilty verdict on this charge if they could not come to a consensus on the charge of assault and battery with intent to kill. The judge said that in the case of assault and battery of a high and aggravated nature, the accused could have been "chargeable or guilty of the crime of manslaughter . . . except that the person did not die."[114] In other words, had Gerald not survived the attack and Stogner not been charged with murder, he might have been charged instead with manslaughter, that is, "the killing of a human being in sudden heat and passion upon a sufficient legal provocation."[115] Manslaughter is not premeditated and does not involve malicious forethought. It is triggered by "sufficient legal provocation . . . for example, a person pulls a person's nose or spits or slaps him in the face."[116]

The judge explained that Terry Stogner should be acquitted of both charges if the jury believed that he was acting in self-defense. As Hughston said, "[The] law recognizes the right of every person to defend himself from death or serious bodily harm; and to do this, he may use such force as is necessary, even to the point of taking a human life."[117] However, the judge said that a self-defense plea must be accompanied by four demonstrations of fact. "First, that he was not at fault in bringing about the immediate difficulty." Second, "he in good faith believed that he was in imminent or immediate danger of losing his life . . . or of sustaining serious bodily harm." Third, "that a person or ordinary firmness and courage situated in like circumstances, should have reached a similar conclusion." Finally, "the defendant must show that he had no other reasonable, safe, adequate, and obvious means of escape."[118]

Summing up his remarks, Judge Hughston declared, "If you have no reasonable doubt as to the defendant's guilt after considering all the evidence, including the evidence of self-defense, then you should find him guilty in regard to one or other of the particular charges."[119] He added that Stogner was "entitled to the benefit of every reasonable doubt arising upon the whole case, after considering all the testimony and evidence for and against any defense relied upon by the accused. It is a matter of no consequence whether or not the preponderance of the evidence is in his favor."[120] The judge said that the jury could not justifiably convict Stogner of either charge "unless his guilt had been established, as I stated beyond every reasonable doubt."[121]

After some requests for the court—the jury wanted to review the testimonies of both Stogner and Douglas, and they asked for additional explanation of the three possible verdicts—the jury was sent to the Jury Room. They began to deliberate the fate of Terry Stogner. They paused at one point to ask the judge for permission to inspect Terry Stogner's ears—presumably to see if there were still marks from the cuttings—but the judge denied the request.[122] After deliberating for two hours,[123] the jury returned to court to announce the verdict. They found Terry Stogner guilty of assault and battery of a high and aggravated nature. He was sentenced to ten years in state prison.

Gerald Jackson's high school friend Linn Johnson believes it was an injustice that Terry Stogner was not convicted of assault and battery with intent to kill since, in her mind, what happened to Gerald Jackson was most definitely a murder. "That's really what it was," she said.

"It just took Gerald a long time to die."[124]

Terry Stogner's claims that Jackson had attacked and then chased him around the parking lot with a pocketknife do not ring true to people familiar with Jackson Station.

"I don't believe that," said Debbie Massey.[125]

Bill Coleman commented, "They would have seen . . . Somebody, some of the clientele would have heard the ruckus, the loud voices out there."[126]

Ben Hawthorne suggested that the idea that Gerald was the instigator in this incident is absurd. "Gerald would not have started a fight," he declared.

Nonetheless, Terry Stogner's very capable attorney Marvin Watson had skillfully planted enough seeds of doubt in the jury's mind to get them to think otherwise. The verdict had to be a unanimous, so any disagreement among the jurors was to the advantage of the defendant. Watson claimed that Gerald had been drinking on the night of the attack, and had a blood alcohol test of .068 to prove it.[127] Stogner, on the other hand, had never been given a blood alcohol test—although he had been drinking for hours prior to the altercation with Gerald. Watson further argued that the police work in this case was shoddy in many respects. For example, the crime scene in the Jackson Station parking lot had never been cordoned off, blood tests were never conducted on any of the evidence collected[128] by the police, and two sets of mugshots taken by the police of Terry Stogner had either been lost or were never developed.[129]

When they were on the stand, Marvin Watson had managed to get both Craig Douglas and Terry Tinsley to admit inconsistencies in their testimony. While Tinsley had initially told police that he had not seen Gerald being hit with the bush axe, in court and on the stand Tinsley said he was certain he had.[130] Despite his testimony to the contrary, Watson managed to get Douglas to essentially agree that Douglas's earlier statement about Gerald trying to cut Stogner with a knife had been correct after all. Watson was adamant that Terry Stogner never intended to pull a bush axe from the truck. He said Terry Stogner's truck was "pretty full of tools."[131] Stogner had simply grabbed the bush axe because it was the object closest to him as he tried to defend himself from Gerald's maniacal rampage.

Thirty years later, Townes Jones is no longer Greenwood County solicitor, but he still practices law. With salt-and-pepper hair, closed cropped beard, and wireframe glasses, he exudes the charm and appearance of a small-town Southern lawyer. In an interview in his office in Uptown Greenwood, Jones recalled that he tried to convict Stogner on a murder charge that would have put him away for twenty years.

"That's what we felt the appropriate verdict and sentence would have been given the nature of the attack, the weapon that was used, and there was really no evidence of any significant provocation on Gerald's part." He said, "Obviously it was a compromised verdict."[132]

However, the fact that the jury found Stogner guilty at all meant that they rejected the defense's claim that he was the victim in this incident and had been acting in self-defense. The jury did not have any doubt, therefore, that Terry Stogner was in fact guilty of assaulting Gerald Jackson at Jackson Station. What the jury could not agree on was whether Stogner had attacked Gerald with an "intent to kill."

Townes Jones had made the argument that it was simply obvious Terry Stogner meant to kill Gerald Jackson with the bush axe. He claimed Stogner was well trained with a bush axe and knew how to handle it as a weapon. Jones pointed out that Stogner did not attempt to use the axe defensively, as a shield across his body perhaps, neither did he hit Gerald in the chest or the leg. When Stogner swung the bush axe, he was aiming for, and made direct contact with, Gerald's skull. He tried to knock his block off.

It was likely that the concept of "legal provocation" swayed the jury away from conviction on the charge of assault and battery with intent to kill and toward the charge of assault and battery of a high and aggravated nature. This allegation is used in the prosecution of people who commit non-premeditated, heat of passion, sorts of crimes. There was no denying that passions were on display in the parking lot that morning at Jackson Station. Indeed, as we saw earlier, Marvin Watson insisted that it was Gerald Jackson who had "passed the first licks."[133] Strangely, Townes Jones did not dispute this.[134] As Judge Hughston instructed the jury, it had to answer the question "whether the state met its burden of proving this man guilty of this charge beyond any reasonable doubt."[135] At the end of the day, the state failed to do this. The prosecutor could not convince the jury that Stogner had intended to kill Gerald Jackson. Members of the jury were effectively on the bubble. Watson, Douglas, and Stogner had put enough doubt in their minds for them to reject the charge that Stogner had deliberately tried to kill Gerald Jackson. "Stogner was incredibly well represented by Marvin Watson," comments Robert Tinsley, an attorney from Greenwood. "Marvin's a great lawyer, no question about it. Marvin won the case."[136]

As Townes Jones comments, "The jury went back there trying to decide between assault and battery with intent to kill, and assault and battery of a high and aggravated nature. Or not guilty, self-defense. And they just compromised on the middle."[137] Jones said his case would have been stronger if Douglas had not been afraid of speaking out against his erstwhile boss and drinking buddy. Douglas had seen Stogner's violence directly and up close. He knew what Stogner could do. "My main witness—Douglas—was hesitant to testify against Stogner," Jones said. "He testified, but he was reluctant. He wasn't as convincing as we had hoped he could have been because of his reluctance and fear."[138]

Terry Tinsley also witnessed the attack, but his testimony was also incomplete.[139] Given that the extant witness accounts of this incident were so different—and that they also varied from accounts of those who were at the club immediately before the attack—significant gaps in the narrative remain. As such, thirty years later, it remains impossible to know what exactly happened the moment before Stogner struck Gerald in the head with the bush axe. As Gerald's accountant and dear friend, Anita Clinton, admits, "Truth is . . . I do not think we will ever know those last twenty minutes of details."[140]

The author contacted both Craig Douglas and Terry Stogner for comment on the incident at Jackson Station. Both men are still living and working in the South Carolina upstate. Craig Douglas first responded to a request for an interview by saying that he would have to think it over. When he got back to the author, he said that he would talk, but only in exchange for payment. He said the whole incident at Jackson Station was "trash" to him. Douglas said that, before the incident, he was just a normal guy looking for a good time. He said witnessing the attack on Gerald and his getting wrapped up in the case had taken a toll on his life. He would talk, but he said he could not do so for free. The author responded that he had interviewed many people for the book, had not paid any of them, and could not start doing so now. The author told Douglas that, without an interview, he would simply rely on the court transcript. Douglas implied that it did not tell the whole story. The author thanked him for his time and for returning his phone call. Douglas said of course he would, he was a man of his word.

Terry Stogner was unavailable when the author called him in the morning of February 28, 2017. In a voicemail, the author expressed that he was interested in speaking to Stogner about the events at Jackson Station. He mentioned that he had talked to Marvin Watson, who had agreed to turn over his notes of the case with Stogner's approval. The author said he hoped Stogner might be willing to do so. He asked Stogner to call him back. In a message left on the author's voicemail machine later that day, Stogner indicated that he was not interested in speaking to the author and what he had to say about the case had already been said in court.

For his part, Terry Stogner's attorney, Greenwood lawyer Marvin Watson, believes the jury's verdict was the correct one. In his view, any handwringing about whether justice was done in this case is beside the point. "Both boys came from good families," Watson told the author during an interview in his office in Uptown Greenwood, in February 2016.[141] Then in his early eighties, Watson had been practicing law in South Carolina since 1956. An alumnus of the University of South Carolina, Watson was a lifetime season ticketholder to Gamecocks football games. He often gave away his spare tickets to local police officers.

Watson first met Terry Stogner when he came to him seeking legal representation in the case involving Gerald Jackson. He said Stogner "seemed to be a pretty nice kid, an intelligent kid." Watson said Stogner's boss at the survey-ing company, Paul Wash, "may have encouraged him to come to me."[142] In meeting with Stogner, Watson found out he "did know some of [Stogner's] mother's relatives, all of them were from Laurens [County]."[143]

Watson told the author that he had no reservations whatsoever about taking Stogner's case. "What do you mean reservations?" Watson barked, seemingly offended by the question.

"Somebody was going to have to represent him, whether he hires me or someone is appointed."

Of Jackson Station, Watson said, "I never went in the place." He went on: "I never knew Gerald Jackson. I knew some of his relatives, and they were good friends of mine. But I did not know Gerald, and I did not know about his life or anything else."[144]

Marvin Watson saw no injustice in the Stogner case. "I think he did get a fair trial," Watson said. "He came out a whole lot less than what they wanted him to have."[145] People who think Stogner got off lightly "don't know a damn thing about the law," Watson declared. "He got the maximum sentence of assault and battery of a high and aggravated nature."[146]

Watson argued it is beside the point that after the attack by Stogner, Ger-ald spent the remaining years of his life in a wheelchair, could barely speak, and needed assistance with his most basic of bodily functions. He saw no problem with the fact that Stogner went free after serving less than five years in prison. Watson insisted Stogner "got the maximum sentence [10 years] for assault and battery of a high and aggravated nature. He was convicted and served the sentence that the jury convicted him of." At the end of the day, Watson said Stogner simply happened to be "at the wrong place at the wrong time under the wrong circumstances." He said Jackson and Stogner were "two tough eggs." He says they got into an argument, which quickly became heated. When he swung at Gerald with the bush axe, Watson said Stogner was just defending himself. "There was no question that there was an argument inside," Watson said. "It got outside. Both of them had weapons, and he killed him, I mean, he hit him with a bush axe."[147]

Three decades on, it seems likely (to the author at least) that Stogner's blow from the bush axe took Gerald completely by surprise. Although during the trial, Gerald would say that he did not remember who hit him, there is at least one recorded recollection about the incident that he gave later in life. During a conversation with a VA Hospital volunteer in 2008, Gerald said he had been "walking in his parking lot one night, and an angry customer hit him in the back of a head with a bush axe."[148] Given that the bush axe swung by Stogner made contact with Gerald on the right side of his head, Gerald's comment indicates that he must have been looking away from Stogner a split second before the blow was delivered. If this is true, he turned around to face Stogner right before the axe made contact with his head. Gerald never saw the blow coming. This would explain why there was no cry or scream or any attempt on Gerald's part to defend himself.

It is almost impossible to fathom the animus behind a swing that could lodge a bush axe nearly four inches deep in someone's skull. To the outside observer, at first glance the attack on Gerald Jackson appears as a vicious hate crime. Indeed, it was this hypothesis that provided one of the motivations for the author embarking on research for this book in the first place. Gerald Jackson was, after all, a proud, gay, Navy veteran, a person who was not scared of anyone. Did Jackson's way of being-in-the-world generate a certain resentment or hostility among some people in the greater Greenwood area? Certainly, the South has not been known as a region that tolerates people who are different, those with a moral code that questions the taken-for-granted-ness of what others take to be unquestionable values and beliefs. Musician Glenn Phillips, for one, remembers moving to Atlanta from the north in the early 1960s, and being "assaulted by the level of bigotry" he found there. Phillips claims that the hegemonic culture at the time was based essentially on hatred. The South he experienced expressed hatred "against Blacks, Jews, Catholics [and] Yankees," Phillips said. "And gays were at the bottom of their stupid fucking list."[149]

As we have seen, there is considerable evidence that Gerald Jackson and Steven Bryant were considered by many to be beloved members of the Greenwood community. To most of their friends and acquaintances, their sexual orientation was a nonissue. However, there are also some disturbing accounts of hatred and violence directed toward them, which were likely due to their being unapologetically gay. As Tersh Harley pointed out, "Gerald and Steve were openly gay in the homophobic rural old South." He said, "Over the years I watched them endure a lot of cruelty. Their property was constantly vandalized. Their pets and animals were killed and assaulted. [Backstabbing] neighbors took advantage of their kindness and generosity."[150] Harley said people would attack Gerald and Steve's animals. Their cows would be shot at from across the field. Dogs would be found with BBs or .22 slugs in their hides. "Anything [Gerald and Steve] had just seemed to get stabbed, cut, and occasionally killed," said Harley, sadly. To add insult to injury, "Gerald knew who did it and these same people were the ones coming in the bar drinking beer. It was a very anti-gay thing . . . It was very mean."[151] Harley said these attacks happened, as far as he could tell, regularly during the entire time Jackson Station was open.

There had been no mention of Gerald Jackson's sexuality or his relationship to Steven Bryant during the trial of Terry Stogner. Musician Billy Wirtz chalks up Stogner's attack on Gerald as being mainly due to "ignorance." As he put it, "I don't think his sexuality helped but I don't think it was the reason the guy attacked him. The guy attacked him because [Gerald] kicked him out of the club and he was just some drunk, local psycho. It is still South Carolina."[152] Wirtz added, "You had to be a real asshole to get kicked out of Jackson Station, okay? Whatever he did, the guy certainly deserved it. It wasn't because he was wearing . . . a bad fashion choice or something like that."[153] On the other hand, Gerald's longtime friend Linn Johnson does think Gerald's sexuality played a role in the attack. "I think all that is involved," she said. "I think between Mama, and the gay thing, and debt. I think, yeah, that had a lot to do with it. You know how rednecks are."[154]

Terry Stogner was sentenced to ten years at the Goodman Correctional Institute in Columbia, South Carolina. Stogner protested the verdict against him. On August 12, 1991, with the aid of Columbia lawyer John G. Delgado, Stogner filed for post-conviction relief (PCR) in Greenwood County court. Stogner requested that his sentence be vacated. Marvin Watson remembered that he "did not recommend that [Stogner] appeal his case and discouraged him from appealing his case." Nonetheless, Watson said "he and his family filed a PCR, and the court gave him the right to appeal his case to the Supreme Court."[155]

In his petition to the South Carolina Supreme Court, Stogner argued that Marvin Watson had "failed to provide him with reasonable professional assistance of counsel at trial."[156] He argued that Watson had been ineffective in challenging the perception of Jackson Station as a peaceful establishment. Stogner mocked the "beautiful picture about how well all different kinds of people got along at this bar; and all of this love and peacefulness was attributed to Mr. Jackson, because 'he was real friendly and outward with everybody and stuff.' What a wonderful person!"[157] Stogner offered a different view. As he argued in the legal brief, "The simple fact-of-the-matter is, Jackson Station is about the roughest bar in town; fights, stabbings, and shots being fired were common place at this red-neck roughhouse. The police received regular disturbance calls and had to respond almost every weekend. More times than not, Mr. Jackson would be actively involved. In fact, it was common knowledge that Mr. Jackson was known as a thoroughly dangerous man because he took dope, was a boozer, carried a knife and had a hair trigger. This was not the first time he had tried to carve-up a patron at his establishment."[158]

Stogner argued that Marvin Watson had "failed to discover this exculpatory evidence and present it at trial."[159] Stogner also claimed that Watson had erred by not securing the mugshots that had been taken "shortly after the disturbance took place."[160] Stogner claimed that such "pictures would have shown the extent of petitioner's injuries and the seriousness of his wounds."[161] Stogner maintained that "the amount of force used" when he swung the bush axe at Gerald "was a major concern," during the trial.[162] Watson had not addressed this in his defense. Stogner claimed that if "this additional evidence had been presented at trial, these concerns would have been put-to-rest [sic] and there would have been *no* question whether the amount of force was justified."[163]

Stogner additionally argued that not only had Marvin Watson failed to provide adequate counsel but so had his own PCR attorney, John Delgado. Stogner demanded a second PCR hearing. He argued that his "PCR counsel was clearly ineffective and obviously in-the-dark or at the very least ignorant of PCR procedure."[164] Stogner continued: "Due to the ineffectiveness assistance of PCR counsel, petitioner has not been able to take a full bite of the judicial apple . . . Not only was there a miscarriage of justice in the original trial, but a fundamental repugnancy in petitioner's attempt to fully and fairly raise and argue *all* of his original PCR claims."[165] The South Carolina Supreme Court dismissed Terry Stogner's appeal on August 28, 1993.[166]

In October 1993, Stogner applied for parole. His request was denied by the South Carolina Parole Board. In 1994, he applied again. Gerald's close friend Reggie Massey attended the hearing in Columbia. He made the case that Stogner should not be released from prison early.[167] Massey told the board:

> I fully understand and appreciate the constitutional guarantees involved in a criminal trial and I cannot find fault with the jury's decision based on the evidence presented in court. I do respectfully request that the members of the board fulfill your obligation to make the judicial system work for Mr. Jackson at least as well as it has for Mr. Stogner. The full facts of the case can now be reviewed and it

seems to me only proper that Mr. Stogner be deprived of the privilege of living in civilized society for as long as the criminal justice system will allow.[168]

Massey remembered that Terry Stogner's old boss, Paul Wash, from the surveying company in Greenwood, was also at the parole hearing, hoping the board would release his employee. Massey said the surveying business was becoming more reliant on technology and Wash needed Stogner's help with the computer programming part of the job. "Paul didn't know how to do that," Massey says. "Terry knew all the new stuff." Because of this Wash "wanted to get him out [of prison, and] back to work."[169]

In 1994, Stogner's petition again was denied. Then, in 1995, the Board approved his application for parole. Terry Stogner was released from the Goodman Correctional Institute on September 29, 1995.[170] Though he had been sentenced by Judge Hughston to spend ten years behind bars, Stogner ended up serving less than half this time. After four years, seven months, and sixteen days in state prison, Stogner walked away a free man. After his release, Marvin Watson said Stogner went on finish the schooling needed to become a licensed surveyor. Watson said, "He did become a licensed surveyor. He was working in Laurens County. I gave him some business when he was a surveyor and he did a decent job with it, a good job with it. I have not heard from him since then . . . But apparently he did well after he served his sentence and went out into the surveying business."[171]

ELEVEN

REHABILITATION

We can be heroes, just for one day.
—David Bowie and Brian Eno[1]

Most people would not have survived a blow to the head like the one suffered by Gerald Jackson. Recovering from such an injury would be agonizingly slow and the prognosis always uncertain. In May 1990, Gerald was moved out of the Intensive Care Unit at Self Memorial Hospital in Greenwood, South Carolina, and given a regular room at the facility.[2] Blues guitarist Mattie Phifer visited Gerald at the hospital a few weeks after the attack and was physically ill during the encounter. "It was so bad," she said, dejectedly. "I actually got sick . . . He was swollen and [had] splotches on his skin. It just overwhelmed me. He was unrecognizable . . . It just overwhelmed me so. I got sick to my stomach when I went in the room. It was just so sad."[3]

With the assistance of his caregiving team, Gerald moved to Columbia, South Carolina, in June 1990 to expand his treatment options. He would never again live in Greenwood.

"Self had reached the limit of what they can do," Eddie Blakely explained to David Godman in a postcard.[4] Gerald was in and out of a number of care centers across Columbia before ending up at the William Jennings Bryan Dorn Veteran's Administration Hospital.[5] When Gerald was admitted to the hospital, he was experiencing extreme speech difficulties, limited vision, complete paralysis on the left side of his body, and had very little functionality in his right hand.[6] For the first few months he was at the hospital, Dirk Armstrong says that he, Steve, and Mrs. Jackson would go and visit Gerald in Columbia every Sunday. Elizabeth Jackson "didn't like to drive that far, and that was really our only chance to do it," said Armstrong. Dirk admitted that "it was difficult to communicate" with Gerald. "It was just heartbreaking to

Gerald Jackson, Elizabeth Jackson, and Reggie Massey, ca. 1995.

see this guy. I mean, he was a medic in the Marines in Vietnam, and here he is and can't even brush his own teeth. It was really, really difficult."[7]

"I could barely understand what he was saying, but you could understand what he was saying," explains Catherine Brickley, recalling when she saw Gerald at a fundraiser she and her bandmates in the Sensible Pumps organized on his behalf in the summer of 1990.[8]

Blues great Bob Margolin visited Gerald at the VA hospital in Columbia. He said Gerald was "badly hurt and his motor skills were impaired and he had a nasty dent in his head, but his mind was all there. In the hospital he communicated by pointing to letters on an alphabet board."[9]

Steve Bryant was at Gerald's side and supported him graciously during every step of his recovery. Bryant took classes at Midlands Technical College to become a Certified Nurse's Assistant,[10] so that he could better take care of his good buddy and longtime companion.[11] Though he held a few bartending jobs when he first got to Columbia, people in the hospital suggested Bryant put in an application to work there. He was hired as an orderly, and although he worked on a different floor, he could spend more time around Gerald and care for him more closely.

Gerald Jackson and Steve Bryant, ca. 1995.

"It gave him good money, and he was able to be there with Gerald the whole time," said Tersh Harley,[12] who Steve lived with during this time. Between working, caring for, and hanging out with Gerald, now Steve spent much of his life at the hospital. "If Steve hadn't been there," said Linn Johnson, "I dare say [Gerald] probably would have died." Johnson is effusive in her praise. "Steve is in heaven with Gerald. He has a crown. He does."[13]

"The best thing that happened to Gerald was Steve," agrees John Sanders.[14]

For the last twenty years of his life, Gerald Jackson lived as a quadriplegic who needed twenty-four-hour attention. Steve helped him eat, bathe, and go to the bathroom. At first, Gerald could not even swallow liquids properly. Dina Boorda, who—with her dog Scuppers—volunteered at the VA Hospital and got to know Gerald in 2008—described the patient's condition this way: "Gerald, a 62 year-old, U.S. Veteran, is lying in his bed, paralyzed, overweight, wearing white towels (instead of clothes), has an oxygen tube running to his nose, drippy eyes, and he sputters when he talks."[15] Steve's mother, Hazel Bryant, said Gerald "couldn't drink water, couldn't drink coffee, couldn't drink anything. All his fluids were in his meals. They had to mix it to make it slushy so he could get some fluids in."[16]

Twenty years before gays and lesbians were allowed to legally marry in South Carolina, "Steve cared for Gerald as a good spouse would do," says former Jackson Station bartender (and Erskine Student) Brand Stille.[17] The devotion Steve expressed for Gerald was "phenomenal," says Glenn Phillips. "Their love was truly legendary," concurs Anita Clinton.[18] Deborah Milling was so "glad [Steve] stuck by Gerald and was there for him."[19]

"He would have done the same for me,"[20] Steve said, when people asked him how he managed to cope caring for Gerald. Steve "never even batted an eye," said Tersh Harley. Steve would simply say, "This is what I'm doing. This is what I'm supposed to do."[21]

"You take a man and a wife . . . ," says John Sanders, reflectively. "A woman wouldn't have stayed. You wouldn't find many women that would have stayed with their husband like Steve did Gerald. He was faithful to his death."[22]

Tersh Harley said that Steve would sometimes "get [Gerald] all cleaned up," and take him out and around Columbia. They would "put him in the Volkswagen and drive him around a little bit." Harley said, "He'd come over to the house, we'd sit out front for a couple of hours."[23] Through it all, Harley said that both Gerald and Steve were "positive and humorous."[24]

About once a month, Steve brought Gerald back to Hodges to visit. They might eat fried bologna sandwiches or get takeout from Rick's Uptown Cafeteria, with Linn Johnson and her daughter Angela Rowland. They occasionally would venture up to Jackson Station to hang out and see the place. People were trying to resurrect the club, and Gerald and Steve wished them all the best. Gerald had insisted, back in the day, on putting in a ramp at the entrance of Jackson Station to make it easier for people in a wheelchair.[25] Now he was the one in the wheelchair.

"He made an incredible comeback in a lot of ways, [but] ultimately [it] killed him, led to his death," says Robert Tinsley. "But he had smile on his face, even afterwards. He had a nice smile on his face. Whenever I saw him, he would light up."[26]

Unfortunately, Gerald's ability to monitor his own body temperature was another consequence of the assault. He had to be kept very cool or he would start sweating profusely. "Whatever part of your body makes you 98.6 was gone," Linn Johnson says. "It was not pretty." Sweat would pour off his body, and his face would turn red. Visiting with Gerald out in his car with the air conditioning on high made things easier.

Although it improved dramatically over the years, Gerald's ability to communicate remained severely strained. Steve played the role of translator.

All conversations would be difficult. There was better understanding when the talk involved stories of people and places Gerald had known prior to the attack.[27] "You know how stroke victims are, the way they talk?" asks Linn Johnson. "If you knew Gerald beforehand, and you knew what he was saying, or you knew what he was laughing about, then you could understand him," she said.

South Carolina guitarist Drink Small recalled going to see Gerald at the VA Hospital on four separate occasions. Small said he was asked by Gerald's friends and family to visit him in the hospital, joking with him: "We think you could do more for him than surgery would."[28] Drink Small said Gerald cried when he saw the musician and that he held his hand tight. "He was so glad to see me," Small said. On his next visit, Small said Gerald "kind of cried," and "couldn't sit up." On the third occasion, Small remembered Gerald's "lip was trembling," but that he could not verbalize. However, on what would be his fourth (and final) visit to the VA Hospital, Drink Small said Gerald had regained the use of both of his hands and was able to "mumble a little something." The two old friends managed to have a brief exchange. Gerald "knew who you were," said Small. Gerald was "in his right mind and everything."[29]

Old friend and Jackson Station DJ Ben Hawthorne said it was "shocking" to see Gerald after the attack. He was "trapped in a shot body." Gerald had lost a ton of weight and his head was "crushed in" on the right side. His "mind was sharp, but he couldn't move and couldn't express himself."[30] Tersh Harley said that, despite his injury, Gerald still had his wits about him. "You can always tell a lot of times when people are still able to make puns," he said, "[or] crack a dirty joke about a situation that they see right there." Harley says, "Gerald was right on top it every time, in other words, just as sharp and just as dirty as ever."[31]

While Linn Johnson happily kept up with Gerald when he came back to Greenwood, she never did visit him at the VA Hospital in Columbia.

"I just couldn't go up there. I could not do it. I could not make myself do it. And Gerald knew I couldn't do it."[32] A similar reluctance befell a number of Gerald's friends. They simply could not muster the courage to see him. Given what a gregarious person Gerald was and how much he had done for others in the past, this must have been torture for him. Gerald was not only physically and physiologically isolated from the world, but with the exception of Steve and a few others, he was socially isolated, as well.

Roland Tranter said, "No, I never saw Gerald after that. [We] would always say, 'We ought to go down there. We need to go see Gerald,' but you know how you say things, but don't do [']em."[33]

"What's the name of that song? 'Nobody know you when you're down and out'?"[34] asks Drink Small? "When you get sick, people won't come see you . . . They love you when you're up, but you get down there, they ain't coming to see you. That's the truth."[35]

However, a number of friends did visit Gerald at the VA Hospital. Anita Clinton said she went there over twenty times. Nic Massey, who visited Gerald often with his dad, Reggie, said the care Gerald received at the facility was particularly good. "You could really tell that the nurses there, like, genuinely loved him. You could tell they were actually friends with Gerald. He always had that effect on people."[36] Tersh Harley gives credit to the VA Hospital for their work with Gerald. He said, "The VA did an amazing job with him. I was so impressed with everything they did over there for him." Because of the problems he had regulating his body temperature, Gerald was allowed a private,[37] individually air-conditioned room so he could keep cool. As such, Gerald's "room was quite different from all the other rooms."[38] Also, the décor in Gerald's area was not what you saw in most rooms. Photographs and post-cards adorned the walls. Gerald also had a refrigerator, a stereo, and not one, but two television sets. "He had everything in that room," said Hazel Bryant.[39]

Linn Johnson said Jackson entertained himself "with a garden, watching birds, music, and painting."[40] Friends occasionally brought him marijuana brownies to ease his mind, which Gerald kept in the freezer. On special occasions, Tersh Harley said, "Gerald liked to get his little pot brownie and ice cream." He would "just sit out in a wheelchair, sit outside where it was nice in the sunshine, and just talk and zone out, basically." Harley chuckled, "All the nurses and everybody knew what was going on. It wasn't a big deal. It's like, 'Yeah, OK, Gerald's going to have a nice afternoon.'"[41] Tim Bradshaw—like Harley, an alumnus of Erskine College—went to visit Gerald in Columbia one Sunday morning. He found Gerald "laughing uncontrollably at some show that was on his television." Initially Bradshaw was confused but later understood when he learned that Gerald had "just consumed more than his share of a plate of brownies a visitor had left the day before."[42]

Gerald also found relief through music. "Music depends on my mood," he told Greenwood *Index-Journal* reporter St. Claire Donaghy in an interview in 2006. "It might be Miles Davis, classical, or The Cure. But no country or hip hop."[43] Painting was also critical to his rehabilitation.

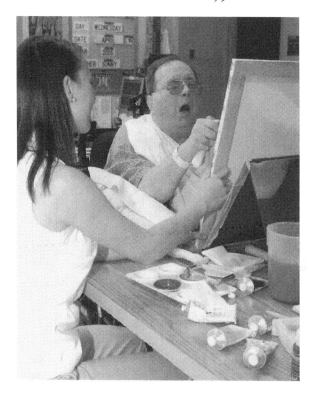

Gerald Jackson, April 6, 2005.

"I'm not as bored when I paint," Gerald admitted. "I paint whatever catches my fancy and I like color."[44]

The very caring staff in the Nursing Home Care Unit of the VA Hospital assisted Gerald's artistry. In April 2005, the staff published an article about Gerald in a spoof newspaper, *Art World News* (vol. 1, no. 1), which showcased Gerald's work. "Artist Claims Fame at Dorn VA," the faux headline announced. The unauthored piece reported that, "Gerald has delighted many with his original, vibrant and colorful creations. His art often has a humorous edge—as does the artist." The article went on to note that Gerald had been assisted by a USC graduate student who "spent many hours enjoying Gerald's sense of humor while setting up his art supplies and mixing paints to his exacting specifications."[45] While painting is hard work under the best of conditions, it was especially so for Gerald, who painted "from his bed, despite limited vision, paralysis on the left side of his body, and limited gross motor control with his right hand."[46] St. Clair Donaghy, reporter with the

Index-Journal, described Gerald's paintings as "mostly abstract, contain[ing] bold strokes, and dabs of color from acrylic paints. Some colors are cheerful and bright while others are subtle and muted."[47]

Despite his injuries, and despite his hospitalization, Gerald nonetheless managed to cobble together a meaningful life. He did so not only with the help of Steve but also with masonic friends and other volunteers at the VA Hospital. Hazel Bryant said Gerald had been in the hospital for a number of years before he started wondering why his old masonic associates had not bothered to visit him.[48] She said a minister came by the hospital one day and Gerald mentioned his consternation to him. The minster said he knew some masons and would get in touch with them. Soon after, as Hazel Bryant said, the "masons started coming in there, and [Gerald] had a ball after that. They took care of that boy after that . . . It meant so much to him."[49]

Gerald's painting at the hospital materially improved. The masons started footing the bills for all of Gerald's art supplies.[50] Soon the room was filled with "paint brushes in cans, canvas boards filling the windowsill, and plastic paint bottles scattered about."[51] The hospital staff initially had made special paintbrushes that would better fit Gerald's broken hands. By 2006, Gerald was painting freehand, using regular paintbrushes and could even open his own paints. Gerald was becoming more independent. "Working with the brushes has helped Gerald learn how to feed himself again," said Steve Bryant.[52]

Over time, Gerald came to accept his plight. He bore no ill will toward Terry Stogner, the man who had very nearly killed him and put him in a wheelchair for the rest of his life.

"I forgive the guy," Gerald said. "It doesn't bother me. I don't think he'll do that kind of thing again."[53] Dina G. Boorda, a Columbia attorney, captured the essence of Gerald Jackson's equanimity and grace when she served as a volunteer at the VA Hospital in 2008. Boorda worked at the facility with her pet therapy dog, a Labradoodle. She says that her first visit with Gerald "unexpectedly brightened my day, and it impacted my life." Boorda, a Dame in the Sovereign Military Order of the Temple of Jerusalem, experienced an epiphany of sorts when Gerald told her, "I am so blessed."

Given his condition and whereabouts, she initially thought this was a very odd thing for Gerald to say. "How can this man feel 'blessed'?" Boorda wrote. "I questioned myself. I am blessed—I have a wonderful family, a good education, beautiful house, a caring church. No, Gerald, I was thinking, I am the one who is blessed." Boorda says she "must have had a confused look on her face because Gerald went on to explain to me how God had blessed him. He says he has it much better off than most of the people 'in this place.'"[54] Boorda says Gerald's word had stayed with her. Gerald had "captured her heart." She viewed Gerald as an example of "God's true blessing . . . His Gift of Life." She said Gerald did "not whine, complain, or any way act or seem resentful for his situation. He is happy, productive, and has a Christian heart. God has blessed Gerald with a gift to make the world a better place through his art and his loving heart."[55] Dina Boorda would be inspired by Gerald to write a poem in his honor, called "Ambiguous Clock":

> What time is it?
> Gerald says:
> Time is what
> you make of it;
> it is whatever
> time you want
> it to be![56]

Back in Hodges, there were a number of attempts to resuscitate Jackson Station. Steve Bryant, Elizabeth Jackson, Dirk Armstrong, and other friends valiantly kept the club going until November 1990.[57] Bill Artiss and Joe Henderson of Greenwood took out a lease from Mrs. Jackson and reopened the club on March 1, 1991.[58] According to Jeffrey Verver, the men "made several changes, creating additional room [on the back of the building] to accommodate more people."[59] Initially, Artiss and Henderson did well bringing the music back to Jackson Station. "Booking bands is no problem," Artiss said in a 1992 interview. "They contact us and tell us when they'll be in our neck of the woods. We've had Nappy Brown, Drink Small, Koko Taylor and a whole bunch of others play here—not so much for the money; they just like the place."[60] However, the good times were not to last. Artiss and Henderson shut down after being "in business for about a year and a half."[61]

The club lay dormant for the next three years before another group of people tried to reopen the club. In October 1995, Bonnie Capps[62] and her then boyfriend Alton Payne made a heroic effort to resurrect Jackson Station.[63] Capps said they asked Gerald's permission before doing so. She said that Gerald was "so excited" and "very happy" about the prospect. Yet by now the age and the wear and tear on the building was becoming apparent. Expensive work was needed to bring the structure back up to code. The couple sunk $70,000 (mostly borrowed on credit cards) into Jackson Station on repairs alone. Over a nine-month period, they put in a new bar, renovated the bathrooms and the kitchen, made upgrades to the lighting and electrical system, and restored the deck. The club strived mightily to replicate what Gerald and Steve had done. "We spent a massive amount of money," Capps said.

Bob Margolin, Nappy Brown, and Noel "Kidman" Riddle played on opening night.[64] Just like in the old days, Jackson Station was "decorated with all sorts of memorabilia. Flags, street signs, replicas of trains, and old railroad lanterns hang from the rafters and the walls."[65] A similar assortment of music, food, and libations could still be found at the club, just like in the old days at Jackson Station. Co-owner Alton Payne said that he "always enjoyed coming to Jackson's. The music is its most interesting feature. I wanted to bring back the same musical format Gerald had here."[66]

Gerald and Steve were thrilled about the club's reopening. "It's wonderful," Steve said of Capps and Payne's effort. "We are very happy that they have kept it the way we had it."[67] Unfortunately, this latest iteration of Jackson Station also did not last for long. It shut down after just a few months. "I used to joke, that's the most expensive party I've every thrown,"[68] Capps says.

Tinsley Ellis played Jackson Station only once after the attack on Gerald, on October 13, 1995. "It just wasn't the same, without Gerald and his mom, and Steve," Ellis laments. "It wasn't the same."[69] Early the following year, the club shut down for good. The last advertised act to play Jackson Station was Common Ground on Friday, February 23, 1996.[70] "It's just a brutal business," comments David Truly of the Truly Dangerous Swamp Band, about the live music industry. He says it is almost impossible for small music clubs to sustain themselves. Truly notes that Jackson Station was "open way longer than most night clubs."[71]

By 1997, Elizabeth Jackson was renting out the depot for purposes other than that of a music venue. A small business that sold various "rubber stamp" products, including "heat guns, stamps, embossing powders and paper" operated out of Jackson Station.[72] From September 2002 to June 2004, "Jackson Station Flea Market" was held at the property. More or less weekly auctions took place there on Thursday nights.[73] Bonnie Capps claims that the final tenants to lease the building tore out the bar, scraped the murals off the walls, and stripped the place clean of all its valuable signage and memorabilia.

Gerald spent the last twenty years of his life at the VA Hospital in Columbia. Many of the artists and musicians who he had booked at Jackson Station (such as the Swimming Pool Qs and Widespread Panic) continued to have successful careers. In 2007, Nappy Brown released an album on Blind Pig Records called *Long Time Coming*, produced by blues guitarist Scott Cable. The album was well received and afforded the R&B singer, now in his late seventies, one last chance in the spotlight. "*Long Time Coming* was the first record he'd done in years," said Scott Cable. "And we had no budget. I just called in a lot of favors other people owed me. And people played on it that normally would never have done the session, for little to no money."[74] A booking on *Prairie Home Companion* with Garrison Keillor followed. After fifty years, Nappy Brown was once again embraced by American popular culture. However, it is doubtful that many in the audience knew that his career had been brought back to life with the help of two gay guys in an old train depot in rural South Carolina.

Nappy Brown passed away on September 20, 2008. In June, he had played a gig in New Jersey and injured himself during the show. For decades, Nappy Brown had been rolling around on the stage as part of his act. His body could no longer take the abuse.

"In western Maryland, he wasn't well," Scott Cable said. "He wasn't 100%. He did the best he could . . . It was scary." A few days later, in New Jersey, Cable said Nappy "almost passed out and ended up on the ground. They had to cut the set short." Brown was in a hospital bed in New Jersey for almost a week. He was discharged and traveled back to Charlotte, North Carolina, by train.

"He was home for about a week or two and then passed away in the hospital," said Scott Cable, who raised money for Nappy Brown's gravesite and headstone in Charlotte. Cable was amazed by the response. Chuck Jackson, Bonnie Raitt, and Bruce Iglauer (founder of Alligator Records) were among the many donors.

Gerald Jackson passed away at the VA Hospital in Columbia, South Carolina, on September 4, 2010, one month short of his sixty-fourth birthday. A memorial service with Masonic Rites was held on Tuesday, September 6, at the Blyth Funeral Home Chapel in Greenwood. "It was somber," said Tersh Harley, who attended the service. "As soon as I walked in, Steve burst out in tears. And I burst out in tears. It was rough on all of us."[75] Gerald was cremated. He was interred at Greenwood Memorial Gardens, just off US 25, a couple of miles south of Hodges.[76]

After Gerald's death, Steve kept working at the VA Hospital. He also started tending bar again. In 2011, Steve was diagnosed with esophageal cancer.[77] He did not realize he was ill before it was too late. "When he got sick, it went down pretty fast," says Tersh Harley, mournfully.[78] Steve moved back to Liberty, South Carolina, in the spring of 2012 to live with his mother in the family home on Flat Rock Drive.

"It got to that point where he couldn't eat anything but liquids," said Hazel Bryant.

Reggie Massey visited Steve about a month before he died. For about three hours, they visited and talked about all the people and good times of the Jackson Station era. "It was sad," Massey said. "He was down and out. He knew he wasn't going to make it."[79]

Steven Bryant died on June 28, 2012. Terry Pierce, Steve's brother-in-law, says that "like Gerald, [Steve] requested that his remains be cremated. There was a memorial service held at Flat Rock Baptist Church in Liberty, where many people who knew Steve found out for the first time that he was gay."[80] Hazel Bryant said that Steve's father never accepted Gerald and Steve's relationship. "He knew, but he didn't admit it," she said. "He didn't even consider it really, he said, 'No, you're not.'"[81] Later in 2012, Terry Pierce accompanied Steve's sister, Kim, and his mother, Hazel Bryant, "to Jackson Station where they scattered Steve and Gerald's ashes."[82]

Elizabeth Jackson died on November 24, 2001. After she died, Jackson Station was inherited by her daughter Ellen Early, Gerald's sister, who was living in Tennessee. In September 2016, Early sold the depot and its three acres of land to Daniel Prince of Donalds, South Carolina, a small town about ten miles northwest of Hodges. Prince is a self-professed jam band enthusiast, and like Gerald is a veteran (Iraq). He says his plan is to someday reopen Jackson Station as a fully functioning music club where, he says, everyone would be welcome.[83]

Currently busy with a full-time job at a textile plant and a wife and growing family, Prince is unsure when, exactly, Jackson Station will open back up to the public. The two most pressing concerns are fixing the roof and putting in an asphalt parking lot. He says these renovations alone will cost over $100,000. Then slowly, everything else at Jackson Station will need to be repaired and brought back up to code. Gone are the days where you could do this yourself. Now everyone on the job site needs to be certified, licensed, and insured, and so on. Prince accepts the challenge of reopening Jackson Station stoically, saying, "Rome was not built in a day." And he might take consolation (as well as inspiration) in the fact that—while fixing up Jackson Station depot will indeed take considerable time and effort—it was the same for Gerald Jackson when he first bought the place for a dollar all those years ago.

: TWELVE :

JACKSON'S 'TIL DAWN

Jackson Station was like reckless youth. That time when you think you can live forever and you can do any damn thing.
—Harris Bailey[1]

This book has told the story of Jackson Station in its glory days as remembered by the musicians and people who went there. Places like Jackson Station are important, in that they allow humans to seek action away from the often-constraining relationships of work and home. They are what sociologists call a "third place"—a place of community.[2] People would not simply go and see "live" music at Jackson Station; they would "live" at Jackson Station. Jackson Station was a part of their lives.

Obviously, the meanings that Jackson Station held for its patrons changed over the years, as the social landscape of Greenwood County was altered by the movements of time, and the people who once frequented Jackson Station grew up, died, or moved away. As can be seen from the accounts in this book, Jackson Station was many things to many different people.[3] Therein lies its charm and distinction.

Driving past Jackson Station today, it is easy not to give the depot much thought—just another crumbling wooden building in the middle of nowhere. One sees many of these dilapidated structures throughout the countryside of South Carolina. They are fascinating to look at and evoke memories of a different era. In the case of the old Hodges Depot, the tin roof is still holding on, but there is now visible rotting wood under the eaves. Gaping holes are in the decking, windows are smashed out, and various ornamental features are missing. Some of the concrete mason bricks that the building sits upon look rather unstable. Yet the inside of the club is dry. The bar and the stage are intact. Despite being closed for close to twenty-five years, there is no evidence of

Jackson Station, May 2014.

any humans or animals living there. There are no foul odors. The floor seems solid. In Bob Margolin's words, looking at Jackson Station now is "like seeing a lively person who has died and is in his coffin at his funeral. The body is there but the life is gone."[4]

Through the promotion and social reproduction of live music (particularly the blues), the diversity it fostered, and its acceptance of people from all walks of life, Jackson Station left a distinct impression on the people who gathered there. As Greenwood attorney C. Rauch Wise puts it, "And if you never went there, sorry, but words will not describe that unique event."[5] The extent of that significance is quite remarkable. After all, isn't this just a nightclub, that we have been talking about? How could something as mundane as a music venue have such a visceral impact on people? For reasons explained in this book, Jackson Station was truly an extraordinary place.

Larry Acquaviva (a.k.a. "Aceman") writes movingly about the power of the music of Widespread Panic, who played Jackson Station nine times. In his account as a roadie traveling with the band during the early stages of their career, Acquaviva has this to say:

From the very beginning, I knew that these boys were speaking to people in a way that was not of this world . . . It would liberate people, alter them, inspire them, and make them wild with promise. It would shake them, rock them, and cause them to lose themselves in the sound. It would turn grown men into maniacs, young women into irresistible temptresses, and young kids into giants who knew no bounds. And Jackson Station, out in the middle of Anywhere, U.S.A., was one of those places where this phenomenon began. In those early days at Jackson Station I began to see this entity, this juggernaut called Widespread Panic, blossoming into the full force of nature they would become.[6]

Jackson Station emerged from the social, historical, and cultural landscape of its time. Were it not for the old railroad depot readily available for purchase in Gerald's hometown at just that moment in history, it is likely that Jackson Station would have never operated as a music club. Certainly, the place would have never opened had there been no Gerald Jackson, or if Gerald's father (and his father before him) had not each had their own version of Jackson Station out on the family property. Even more so than for South Carolina, Jackson Station can be better seen as a peripheral node on the outer limits of the Georgia music scene. The Georgia Satellites, Love Tractor, Tinsley Ellis, the Swimming Pool Qs, Fats Jackson, Sweet Betty; these all were regular acts at Jackson Station and all hailed from Georgia. Located in the northwest portion of the state, Jackson Station was only thirty miles from the Georgia/South Carolina state line. This made it accessible to bands and people from Georgia. The University of Georgia is closer to Jackson Station than the University of South Carolina in Columbia. In fact, it is likely that most of the late-night people who used to frequent Jackson Station drove in from Athens after the bars shut down and they still wanted to party.

Although Jackson Station featured many kinds of music and their support of independent or New Wave bands was very strong, blues was the genre of choice at the club. Jackson Station was known across the Southern Piedmont as an authentic, down-home blues club. Jackson Station was part of a broad revival of the blues during the decade it was in existence.[7] This blues revival culminated in the luminous career of guitarist Stevie Ray Vaughan who tragically died young and well before his time in 1990—the year Gerald was assaulted.

"We've definitely gotten a strong reputation as a blues club,"[8] Gerald Jackson said in an interview one year prior to the attack. Gerald was as an important patron of the blues in the upstate region of South Carolina. "You could see old blues guys in there tearing it up, old school," remembers Armistead Wellford of Love Tractor.[9] Gerald was especially generous at extending performance opportunities to Black artists such as Drink Small, Fats Jackson, and Nappy Brown; and female artists such as Sweet Betty, the Sensible Pumps, and Sheila Carlisle of the band Arhooly (we could also mention other all-female bands such as the Blind Dates and In Pursuit). Jackson Station Rhythm & Blues club provided significant employment opportunities (a.k.a. "gigs") for blues musicians, gave the public a place to listen to the blues, but most importantly, it was a site to experience the blues.

Of the blues acts who played at Jackson Station most exhibited upbeat, celebratory, Chicago style of blues music. "I'm a rhythm and blues person myself," Gerald said. "I've always liked old rock 'n' roll, R & B—the old Black, gritty stuff."[10] However, Jackson Station also featured sultry, jazzy sorts of blues. Sheila Carlisle's band Arhooly—formed with guitarist Max Drake in Union Grove, North Carolina, in 1973—is representative of this style.[11] They played Jackson Station about seven times from 1984 to 1988. The band centered around Carlisle's Janis Joplin–esque vocals and stage presence and Drake's delicate guitar work. Arhooly performed compelling covers of classic blues songs such as "Drinking Again," "Sweet Virginia," "Wang Dang Doodle," and "Love Me Like a Man."[12]

In an interview in early 2019, Sheila Carlisle said Jackson Station was a "very cool place," ranking it in the top five of her most favorite clubs of all time. She recalled Jackson Station as being friendly, welcoming, and enthusiastic. "There was always a big turnout and a very receptive audience," she remembered. "And everybody danced."[13] Russ Fitzgerald—Greenwood musician and erstwhile Jackson Station bartender—places Arhooly in the pantheon of legendary artists to play Jackson Station. He declared: "Bob Margolin might have had gravitas, Nappy Brown may have had majesty, Tinsley Ellis may have had flash and technique, but Max and Sheila as Arhooly were glorious and molded my sensibilities forever."[14] Bonnie Capps, a close friend to Gerald and Steve, who briefly reopened the club in the early 1990s, said Jackson Station "attracted so many people from so many walks of life." "Everybody was happy," she said. "It was blues that brought it all together."[15] The Reverend Billy Wirtz reminds us that the blues originated in "after hours clubs [like Jackson Station]. It came from places that were considered sinful." Jackson Station "was a continuum of that which had gone before, and a very good one at that."[16]

Widespread Panic bassist Dave Schools speaks for many when he says that while the "terrible shit" that happened to Gerald "sort of tarnishes the good times, it's kind of the price one might have to pay for all of that freedom. And it was all in the name of a good time."[17] In a world before the advent of smart phones and other technologies that steal the energy out of a room and work to channel and refocus the gaze of people elsewhere, folks ventured to places like Jackson Station to socialize and connect with others.

The social vibe at Jackson Station ran the gamut from rational conversation to ecstatic communion. It provided opportunities for both association and dissociation. Today, there are regrettably few places in society where people may experience either, let alone both. Perhaps most importantly, people went to Jackson Station—this would usually happen on the slower, non-music nights during the week—to tell stories to and about each other. In the process, they would create memories and generate other stories to tell. Most of what patrons did at Jackson Station—once one looks beyond the consumption of food, drugs, and alcohol—was talk. The purpose of such communication was "not to exchange information" or engage in "shop talk or a form of one-upmanship." Rather, it was to talk out of "pleasure, to divert themselves by telling stories and recounting the day's events."[18] In *The New Mind of the South*, Tracy Thompson observes, "[T]he South has virtually no tradition of public space—no Central Parks, no Public Gardens, no custom of the neighborhood pub." Instead, as she points out, Southern social life is to be found mainly "within the walls of private homes."[19] Jackson Station is noteworthy because although it was a private space, it still had elements of publicness about it. For individuals such as Tersh Harley, the Jackson Station experience was all about "chatting, over hours and hours and hours, just sitting around drinking beer and chatting."[20]

In addition to its associative function, Jackson Station also facilitated social dissociation. Jackson Station allowed people to cut loose, to push the boundaries of expression, and engage in liminal experiences. Such dissociation was present at Jackson Station mainly during the weekend or on other big band nights. Musicians and patrons alike would "jam out" or "rock out," dancing and writhing to the music in an eccentric, idiosyncratic, and almost primitive way. It is a dance of letting oneself go, of accepting difference, and experiencing the joy of being in a community of others. This is music at its most powerful. In a recent interview, Afro-Latin-blues-rock guitarist Carlos Santana calls this kind of musical experience "the best medicine there is."[21] He says that the joyous experience of music, especially African music, allows people to "shake off, ward off, fear, resentment, guilt, remorse . . . .They shake it off. Because joy immediately dismisses fear."[22] Santana never played Jackson Station (though he may have heard about it), but the sentiments he describes could surely be found there. "As wacked-out as the place was," writes Larry Acquaviva, "there was never a negative experience" at Jackson Station. "The place was like a sanctuary out in the middle of the wilderness." He vividly remembers Jackson Station "shows for the palpable feeling of acceptance that seemed to envelop everyone in attendance." Acquaviva admits to "sounding too cheesy," but nonetheless claims that "the experiences at Jackson Station were beautiful, uniting all those present with a feeling of brotherhood."[23]

Though music remains a very important social force in society and one that is central to people's identity, it is nowadays experienced more remotely than it was in the past—often digitally through ear buds, without any other humans involved. The emergent, effervescent, contingent nature of musical experience found at places like Jackson Station is often missing in the social landscape. However, one may find glimpses of the spirit of Jackson Station in contemporary music clubs and festivals.[24] For example, consider Tipitina's in New Orleans, the Crescent City's iconic rock and roll venue. The fact that members of the hugely successful jam/funk band Galactic[25] recently took over ownership of Tipitina's indicates a commitment to the continued value and relevance of live music. One could also point to the tens of thousands of persons who take time out of their busy lives to attend festivals such as Burning Man and Bonnaroo.[26] Just what is the source of meaning that these events provide contemporary Americans (and others from around the world) that motivates them to make pilgrimages to these sites year after year?

The sort of musical community found at these mega musical events share a family resemblance to what Gerald Jackson and Steve Bryant were trying to build at Jackson Station. Clubs like Jackson Station provided a minia-ture version of the ecstatic communal experiences found at the best music festivals.[27] In Burrows's words, attending festivals "is like escaping the daily trudge to enter a fantasy town, particularly if aided by inebriation . . . People wander around [and] watch bands for hours on end. They dance with others who share their passions. For a while the world looks good."[28] Such festival experiences become a part of the story people tell about themselves. Memories generated at these events become part of their identity, of who they are. Jackson Station offered a similar experience at the local level.

As Robert Tinsley says, "There was nothing like going to Jackson Station. It was an event. And I didn't go every Friday night because I was working, of course, and it took a good bit out of you. Like I say, you had to plan around it."[29]

Perhaps Jackson Station was simply an attempt to bring something like Mardi Gras to Greenwood County. Gerald and Steve loved New Orleans and tried to travel there each year. It is a city where even today one might stumble across phenomenal hole-in-the-wall blues club like Jackson Station.[30] "They got me interested in New Orleans," said Reggie Massey, "And I have been trying to go back ever since."[31] Guitarist David Truly said Jackson Station reminded him a good deal of his "hometown of New Orleans. It's a place where, in the midst of this very conservative part of the south, you saw this eclectic, eccentric mix of everything that is right and wrong according to the different groups of people, you know, but everybody [was] together." In New Orleans, Truly said, "[m]usic was one of those areas where size, shape, color, in a lot of ways didn't matter. It was one of the few areas, even though you are in the super conservative South, everybody came together."[32]

For musicians lucky enough to have a paying gig, the act of performing has changed considerably from when Jackson Station was at its peak. Live music shows are a different animal than they were a generation ago. As Tinsley Ellis says, "We were much younger then, 35 years ago." In reference to the long, grueling gigs at Jackson Station, he said, "I don't think I could do that now. I'm pretty sure I couldn't, unless I had a lot of caffeine or something, coffee . . . Back then, we were young and wild."[33] Ellis continues, "At the time, we were all in it for the music. Nowadays, if you told you know, your band, 'We gotta' play [']til 4:00 am,' they'd expect to be paid more, or something like that. But we were all in it for the music."[34] David Truly concurs. "The days of 'Hey man, you want to play one more?' '*Sure, you know, let's just keep playing until the sun . . .*' You know? You don't see that shit. I mean it's hard to find that anywhere."[35] On the other hand, harp player Freddie Vanderford thinks audiences are listening more carefully to the live music these days. He says people who come to his shows today are "more attentive." Thirty years ago, he says, the music was loud and you had people "jumping around and this, that and the other." Today, he says, "[t]hey actually sit down, listen to what you are doing."[36]

What is especially interesting about Jackson Station was not only that it was a blues bar, but also that it was a blues bar where gays and lesbians in particular would congregate, at a time when simply being gay was socially (and often legally) forbidden.[37] Jackson Station was no Stonewall Inn; in fact, some locals insist it was *never* in fact just a gay bar—rather, a bar run by gay men. However, there can be no denying that Jackson Station was an inclusive place, providing a highly a tolerant, cosmopolitan, quasi-urban experience in a rural setting.

"Gerald and Steve were out; very obviously gay," said the Reverend Billy Wirtz.[38] Unashamed of who they were, they offered a model of being gay in the South.[39] While life may be easier in some respects for gays and lesbians today than it was in the 1970s and 1980s, many still have difficulty "making sense of their sexual identities and struggle in a hostile world."[40] Gay marriage has come to America and even now, to Hodges, South Carolina, but old habits die hard. It might even be argued that gays and lesbians are less accepted than there were during the days of Jackson Station. Culture wars continue to be waged across the country, and the Palmetto State is no exception. The South may turn a blind eye to the lives of gay people in certain places, but the dominant culture does usually allow it to be publicized.[41] "In the South, we have this one front that we put up" while things go on "right under everybody's nose," says Billy Wirtz. "You just kind of go about your business quietly and don't make a big deal out of it. Just mind your manners, just do what you do, and we'll be okay." Jackson Station offered a safe space and a degree of social protection against homophobia and other forms of bigotry.

"Gerald and Steve were so brave," said Deborah Milling.[42] She admires the "financial and personal risk" they took "to follow their hearts and open together as an openly gay couple a fun, creative place that one would not expect to find in a highly conservative rural area."[43]

Obviously more could be said—and should be said—about Jackson Station as a gay space. The HIV/AIDS crisis of the 1980s coincided with the life of Jackson Station. Little was known about the disease back then, and a positive diagnosis was often a death sentence. The Jackson Station clientele was predominantly made up of younger baby boomers and older members of Generation X. At the time of writing, many people of the boomer generation are already starting to pass from the scene. Unfortunately, it is possible that a high proportion of the gay men who did frequent Jackson Station died prematurely (as did Gerald and Steve) and took their stories with them.

In a Southern culture fractured by race, class, gender, and sexual orientation, Jackson Station brought people of all backgrounds together while acknowledging and at times celebrating difference. Presently, in the South and across much of U.S. society, there seems to be a disheartening opposite trend of increasing xenophobia and self-segregation of people away from those who are different. Rather than seeking out and trying to understand other cultures, too often people now surround themselves with those who look and think like them. At Jackson Station this simply could not happen. Thinking of the diversity at Jackson Station, one cannot but conclude that present-day American society—particularly Southern society—is becoming dangerously tribalistic. To the extent that Jackson Station broke down such barriers, it showed what an inclusive, alternative community might look like.

While the social acceptance of sexual orientation did mark the experience at Jackson Station, the story was perhaps more complicated regarding race. In terms of the extent of racial integration, certainly Jackson Station did not provide a similar experience to a venue like Charlie's Place,[44] which operated in Myrtle Beach, South Carolina, as part of the so-called "Chitlin' Circuit" during the first half of the twentieth century. For one thing, the proprietor of Charlie's Place, Lucius Drucker (a.k.a. Charlie Fitzgerald) was a Black man from New York City. Gerald Jackson was a White (gay) man from Hodges. Despite many stories of acceptance at Jackson Station, it is likely that many African Americans in the Greenwood area were wary of venturing up to Hodges due to an inherent distrust of Whites. The larger-than-life George Wallace photograph that was by all accounts prominently featured inside the club might have initially confused Black customers.

Blues guitarist Mark "Buddyro" Harrison recalls playing Jackson Station with his band the Fairlanes in the late 1980s. The band's bassist, Chris Carroll (who was Black), was at first shocked to see that George Wallace photo in Jackson Station. As Harrison recounts:

> It was about a five-hour trip for us to get down there. We didn't start playing until at least midnight, but we played until four thirty or five in the morning. I remember the first time Chris went with us, we told him, "This place is different, man. They get a really good crowd." And they did play some big slam all night long. But we went there with Chris, and they had all this weird stuff.[45]

He continues: "Just a bunch of old Southern stuff. But they had this photograph of George Wallace that was blown up. And that photograph took up just almost a whole side of one of the walls; it was huge. So Chris walks in there and he sees this big photograph and says, 'Man, that's George Wallace, man. You know who he is?'" Harrison replied, "'Yeah, man, it's all right, man. These people are cool.'"[46] However, Harrison said "it freaked Chris slap out, initially, to see that picture of George Wallace. Chris thought he'd landed in Klan territory; he thought we were playing in some kind of Klan headquarters or something." However, Harrison said that "once [Chris] met the owner of the bar, and actually the owner of the place—his name was Gerald Jackson,"[47] the bassist relaxed and realized he had nothing to fear.

Jackson Station regular and close friend of Gerald, David Goldman, suggests Gerald had one simple reason for featuring George Wallace in his bar. "The Wallace poster, and the 8 x 10 of Lester Maddox, were displayed, I believe, to indicate 'You are in Rebel country.' They were Gerald's way of saying, 'Screw you, if you can't take a joke.'" He also notes that: "It's worth mentioning that numerous very liberal professors from Lander drank and laughed in the shadow of those pictures, as did the many Black people Gerald welcomed in through the years."[48]

It is impossible to know the exact nature of racial integration at Jackson Station, which of course should not be overstated. One reader who reviewed this book prior to publication asked if *Live at Jackson Station* is "ultimately a story about the way in which White South Carolinians in the 1980s used blues and other forms of danceable music to create their own one-off Wonderland in which they could drink, dance, shout, bond, and purge their blues in a way that mirrored what Black juke joint life had enabled their Black peers to do for many decades?" There is undoubtedly some truth to that statement. However, it was never an entirely White crowd at Jackson Station, and it is likely that the African American musicians who played there were treated much better than they were at other gigs.

Whereas the original Chitlin' Circuit was "the launching pad for many of America's greatest Black entertainers,"[49] when they started out in the music business, Jackson Station provided a space for great Black entertainers in the denouement of their careers. Artists like Nappy Brown, Sweet Betty, and Drink Small all developed sincere, enduring friendships with Gerald and Steve. I do not think this would have happened if the club had embodied or tolerated a racist culture. This is not to claim that Jackson Station was a utopia of tolerance. In addition to all sorts of other Southern memorabilia, it is indeed troubling to see the Confederate Flag hanging on the wall of the depot in an old photograph of Jackson Station taken in 1983.[50] Gerald was, of course, a White Southerner. Like all of us, he was a product of his time. Does the presence of the rebel flag at Jackson Station suggest that, at least as far as race relations goes, perhaps Jackson Station was not the tolerant, pluralistic place that this book has made it out to seem?

"The rebel flag was still flying atop the state capitol,[51] for goodness sake," notes David Goldman. He says that back then, "seeing it in a bar—especially one that catered to a college crowd—was not unusual."[52] If one measure of the quality of race relations is the extent of racial integration within a particular social space, then Jackson Station would certainly score in positive territory. Jackson Station welcomed all sorts of people. The story of race at Jackson Station is a complex one. Judged in terms of its own time and place, Jackson Station should be viewed as being a racially tolerant space. This seems especially true when considered in relation to other institutions in the greater Greenwood Community such as churches, schools, workplaces, restaurants, and neighborhoods that were, and continue to be, highly segregated. Jackson Station represented something different. It is an alternative South, albeit one still rife with contradiction and complexity.

The most important symbol at Jackson Station was the South Carolina flag mural that Gerald had painted on the back wall behind the stage. The distinctive image of white crescent and Palmetto Tree was based on the Liberty Flag (the Moultrie Flag) that had flown during the Revolutionary War. The first definition of the word "liberty" in Merriam-Webster's dictionary is "the quality or state of being free." More specifically, it means the power to do as one pleases; freedom from physical restraint; freedom from arbitrary or despotic control; the positive enjoyment of various social, political, or economic rights and privileges; [and] the power of choice.[53] "Liberty" is the perfect word to capture the essence of Jackson Station. Practicing liberty involves embracing an ethos of live and let live, of not imposing one's views on others; of leaving people alone to mind their own business; of tending to one's own garden. Today, more than ever, it seems we could all do with a lot more of this kind of liberty.

Ultimately, it was the music at Jackson Station that made the magic happen. At the depot, one witnessed, "bluesmen practice their craft in the most natural of settings."[54] Jackson Station was not simply a blues club, but a rhythm and blues (R&B) club.[55] As Jeffrey Verver writes, "Jackson Station is first and foremost an R & B roadhouse."[56] It should also be remembered, as Robert Tinsley says, "that Greenwood became a blues town because of Jackson Station."[57]

In philosophical terms, blues is to concept what rhythm is to intuition. Both are needed.[58] Blues is often inward looking, despondent, plaintive. It speaks to segregated worlds. Rhythm is drums, beats, and dancing together. In contrast to the more traditional blues, R&B is happier, more celebratory.[59] Jackson Station offered a representation of such a world in motion. Writer Richard Wright referred to the uplifting nature of blues music as "the most astonishing aspect of the blues." He wrote that blues songs, "though replete with a sense of defeat and down-heartedness, they are not intrinsically pessimistic; their burden of woe and melancholy is dialectically redeemed through sheer force of sensuality, into an almost exultant affirmation of life, of love, of sex, of movement, of hope."[60] These qualities and more would all be found at Jackson Station.

"Jackson Station was the end of the world, after hours place," comments Russ Fitzgerald.[61] It was the only late-night drinking establishment in the county. It was one of the few locations in the vicinity where one might encounter an interesting person and have a decent conversation. People partied and barhopped around Greenwood earlier in the evening, getting ready to head up Jackson Station at the end of the night. Everyone knew where he or she would end up. There was only one option. There was no uncertainty. If you lost track of a friend or wanted to see the person you met last week again this week, just head up to Jackson Station. Eventually you would find them.

As W. Townes Jones IV stated in his closing remarks to the jury during the trial of the *State of South Carolina v. Terry Daniel Stogner*:

> What's the composition of the crowd out there? What's the composition of it? What was testified to by the state's witnesses about who comes out to Gerald Jackson's? Did they say that white people and Black people come out there? Did they say that old and young? Did they say the bikers and preppies and college students and anybody and everybody, a mixture, an entire mixture of this community and this population and this segment of Greenwood can go out there and do what? Get along.[62]

At Jackson Station, the emphasis was on "connecting with people," Glenn Phillips says. "It wasn't about closing things out; it was about opening things up."[63]

It was through this act of "opening things up," which, at the end of the day, made going to Jackson Station so valuable. After spending time at the club, the "little hole in the wall that we could barely find seems so unbelievably bigger."[64] For a few hours, folks at Jackson Station, guided by the theatrics of the musical shamans[65] onstage, communed with something bigger, louder,[66] and more powerful than themselves. They would leave the club as changed people.

According to Dave Schools of Widespread Panic, Jackson Station offers "a really good window into the formation of a band that became Widespread Panic. That was the formative years of us struggling through shitty gear and no monitors and experimenting with our sound. And experimenting with our group mind. Learning how to be a band together onstage. It's great stuff, because to me, that's where the story really is." Schools says that the musical spirit that can be found at Widespread Panic's later shows, at their "big gigs, the pilgrimage gigs"[67] (at places like Red Rocks Amphitheater in Morrison, Colorado, for example)—has its origins, in part, at Jackson Station.[68]

Like a real train station, Jackson Station was a social hub that brought people together. Patrons would arrive at the club from places near and far. Regardless of where they originated, Jackson Station helped everyone on their particular journey. Some folks came to Jackson Station immediately from work; others left Jackson Station and went to work (without having slept). Some people came to Jackson Station from out of state; some lived across the street. Some visitors spent only a few minutes at Jackson Station; others spent half their lives there.

Jackson Station also provided a space for people to come together who might normally be on opposite sides of the tracks; for example, Blacks and Whites, gays and straights, lawyers and criminals. In doing so, it provided a model of social integration, not only for a few hours late on a Friday night, but cumulatively, over weeks, months, and years. Jackson Station built community. It fostered social recognition despite inequality and difference. The vivid memories people have of Jackson Station attest to this power. Such memories can become the basis for the creation of likeminded spaces of sociality in the here-and-now.

As Bruce Cobb observed, "Some nights you'd walk in there, you would see one hundred people you knew. Another night you'd walk in, you wouldn't see a soul you knew."[69] There was tremendous diversity at Jackson Station. Everyone was on his or her own trip. Jackson Station was a crossroads, a place where "choices and opportunities wait" at "an exciting but uneasy spot."[70] Tim Bradshaw says the culture at Jackson Station was a roughly even mix of four subcultures: college students from Erskine College and Lander University, rednecks, gays and lesbians, and countercultural types.[71] Individuality

Gerald Jackson at Jackson Station, 1986.

was encouraged. Jackson Station facilitated powerful, contingent, moments. You never knew who might be coming through the door. As David Truly says, there would be "pretty in-depth conversations about politics, and about where South Carolina was going. And in the midst of this, somebody else would come up and talk about his new Harley."[72]

"Jackson Station was rustic, welcoming, and filled to the brim with every whack-o-, nut job, and freak in the vicinity," remembers Larry Acquaviva. "There were average joes, working-class folks, lesbians, hippies, professional people such as doctors and lawyers, homosexuals, crusty old rock and rollers, drug dealers, cowboys, alcoholics, and bikers."

Roland Tranter recalls being at Jackson Station early one morning and having a conversation with a "female veterinarian—a large animal vet." He says, "We were talking to her [and] then she started reciting poetry to us." Tranter said, "Anything could happen there. You just never knew what was going to take place."[73]

Sometimes Jackson Station put people from different cultures on a collision course with each another. One of the best parts of Jackson Station was that people were called out on their bigotry. David Goldman recalls being in Jackson Station one evening in 1978 or 1979 and witnessing an exchange between a drunk redneck and a now-retired female Lander University professor. The man asked her: "What do you call a shame"?

"What?" the professor replied.

Jeff Calder and Billy Burton at Jackson Station, ca. 1983.

"Two empty seats on a busload full of n***gers going off a cliff," guffawed the man.

The professor was not amused. She looked him straight in the eye and said pointedly: "You are one dumb son of a bitch." Goldman remembers the drunk redneck was "clearly shocked by her response." He "struggled to his feet and staggered off to another part of the depot."[74]

Russ Fitzgerald recounted a similar culture clash one night during a set break at a Bob Margolin show. "There was one night when [some] good old boy walks up and says to Margolin *'Play us some of that good ol' n***ger blues!'* And Bob was actually reasonably gentle with him but, you know, set him straight and sent him on his way, but then he's like, after the guy's gone off, Margolin was just like, *'You know, I played with guitar with Muddy Waters for seven years. Man . . . ,'* and that was it, and then shakes himself off and goes and plays."

On other occasions, fate provided quite wondrous moments at Jackson Station. Dave Schools says, "To be on the stage and watch our crowd under the influence of whatever sparkles they had acquired as they merged into the late-night crowd was a spectacle to behold." He says, "It wasn't just our people who were taking up all the room on the dance floor whirling like dervishes, being sort of freaked out when suddenly there is a motorcycle guy standing beside them grooving on the music with his arms crossed. It was the motorcycle guy coming in, and you see them come in the door at the back of the place, 'What the hell is going on up there in front of that band? Give me a drink!'"[75] Tinsley Ellis remembered playing Jackson Station one night when the circus came to town. "There was a circus in the area . . . maybe a regional circus. And at one point during our show, people were doing acrobatics in there, and a guy jumped up on the bar and was the fire-eater, and he was eating fire on the bar. And I thought, I remember at the time, this is one of a kind."[76] Larry Acquaviva writes: "The further the night went on—usually through three, sometimes four full sets of music—this place would only get wilder: lawyers dancing with bikers, pretty little hippy chicks making out with cowboys, and every freak imaginable becoming so engrossed in the music that they'd forget where they even were."[77]

Jackson Station provided the greater Greenwood community with a vibrant, diverse, and inclusive social space. "They created this environment where everybody was welcome," said Glenn Phillips. "They gave everybody what they wished they had had." This took work and it was a matter of agency. "Gerald had a way about him," Ben Hawthorne said, pondering the success of the club. "Everyone liked him. Everyone respected him. Without Gerald, it couldn't be Jackson Station. Gerald made it happen."[78] Gerald had the ability to talk to anybody. In our own day and age, it is a shame that so many people have lost the art of conversation. In explaining his business philosophy, Gerald once said, simply: "Treat them right."[79] For Gerald Jackson, the category "them" was absolutely inclusive. His treatment of others was genuine. Liberty-loving people should be inspired by his life and work. In Reggie Massey's words, Gerald Jackson "created a business that became a local legend which cannot be replaced."[80] As we have seen, Gerald Jackson was a complicated, colorful individual. Long-time friend David Goldman captures the core of his character when he describes Gerald as a: "Vietnam Vet, macho guy who could flame out gay at the drop of a hat, Mama's boy, cock hound, sophisticate, rube, Jesus lover, proud Rebel, [and] proud American."[81] It was this combination of seemingly disparate identities that made Gerald Jackson such a fascinating person and Jackson Station such an extraordinary place.

As Rolling Stones guitarist Keith Richards once said, "For me, music is at the center of everything. It is something that binds people together, through centuries, through millennia. It's undefinable. And no one's going to have the answer to it, but it's fun exploring."[82] This book has described the impact of a live music venue called Jackson Station on a small community in rural South

Carolina. It does not pretend to have all the answers, but like Keith Richards says, it has been fun exploring.

Jackson Station brought fascinating sound to the South Carolina upstate in the 1980s and early 1990s, captivating and cultivating the musical tastes of the listening public. It provided a space for music fans and amateur musicians to observe, listen, dance, and talk about music. The title of this book, *Live at Jackson Station*, not only represents the fact that there was live music at Jackson Station, but also that Jackson Station provided a place for people to live their lives. It offered them life. Philosophically speaking, Jackson Station gave people—as we have seen throughout this book—a space to let Being be.[83] In the words of Tinsley Ellis, "Jackson Station was the great unifier. An oasis of liberalism out in the country."[84]

Appendix

Musicians at Jackson Station

The following is a list of musical acts for whom there is documentary evidence (usually from the Greenwood *Index-Journal,* or from extant Jackson Station fliers and concert calendars) that they played at Jackson Station. It should not be taken as a comprehensive compendium of Jackson Station musicians, but rather as a work in progress. It is presented for illustrative purposes only. If a band is not mentioned here, it does not necessarily mean they did not play Jackson Station.[1] Furthermore, an act that appears on this list may have played the club more times (in some cases, many more times) than just dates shown. If any readers would like to add or suggest an entry (which will be posted on the website companion to this book), please contact the author directly.

ACCELERATORS: February 24, 1984

AGENTS: May 2, 1984

ALKAPHONICS: July 13, 1984; April 5, 1985; August 15, 1986

ALLGOOD MUSIC CO.: January 20, 1989; March 9–10, 1989

ANDREW & THE UPSTARTS: October 11, 1985

ARHOOLY: May 31, 1984; June 1, 1984; August 9–10, 1984; February 9, 1985; April 26, 1986

ATLANTA UNDERGROUND: July 29, 1988; July 29–30, 1988

AUSTIN BRASHIER: December 9, 1995

BEDROCKERS: October 15, 1987

BELMONT PLAYBOYS: October 20, 1989

BIG BUMP AND THE STUN GUNZ: August 22, 1986; August 29, 1986

BIG CITY BLUES BAND: April 28, 1989; May 19, 1989

BILL BLUE BAND: May 4, 1984

BILL HANEY & THE ZASSOFF BOYS: June 14, 1985; August 30, 1985; February 5, 1987; March 4, 1988

THE BLIND DATES: February 14, 1987; March 21, 1989

THE BLUES CLUB: June 20, 1986; March 27, 1987; April 8, 1988; June 24, 1988; November 10, 1988; December 23, 1988

BLUE NOTE SPECIAL: September 23, 1988; December 16, 1988; March 24, 1989; April 20 & 21, 1989; August 18, 1989; October 6, 1989; February 16, 1990; May 11, 1990; August 10, 1990

THE BLUZBLASTERS: May 4, 1990

BOB MARGOLIN: April 8, 1983; August 26, 1983; August 26, 1983; October 28, 1983; January 27, 1984; June 28 & 29; 1984; January 4, 1985; July 5, 1985; October 4, 1985; November 1, 1985; January 3, 1986; March 6, 1987; June 25, 1987; January 22, 1988; March 4, 1988; July 29, 1988; January 6, 1989; March 3, 1989

BRIGHT COLORS: April 17, 1986

CATHY PONTON: 1984

CHICAGO BOB NELSON: February 22, 1985; May 23, 1985; May 22, 1987 July 2, 1988; April 20, 1990; May 24, 1990

THE COOLIES: May 13, 1988

THE COPPERHEADS: January 13, 1989; January 26, 1989; January 27, 1989

DESTINY: June 23, 1990

DR. HECTOR AND THE GROOVE INJECTORS: May 8, 1987

DOUBLE SHOT: May 13, 1988; December 9, 1995

DRINK SMALL: July 15, 1982; December 22, 1983; April 27, 1984; June 15, 1984; July 20, 1984; January 4, 1985; January 3, 1986; June 25, 1987; January 22, 1988; July 15, 1988; February 10, 1989; March 3, 1989; April 14, 1989; October 13, 1989; March 2, 1990; April 6, 1990

THE DROVERS: May 18, 1989; October 26, 1990

DRY ICE: February 22, 1985; May 23, 1985; May 22, 1987; May 24, 1990

DUTCHESS AND DIRTY WORK: March 31, 1986

DUTCHESS AND THE DUKES (WITH SCOTT CABLE): 1986

EX-CALIBUR: April 29–30, 1982

THE FAIRLANES: August 5, 1988; April 14, 1989; September 9, 1989; January 19, 1990; April 13; 1990; July 6, 1990

FATS JACKSON: July 27, 1985; March 6, 1987; June 5, 1987; June 25, 1987; January 22, 1988; July 8, 1988; February 10, 1989; March 3, 1989; April 14, 1989; October 13, 1989; April 6, 1990

THE FINS: June 17, 1983; July 7, 1983; December 20, 1983

FIVE RIVER BAND: October 3, 1986

FOOLS IN LOVE: June 28, 1985

FRANK SMOKE & THE DUCKS: June 10, 1983; September 30, 1983; December 15, 1983

FREEDOM OF EXPRESSION: February 13, 1987

FREEFALL: September 9, 1990

GLENN PHILLIPS: January 14, 1983; February 4, 1983; March 11, 1983; May 13, 1983; July 22, 1983; September 9, 1983; February 3, 1984; May 18, 1984; September 7, 1984; January 30, 1987; February 23, 1990; August 24, 1990

GRAVITY CREEPS: August 10, 1989; October 19, 1989; December 1, 1989

GRUBWORM: Spring 1990

GUITAR & DRUMS: late 1984/early 1985

THE HEARTFIXERS: July 1, 1983; September 11, 1983; November 4, 1983; July 27, 1984; May 31, 1985; August 16, 1985; April 13, 1986; January 1, 1988; February 25, 1988; March 25, 1988

THE HUMMINGBIRD TREE: March 27, 1987

JACK SPARKMAN: June 28, 1990

JAH RICHIE & THE ZION STEPPERS: June 6, 1986; September 15, 1986; August 4, 1990

JAKE SHAKE AND THE RHYTHM BUSTERS: October 23, 1986

JEFF SARLE: December 1986/January 1987

JIMMY MARKHAM & THE DIRTY DOGS: May 25, 1990

JIMMY THACKERY & THE DRIVERS: December 8, 1995

JOHN MOODY: December 1986/January 1987

JOHNNY WINTER: April 9, 1983

KILLBILLYS: Spring 1990

THE KILLER WHALES: May 3, 1985; July 12, 1985; May 22, 1986

THE KING BEES: April 20, 1990

KOKO TAYLOR: ca. 1991

THE LEAGUE OF DECENCY: May 26, 1989

LEE MOSES AND THE SHOE STOMPERS: February 25, 1988; February 26, 1989

THE LEGENDARY BLUES BAND: March 3, 1989; April 6, 1990

THE "LIGHTNING BUG" RHODES BLUES BAND: December 30, 1988; December 8, 1989; February 2, 1990

LOOSE CHANGE: December 9, 1988

LOS PISTOLERROS: June 29, 1990

LOVE TRACTOR: Winter 1982 to Fall 1983

LUTHER "HOUSE ROCKER" JOHNSON: February 20, 1987

MAC MCCLOUD AND THE NIGHT STOMPERS: October 14, 1988; February 24, 1989; April 7, 1989; May 5, 1989; November 3, 1989

MARK WENNER: December 1986/January 1987

MOON PIE: Fall 1982

MOXIE: April 12, 1990

MR. RESISTOR: March 24, 1989.

MYSTERY: late 1984/early 1985

NANCY JOINER: November 9, 1989; December 14, 1989

NAPPY BROWN: May 31, 1985; July 14, 1985; October 4, 1985; August 16, 1985; November 11, 1985; January 3, 1986; February 14 & 15, 1986; April 10, 1986; May 30, 1986; March 6, 1987; June 27, 1987; March 4, 1988; March 3, 1989; May 12, 1989; April 14, 1989; September 1, 1989; February 16, 1990

NAPPY BROWN (WITH BLUE NOTE SPECIAL): February 16, 1990

NOBLE JONES: February 15, 1990; March 23, 1990

NOT SHAKESPEARE: August 1984

THE OTHERMOTHERS: May 1, 1986

PEACH PUFFS: January 23, 1988

POCO: October 11, 1986

IN PURSUIT: September 11, 1983; November 18, 1983

PHYDEAUX: March 1, 1990

THE PLUGS: June 3, 1983

REVEREND BILLY C. WIRTZ: September 17, 1982; June 3, 1983; January 3, 1986

RHYTHM MASTERS: August 1984; late 1984/early 1985, December 1986/January 1987

THE RIGHT PROFILE: January 6, 1984

ROCK-A-BILLY-88: May 10, 1985; August 9, 1985

ROCK BOTTOM AND THE CUTTAWAYS: October 17, 1986; December 18, 1986

RONEY AND THE ELDORADOS: November 10, 1989

ROUGH MIX: January 19, 1989; March 16, 1989

THE ROULETTES: March 1, 1985; April 26, 1985; June 21, 1985

ROY'S REGGAE BAND: March 3–4, 1983

SARASOTA SLIM & THE BLUE GILLS: June 17, 1988

THE SATELLITES: October 22, 1982; March 25, 1983; May 27, 1983

SENSIBLE PUMPS: January 9, 1987; May 18, 1987; July 3, 1987; August 28, 1987; March 11, 1988; July 22, 1988; November 25, 1988; March 31, 1989; April 28, 1989; October 27, 1989; June 15, 1990

THE SHADES: April 15, 1988; February 3, 1989; May 12, 1989, September 1, 1989

SIMON SEZ: March 8, 1990; May 17, 1990; July 19, 1990

SMOKEY LOGG AND THE FLAMETHROWERS: August 11, 1989

SNIT & THE KICKERS: May 25, 1990; July 20, 1990

STONEY B BLUES BAND: June 5, 1987; December 17, 1987; February 17, 1989

THE SUPREME COURT (JEFF CALDER & GLENN PHILLIPS): February 23, 1990; August 24, 1990; October 19, 1990

SWEET BETTY: October 9, 1987; January 22, 1988; July 8, 1988; February 10, 1989; March 3, 1989; April 14, 1989, October 13, 1989; April 6, 1990

SWIMMING POOL QS: December 10, 1982; February 11, 1983; May 13, 1983; May 20, 1983

TINSLEY ELLIS: July 1, 1988; September 1, 1989

TONE POETS: August 31, 1989; September 14, 1989; September 28, 1989; October 12, 1989; November 2, 1989; February 22, 1990; April 5, 1990; June 7, 1990

TOOLS OF FREEDOM: September 9, 1988

TORNADO: August 3, 1984

TOTTAS BLUESBAND (WITH MATS BOLANDER): February 17, 1984

TRANSPORT BLUES BAND: March 20, 1987

TREVA SPONTAINE & THE GRAPHIC: October 28, 1983; June 8, 1984

TRIPLE PLAY: August 12, 1988; August 13, 1988; October 21, 1988; December 2, 1988

TRULY DANGEROUS SWAMP BAND: March 6, 1986; May 1, 1986; May 23, 1986; May 29; 1987; June 26, 1986; August 7, 1986

XLS: April 29, 1983; August 12, 1983; December 21, 1984

WALK THE WEST: May 7, 1986

WALTER "LIGHTNING BUG" RHODES: March 30, 1990

WIDESPREAD PANIC: April 17, 1987;[2] June 12, 1987;[3] August 21, 1987;[4] March 18, 1988;[5] April 1, 1988;[6] June 3, 1988;[7] October 7, 1988,[8] November 18, 1988;[9] April 7, 1989[10]

WILL "SMOKEY" LOGG: August 11, 1990

ZACK ZAPPIN' AND THE SITUATION: July 12–13, 1990

Z GULP: April 20, 1984

THE ZASSOFF BOYS & BUDDY RAY: September 16, 1988

Notes

INTRODUCTION

1. "Beat It on Down the Line," on the 1967 album *The Grateful Dead*.

2. There is debate about whether the club should be called "Jackson Station" or "Jackson's Station." Most of the time Gerald called his club "Jackson Station." This is how the name appeared on the signs outside the club and in and many marketing materials. However, there were other times when he and others also referred to the club as "Jackson's Station." My preference is to use "Jackson Station," simply because that is the variant that was more common (and the possessive seems a bit awkward to the eye). However, if I quote someone saying "Jackson's Station" or if it appears as such in some sort of published text (e.g., newspaper article), I do not correct it.

3. Verver, "Next Stop: Jackson Station," 53.

4. "We at Jackson Station . . . ," Jackson Station Depot, bar pamphlet, circa 1981, author's collection.

5. The Sensible Pumps were an all-female blues band that played Jackson Station many times from 1986 to 1990. The band members included Mattie Phifer, Catherine Brickley, Susan Cree, and Mindy Harvey.

6. Mattie Phifer, phone interview with author, July 30, 2018.

7. Verver, "Next Stop: Jackson Station," 53.

8. See South Carolina Code of Laws, "SECTION 16–15–120. Buggery. Whoever shall commit the abominable crime of buggery, whether with mankind or with beast, shall, on conviction, be guilty of felony and shall be imprisoned in the Penitentiary for five years or shall pay a fine of not less than five hundred dollars, or both, at the discretion of the court."

9. While the buggery statute remains on the books in the South Carolina Code of Laws (and indeed, it will take a very brave set of politicians to remove it), the Supreme Court ruling makes the state law unenforceable.

10. In her obituary, it was written that Elizabeth Jackson "owned and operated Jackson Station." See "Deaths and Funerals," *Index-Journal*, November 21, 2001, 4.

11. Donaghy, "Kinfolk still Kicking," 2

12. For an approximate listing of musical acts which played Jackson Station over the years, please see the Appendix.

13. Reverend Billy Wirtz, phone interview with author, February 25, 2017.

14. Glenn Phillips, phone interview with author, June 3, 2014. This Glenn Phillips is not to be confused with Glen Phillips of the band Toad the Wet Sprocket.

15. Dave Schools, phone interview with author, March 14, 2017.

16. Schools, interview.

17. Tinsley Ellis, phone interview with author, February 18, 2017.

18. Patoski and Crawford, *Stevie Ray Vaughan*, 84.

19. Patowski and Crawford, *Stevie Ray Vaughan*, 69.

20. Stevie Ray Vaughan (1954–1990) was a famous electric blues guitar player from Texas, known for revolutionizing and popularizing blues music before his premature death.

21. Patoski and Crawford, *Stevie Ray Vaughan*, 69.

22. Spera and Jerry Dicolo, "Tipitina's Bought."

23. Brown, "The Story of LA Club."

24. Hogan, "The Last Best Party."

25. Miller, "The Blues Station," 1D.

26. So says WillieB69, a music fan on an Allman Brothers Band message board, after the death of Nappy Brown in September 2008. Available at http://allman brothersband.com/modules.php?op=modload&name=XForum&file=viewthread&tid =81239.

27. Edwards, *Bars, Blues, and Booze*, 297.

ONE : CAROLINA DRAMA

1. See the song "Jim 3:16" on the album, *Take it Like a Man* (2015) by Jim White v. the Packway Handle Band.

2. Personal conversation with author, June 20, 2015.

3. Verver, "Next Stop: Jackson Station," 53.

4. Four days later, on April 11, 1990, Drink Small would receive the South Carolina Folk Heritage Award at the South Carolina Statehouse. For more on Drink Small's life and music, see Wilson-Giarratano, *Drink Small*.

5. The Legendary Blues band was comprised of past members of the Muddy Waters backup band and had appeared in the popular movie *The Blues Brothers* (1980).

6. Drink Small, phone interview with author, July 27, 2014.

7. So named, Dirk Armstrong says, in a phone interview, because the Station was "on the Spur," of the railroad from Hodges to Abbeville. Armstrong says the Spur Burger "got lots of interesting and awkward jokes about it."

8. Drink Small, interview with author, Columbia, SC, October 17, 2014.

9. South Carolina v. Stogner.

10. Incident Report, Greenwood County Sheriff's Department. April 7, 1990.

11. South Carolina v. Stogner, 41.

12. Untitled Police Notes, Gerald Jackson File, Greenwood County Sheriff's Office.

13. Dirk Armstrong, phone interview with author, March 8, 2017.

TWO : GERALD JACKSON

1. Jeff Calder, phone interview with author, May 9, 2019.
2. "Deaths and Funerals—M. Edgar Jackson," 8.
3. "Marriages and Engagements," 2.
4. Sheehan, "An Afternoon Ride in the Country," 1B.
5. "South Carolina Deaths," 5.
6. Gerald appears to be speaking of the Piedmont & Northern Railway network here, which operated service from Charlotte to Spartanburg and then on to Greenwood from 1911 to 1969. See Wade, *Greenwood County and Its Railroads*.
7. Miller, "The Blues Station," 1D.
8. John Sanders, interview with author, Hodges, SC, July 25, 2018.
9. Sanders, interview, 2018.
10. "I'm thinking of a clever way . . ."
11. Sometimes the numbers would change in the flyers. On one occasion, Jackson stays "there were 2 hotels, 8 saloons and NO churches in the old days." See "The size and the width of the old train depots."
12. "I'm thinking of a clever . . ." In an interview, Hodges local Butch Riddle says this is a quote from his grandfather, Guy Emerson, who used to own Emerson's Store. For more on Emerson's Store, see Sims "At the Museum," 15.
13. "The size and the width of the old train depots . . ."
14. "I'm thinking of a clever way."
15. Calder, phone interview, 2019.
16. Butch Riddle, interview with author, Hodges, SC, March 8, 2019.
17. Thomas, "Hodges Depot," 9.
18. From 1824 to 1834, the community was known as Mt. Ariel and was one of South Carolina's first planned communities. See https://www.scpictureproject.org/greenwood-county/cokesbury-college.html. It is located two miles northwest of the original settlement in the area, which had grown up around the founding of the Old Tabernacle Methodist Church in 1812.
19. "Progress of Improvement in the District—Improvement at Hodges," 2
20. Thomas, "Hodges Depot," 9.
21. Thomas, "Hodges Depot," 9.
22. John Sanders, interview with author, Hodges, SC, July 25, 2018.
23. Miller, "The Blues Station," 1D.
24. Otis Harvley, interview with author, December 13, 2018.
25. Gerald had perfect attendance in the 1957–58 school year. See "162 Pupils Had Top Attendance Records."
26. "Deaths and Funerals—M. Edgar Jackson."
27. Gerald Jackson "really missed his Dad," said Hazel Bryant, in an interview. "He was real fond of his dad."

28. Sanders, interview, 2018.

29. "Music Program to be Tonight at West Hodges," 3.

30. "West Hodges Pupils to Give Musical Play," 5.

31. "$1400 Raised by Northside Pancake Event," 5.

32. "Their Posters Won," 6.

33. "Carols at Hodges," 1.

34. "Hodges Program," 1.

35. "Local Boys to Attend T & I Convention," 6.

36. "Gerald Thomas Jackson."

37. "Student Assistants Are Selected," 2.

38. "Talent Show," 12.

39. "High School Junior Prom is Scheduled Next Friday." 13.

40. "Annual Midwinter Ball Set," 12.

41. "Judge Says More Understanding Needed of US Court Decisions," *Index-Journal*, August 12, 1968, 9.

42. "Gerald Thomas Jackson."

43. "Gerald Jackson," August 6, 1969, 27.

44. "Gerald Jackson," August 27, 1969, 3.

45. Chandler, "Their Brother's Keepers."

46. Rusavskiy, "Face of Defense."

47. Bill Coleman, interview with author, Greenwood, SC, September 4, 2018.

48. Jack McConnell, phone interview with author, September 21, 2018.

49. Cornelison, "Jackson Station Depot," 5B.

50. "Code of Conduct."

51. Roland Tranter (*pseud.*), interview with author, Greenwood, SC, March 6, 2015.

52. Anita Clinton, email to author, December 2, 2018.

53. David Goldman, email to author, March 7, 2015.

54. David Goldman, email to author, January 14, 2015.

55. "Oh he dilly-dallied on the side, yeah," Linn Johnson said of Gerald. Interview with author, Greenwood, SC, September 22, 2015.

56. Johnson, interview.

57. Bonnie Capps, phone interview with author, July 16, 2014

58. Billy Wirtz, phone interview with author, February 25, 2017. He says the exact quote from Gerald was, "I don't do much, I just hang out and fuck a few farm boys every now and then."

59. Wirtz, interview.

60. Johnson, interview.

61. Retired Lander University English professor Bill Poston adds important context: "'Now Lucy looks sweet 'cause he dresses like a queen / But he can kick like a mule it's a real mean team'—from Mott the Hoople's version of a David Bowie song (the group had the hit)." Email to author, July 7, 2017.

62. See Vito Russo, *The Celluloid Closet: Homosexuality in the Movies.* New York: Harper and Row, 1987.

63. Brand Stille, phone interview with author, June 16, 2014.

64. Tranter, interview.

65. Sanders, interview.

66. George Singleton, email to the author, August 23, 2018.

67. Joe Cabri, interview with author, Greenwood, SC, February 27, 2017.

68. Tommy Kidd (*pseud.*), interview with author, Greenville, SC, May 3, 2018.

69. Cornelison, "Jackson Station Depot," 5B.

70. Anita Clinton, email to author, December 2, 2018.

71. Joe Cabri, interview, February 17, 2017.

72. A band that helped usher in the New Wave music revolution in the South in the 1980s. For more on the Qs, see chapter 5.

73. Calder, interview, 2019

74. Jeff Calder, phone interview with author, May 28, 2014

75. David Goldman, interview with author, June 20, 2014.

76. Deborah Milling, phone interview with author, July 8, 2014.

77. Harris Bailey, email to author, June 30, 2014. In using the term "Golden Age," Harris was referring to the Larry Jackson presidency (1973–1992) which was when Lander transitioned from being a struggling private school to a thriving public institution. See Megan Price, "Remembering Lander President."

78. Harris Bailey, interview with author, Greenwood, SC, July 10, 2014.

79. Gay Coleman, interview with author, Greenwood, SC, September 4, 2018.

80. McConnell, interview, 2018.

81. McConnell, interview, 2018.

82. Calder, interview, 2019.

83. Anita Clinton, email to author, November 30, 2018.

84. Stille, interview, 2014.

85. Capps, interview, 2014.

86. Capps, interview, 2014.

87. Bruce Cobb, interview with author, McCormick, SC, September 5, 2018.

88. Cobb, interview, 2018.

89. Kidd, interview, 2018.

90. Karen Miller-Johnson, personal communication to author, July 24, 2014

91. Ralph Campbell, interview with author, Shoals Junction, SC, August 7, 2015

92. Goldman, interview, 2014.

93. Otis Harvley, interview with author, December 13, 2018.

94. Goldman, email to author, January 14, 2015.

95. Tinsley Ellis, phone interview with author, February 18, 2017

96. "Gerald Thomas Jackson."

97. Reggie Massey, interview with author, August 12, 2015.

98. Reggie Massey, interview, 2015.

99. Reggie Massey, interview, 2015.

100. Dirk Armstrong, phone interview with author, March 8, 2017.

101. Reggie Massey, interview, 2015

102. "Code of Conduct," Jackson Station Depot.

103. A blues band from Hilton Head Island in the 1980s and played at a placed called the Old Post Office Emporium. They would play Jackson Station regularly over the years.

104. David Truly, phone interview with author, September 18, 2018.

105. Goldman, interview, 2014.

106. Goldman, interview, 2014.

107. Benjamin Hawthorne, interview with author, Greenwood, SC, July 18, 2014.

108. Guran Blomgren, "We'll Show Them What the Blues Is," 15.

109. David Goldman, email to author, January 26, 2019.

110. Goldman interview.

THREE : STEVEN BRYANT AND ELIZABETH JACKSON

1. "Bizarre Love Triangle," from their album 1986 album *Brotherhood.*

2. "Gerald Thomas Jackson."

3. Glenn Phillips, phone interview with author, June 3, 2014.

4. Gerald's older sister.

5. Hazel Bryant, interview with author, Liberty, SC, March 6, 2017.

6. Bryant, interview, 2017.

7. Tommy Kidd, interview with author, Greenville, SC, May 3, 2018.

8. Terry Pierce, email to author, February 28, 2017.

9. Kidd, interview, 2018.

10. Bryant, interview, 2017.

11. A state mental hospital in Greenville, SC.

12. Bryant, interview, 2017.

13. Kidd, interview, 2018.

14. Bryant interview, 2017. Bryant said, "Steve worked all those years at the depot without a dime."

15. Terry Pierce, email to author, February 28, 2017.

16. David Goldman, email to author, January 14, 2015.

17. Bob Margolin, email to author, July 3, 2014.

18. Brand Stille, phone interview with author, June 16, 2014.

19. Anita Clinton, email to author, December 1, 2018.

20. Anita Clinton, email to author, November 30, 2018.

21. David Goldman, email to author, January 15, 2015.

22. Benjamin Hawthorne, interview with author, Greenwood, SC, July 18, 2014.

23. John Sanders, interview with author, Hodges, SC, July 25, 2018.

24. Lee and Susan Rush, email to the author, July 17, 2017.

25. Bryant, interview, 2017.

26. Catherine Brickley, phone interview with the author, September 11, 2018.

27. Bryant, interview, 2017.

28. Gerald would also turn people away from the door. "If someone was really inebriated, he wouldn't let 'em in," says Tinsley Ellis in an interview with the author. "He was tough."

29. Jack McConnell, phone interview with author, September 21, 2018.

30. Brickley, interview, 2018.

31. Sanders, interview, 2018.

32. Sanders, interview, 2018.

33. Sanders, interview, 2018.

34. David Goldman, phone interview with author, June 24, 2014.

35. Anita Clinton, email to author, November 30, 2018.

36. Cornelison, "Jackson Station Depot," 1B.

37. David Truly, interview, September 18, 2018.

38. David Truly, interview, September 18, 2018.

39. Margolin shot to prominence backing up the legendary Muddy Waters from 1973 to 1983, before striking out on a solo career.

40. Margolin, email to author, July 3, 2014.

41. Cora Garmany, interview with author, Pomaria, SC, November 19, 2016.

42. Garmany, interview, 2016.

43. Phyllis Free, phone interview with the author September 4, 2015.

FOUR : THE EARLY YEARS

1. From the song "Fortunate Son," on the album *Willy and the Poor Boys* (1969).

2. "Discharges," 11.

3. Sheehan, "An Afternoon Ride," 1B.

4. This claim about a fire is disputed by Otis Harvley, who says in an interview that the Jackson General Store was simply knocked down when the new highway was constructed. Years before, Gerald had actually admitted that he had demolished the old Jackson family store when they expanded the highway. "I had to tear it down when the road was widened," Gerald said told Carey Hayes of the *Greenville News*. "Now I'm going to put something back," See Hayes, "Hodges Depot," 43. It is not clear why Gerald would change the story eight years later.

5. Miller, "The Blues Station," 11D.

6. John Sanders, interview with author, Hodges, SC, July 25, 2018.

7. Guran Blomgren "We'll Show Them What the Blues Is."

8. Reggie Massey, Letter to SC Department of Probation, Parole, and Pardon Services, August 24, 1994. Author's collection.

9. Milward, *Crossroads*, 115.

10. Hughes, *The Dream Keeper*, 26.

11. Wright, "Foreword," x. Wright also mentions that "the most striking feature of [blues] songs is that a submerged theme of guilt, psychological in nature, seems to run through them."

12. Wright, "Foreword," x.

13. Reverend Billy Wirtz, phone interview with author, February 25, 2017.

14. In Edwards, *Bars, Blues, and Booze,* 74.

15. Edwards, 74.

16. Fahey, 2000, 215.

17. For the importance of Muddy Waters for the development of both the blues and rock 'n' roll, see Milward, Crossroads.

18. See the 2015 documentary, *Keith Richards: Under the Influence,* directed by Morgan Neville.

19. See the documentary, *Remastered: Devil at the Crossroads* (2019), directed by Brian Oakes.

20. As we have seen, Gerald would often joke that the "entrance to hell is not far from Hodges, South Carolina." Jeff Calder, phone interview with author, May 9, 2019.

21. Tinsley Ellis, phone interview with author, February 18, 2017.

22. Nick Hyduke, email to author, January 9, 2019.

23. See DeLune, *South Carolina Blues.*

24. Freddie Vanderford, phone interview with author, September 5, 2018.

25. David Goldman, phone interview with author, June 24, 2014

26. Miller, "The Blues Station," 1D.

27. Verver, "Next Stop: Jackson Station," 54.

28. This was one of two railroad depots in Hodges. The other depot serviced the electricity powered Piedmont & Northern Line which ran from Greenwood to Durham (via Spartanburg) and was a Self-Duke enterprise.

29. This is known today as the Hodges One Stop—arguably the best place to get a sausage biscuit in Greenwood County.

30. Ellis, "Rail Depot Closes,"

31. Hayes, "Hodges Depot," 43.

32. Miller, "The Blues Station," 11D.

33. Miller, "The Blues Station," 11D.

34. Miller, "The Blues Station," 11D. Gerald would say, "I bought it for a dollar in April 1975. And the person I bought it from gave me the dollar back" (Donaghy, "Jackson Station," 1C).

35. Cornelison, "Jackson Station Depot," 1B.

36. Hayes, "Hodges Depot," 43.

37. Wade, *Greenwood County and Its Railroads,* 24.

38. *Index-Journal* reporter Vicki Thomas mentions in her story that Hodges locals "did not know when the building was constructed." See Thomas, "Hodges Depot," 9.

39. Jack Graves and Charles Hershey, interview with author, Greenwood, SC, October 24, 2018.

40. Ellis, "Rail Depot Closes"

41. The G&C Railroad was developed with the assistance of noted South

Carolinian and U.S. diplomat Joel Roberts Poinsett (1759–1851)—for whom the Poinsettia plant is named—as one of his last acts of public service.

42. "Thanks for taking the time . . ." Jackson Station Depot, bar pamphlet, circa 1981, author's collection.

43. See "An Old Map," 4.

44. "Thanks for taking the time . . ."

45. "Another Atrocious Murder," 2.

46. *Keowee Courier*, 2.

47. I am indebted to Harris Bailey for first informing me of the Randolph assassination at Hodges and for providing some key sources about this event.

48. Foner, Freedom's Lawmakers.

49. Joel Williamson, After Slavery, 182.

50. In his book Ben Tillman & the Reconstruction of White Supremacy, historian Stephen Kantrowitz erroneously claims that Randolph had been killed at the "Abbeville train station" (2000, 54). In his book After Slavery, Joel Williamson (1965, 260) incorrectly states that Randolph had been killed in Donaldsville.

51. "Liberal with the People's Money," 4.

52. "Testimony of W. K. Tolbert in the Contested Election Case," 3.

53. "Extracts from a Trip to the South," 1.

54. See the *Abbeville Press and Banner,* February 19, 1869, 1.

55. *Abbeville Press and Banner,* February 26, 1869, 3.

56. See Kantrowitz 2000, 54–55.

57. "The Condition of the State," 1.

58. *Edgefield Advertiser,* March 2, 1871.

59. "The size and the width of the old train depots . . ."

60. "Thanks for taking the time . . ."

61. In Kantrowitz 2000, 207.

62. See James Bouie, "The Trump Strain in American History."

63. Thomas, "Hodges Depot," 2.

64. "Horrible Crime at Hodges," 2.

65. "Horrible Crime at Hodges," 2.

66. There was an advertisement on page 2 of the *Abbeville Press and Banner* on June 17, 1859 for J. L. Clark, "repairer of watches, clocks and jewelry," who operated at Hodges Depot.

67. Gerald was probably referring to an advertisement for a new dry goods and groceries business which had appeared on page 1 of the October 5, 1865, *Abbeville Press and Banner*. The ad read, "Come to Hodges' Depot! Here you can get your horse shod or buggy mended, your hat dressed or made, hoop skirts, made or mended, or buy new ones. Here is the railroad, and here is your Dinner House, by D. B. Glymph. Terms cash or marketable. Produce at current rates."

68. "We have a new addition to our gallery . . ."

69. Verver, "Next Stop: Jackson Station," 54.

FIVE : SETTING UP SHOP

1. "Walk on the Wild Side" (1972)
2. Wade, Greenwood County and Its Railroads, 24.
3. Wade, Greenwood County and Its Railroads, 24.
4. Wade, Greenwood County and Its Railroads, 35.
5. Thomas, "Hodges Depot," 9.
6. Piedmont & Northern Railroad timetable courtesy of Ralph Campbell (Shoals Junction, SC).
7. Thomas, "Hodges Depot," 9.
8. Simon, "Cabaret Crowd," 19.
9. Hayes, "Hodges Depot," 43.
10. Hayes, "Hodges Depot," 43.
11. Simon, "Cabaret Crowd," 19.
12. Sheehan, "An Afternoon Ride,"1B.
13. Sheehan, "An Afternoon Ride,"1B.
14. Miller, "The Blues Station," 11D.
15. Sheehan, "An Afternoon Ride,"1B.
16. John Sanders, interview.
17. Bill Coleman, interview with author, Greenwood, SC. For more on the Waterhole, see Hughes, "Second Home."
18. Massey, interview.
19. Otis Harvley, interview with author, Hodges, SC, March 17, 2017.
20. Otis Harvley, interview with author, Hodges, SC, December 13, 2018.
21. Sheehan, "An Afternoon Ride," 1B.
22. Thomas, "Hodges Depot," 9.
23. Anita Clinton, email to author, December 2, 2018.
24. Patoski and Crawford, Stevie Ray Vaughan, 56.
25. Coleman, interview.
26. Bryant, interview.
27. Reggie Massey, interview with author, Greenwood, SC, August 12, 2015.
28. Hayes, "Hodges Depot," 43.
29. Bryant, interview.
30. Thomas, "Hodges Depot," 9.
31. Thomas, "Hodges Depot," 9.
32. Simon, "Cabaret Crowd," 19. In addition to being known for hosting the headquarters of the National Wild Turkey Federation, Edgefield, SC, is probably most famous (outside of their pottery) for being the birthplace of Senator Strom Thurmond, the iconic erstwhile segregationist Dixiecrat (later to become Republican), who, living to 100, has the distinction of being the oldest and longest-serving politician in the history of the country. For literary types, Edgefield, South Carolina, might also be familiar as the birthplace of Edgar "Bloody" Watson, the central character in

Peter Matthiessen's masterwork novel about the Florida Everglades, Shadow Country. The Watson saga begins in Edgefield.

33. Simon, "Cabaret Crowd," 19.

34. Simon, "Cabaret Crowd," 19.

35. Simon, "Cabaret Crowd," 19. Jackson told the reporter the ramps were "for the benefit of disabled veterans and others confined to a wheelchair." Twenty years later Jackson himself would be using the ramps in exactly this capacity.

36. Simon, "Cabaret Crowd," 19.

37. Simon, "Cabaret Crowd," 1975, 19.

38. Miller, "The Blues Station," 11D.

39. Miller, "The Blues Station," 1D.

40. Linn Johnson, interview with author, Greenwood, SC, September 22, 2015.

41. Michael Rothschild, phone interview with author, September 13, 2018.

42. Lee and Susan Rush, email to author, July 17, 2017.

43. Goldman, interview.

44. Glenn Phillips, phone interview with author, June 3, 2014.

45. This would continue even after Jackson Station started having bands. On March 19, 1983, the *Index-Journal* reported on plans for the Cokesbury Spring Fling the following month. Jackson Station was the first on a three-part progressive dinner. The other two locations were the Gary House in Hodges (later known as Somebody's House) and Cokesbury College.

46. Ann Shield Bishop, telephone interview with author, November 4, 2019.

47. David Goldman, email to author, October 27, 2019.

48. Miller, "The Blues Station," 1D.

49. "Eight Charged in Raid of Gambling House." *Index-Journal*, November 7, 1978.

50. Leslie Brooks, "Man Receives Suspended Sentence for Bomb Threat," *Index-Journal*, January 13, 1979.

51. Coleman, interview, 2018.

52. Donaghy, "Jackson Station," 2C.

53. Donaghy, "Jackson Station," 1C.

54. Sanders, interview, 2018.

55. McConnell, interview, 2018.

56. Sanders, interview, 2018.

57. Catherine Brickley, phone interview with the author, September 11, 2018.

58. Bryant, interview Hazel Bryant, interview with author, Liberty, SC, March 6, 2017.

59. Miller 1989, "The Blues Station," 11D

60. Donaghy "Jackson Station."

61. Miller, "The Blues Station," 1D.

62. Miller, "The Blues Station," 1D.

63. Nic Massey, interview with author, Greenwood, SC, February 4, 2016.

64. Tommy Kidd (*pseud.*), interview with author, Greenville, SC, May 3, 2018.

65. Miller, "The Blues Station."

66. Cornelison, "Jackson Station Depot," 1B.

67. Reggie Massey, interview, 2015.

68. Dave Schools, phone interview with author, March 14, 2017.

69. Schools, interview, 2017.

70. "Door Charges."

71. Bruce Cobb, interview with author, McCormick, SC, September 4, 2018.

72. David Goldman, email to author, January 27, 2015. Goldman adds: "I doubt pennies were accepted in that jar. Gerald would not have fooled with rolling up other people's pennies." Email to author, July 30, 2019.

73. "Thanks for taking the time . . ."

74. At first, I hoped to find an entire archive of these pamphlets. However, one does not seem to exist. There are some flyers that date from 1980 to 1981 and others from the late 1980s. There is not a lot in between. The stories in the pamphlets are missing citations. Some of the tales repeat themselves with the facts slightly changed. Like a good salesperson, it seems that Gerald stretched the truth in places.

75. "Stage Notes," March 1989.

76. Tinsley Ellis, phone interview with author, February 18, 2017.

77. Reggie Massey, interview, 2015.

78. Reggie Massey, interview, 2015.

79. Will Holloway, phone interview, September 4, 2015.

80. Russ Fitzgerald, interview with author, Greenwood, SC, March 9, 2017.

81. Benjamin Hawthorne, personal conversation with author, February 24, 2015.

82. Nic Massey, interview, 2016.

83. Bill Coleman, interview, 2018.

84. A fine 1980s alternative rock band, precursor to Son Volt, Wilco, and the Bottle Rockets.

85. For another excellent example of a Southern porch song, listen to the "Front Porch Song," written by Robert Earl Keen and Lyle Lovett.

86. Reggie Massey, interview, 2015.

87. Dave Schools of Widespread Panic implies the cows might have also been useful to Gerald in the cultivation of psychedelic mushrooms. "They did have old Bessie out there for a reason other than milk," Schools chuckles.

88. "Stage Notes," March 1989.

89. Roland Tranter (*pseud.*), interview with author, Greenwood, SC, March 6, 2015.

90. Kidd, interview, 2018.

91. Goldman, interview, 2014.

92. Holloway, interview, 2015.

93. "Beer Prices."

94. Anita Clinton, email to author, December 2, 2018.

95. Fitzgerald, interview, 2017.

96. Bryant, interview, 2017.

97. Reggie Massey, interview, 2015.

98. Reggie Massey, interview, 2015.

99. "Gerald Thomas Jackson."

100. David Goldman, email to author, January 14, 2015.

101. Lila Noonkester, email to author, February 11, 2017.

102. Cornelison, "Jackson Station Depot," 1B.

103. Miller, "The Blues Station" 1D

104. Jeff Calder, phone interview with author, May 28, 2014.

105. Jeff Calder, phone interview with author, May 9, 2019.

106. Phyllis Free, email to author, August 10, 2015.

107. Schools, interview, 2017.

108. Scott Cable, phone interview with author, October 24, 2018.

109. Bob Margolin, email to author, July 3, 2014.

SIX : PLAYING AT THE STATION

1. From the song "Tall Boy," released on the 1997 album *Bombs & Butterflies*.

2. No comprehensive record exists for the musicians who played at Jackson Station. An Appendix at the back of this book lists the names of all the musical acts encountered by the author while researching this project.

3. Mattie Phifer, phone interview with author, July 30, 2018.

4. Bob Margolin, email to author, July 3, 2014.

5. The Reverend Billy C. Wirtz, phone interview with author, February 25, 2017.

6. Tinsley Ellis, phone interview with author, February 18, 2017.

7. David Truly, phone interview with author, September 18, 2018. Truly says that the odd names of other small towns in the area (e.g., Due West, Ninety-Six, Shoals Junction, etc.) added to the mystery of Jackson Station.

8. Blomgren "We'll Show Them What the Blues Is."

9. David Truly, interview, 2018.

10. Scott Cable, phone interview with author, October 24, 2018.

11. Blomgren, "We'll Show Them," 15.

12. Ellis, interview, 2017.

13. Legendary Blues Band Contract with Jackson Station, March 3, 1989. Author Copy.

14. Wirtz, interview, 2017.

15. Michael Rothschild, phone interview with author, September 13, 2018.

16. Rothschild, interview, 2018.

17. Margolin, email, 2014.

18. Blomgren, "We'll Show Them," 15.

19. Blomgren, "We'll Show Them," 15.

20. Dave Schools, phone interview with author, March 14, 2017.

21. Dave Schools, interview, 2017.

22. Dave Schools, interview, 2017.

23. Schools is referring to the legendary music promoter Bill Graham (1931–1991).

24. Dave Schools, interview, 2017.

25. For more on the sociology of scenes, see Grazian, *On the Make.*

26. Billy Wirtz interview. For more on the Chitlin' Circuit, see Lauterbach, The Chitlin' Circuit.

27. Quoted in Brown, "The Origin (and Hot Stank) of the Chitlin Circuit."

28. For an introduction to the "backbone of the Chitlin' Circuit," see http:// www.gatecitysoul.com.

29. Another example is the Littlejohn Grill in Clemson, SC. See Vince Jackson, "In Era of Segregation . . ."

30. There is also a documentary film about Charlie's Place. See https://www.scetv .org/stories/Carolina-stories/2018/charlies-place.

31. The question of why so many of the great original blues artists hailed from Mississippi is an interesting one. In *I'd Rather Be the Devil,* Stephen Calt (2008, 10) suggests the association stems from "an article of faith that because blues arose from the oppressed conditions of Blacks, the repressive state of Mississippi necessarily produced the most intense blues singers."

32. Ellis interview. Stoney B, Howlin' Wolf's grandson, played Jackson Station several times.

33. You can learn more about Margolin's experiences with the film here: https:// bobmargolin.com/the-original-last-waltz.

34. Bob Margolin promotional flyer. No date. Author copy.

35. Tinsley Ellis also says that he usually played three sets at Jackson Station, starting at 11:00, with an hour break between them. The second set would start at 1:00. The last set would start around 3:00 in the morning.

36. Dave Schools of Widespread Panic says, "On a normal night, we could do four or five sets."

37. Bob Margolin, email, 2014.

38. Margolin said: "I still do some gigs with Betty, she has been a dear friend for decades now." For more on Sweet Betty, see her website, http://www.sweetbettyblues .com/sb_bio.htm, where she mentions the importance of Jackson Station to her career.

39. Margolin, email, 2014.

40. Margolin, email, 2014.

41. Freddie Vanderford, phone interview with author, September 5, 2018.

42. Russ Fitzgerald, interview with author, Greenwood, SC, March 9, 2017.

43. Fitzgerald, interview, 2017.

44. Fitzgerald, interview, 2017.

45. Fitzgerald, interview, 2017.

46. Fitzgerald, interview, 2017.

47. Fitzgerald, interview, 2017.

48. I say that Ex-Calibur seems to be the first band to play Jackson Station since it appears to be the first time Gerald took out an advertisement in the Greenwood *Index-Journal* to promote a show. It is possible other bands had played the club before this and they were not listed in the newspaper.

49. Wirtz, interview, 2017.

50. Wirtz would often play at Jackson Station until September 1984 when he stopped drinking. Wirtz said, "I remember going, 'Ah, maybe we shouldn't be playing Jackson Station.' Jackson Station was one of those that went along with a lot of the partying and that sort of thing."

51. See Lollis "Faith Healer."

52. Father of the solicitor in the Gerald Jackson case, Townes Jones IV.

53. Leslie Brooks, "Jenkins says federal agent framed him."

54. Mark Cline, phone interview with author, January 31, 2020.

55. Armistead Wellford, personal communication to author, February 3, 2020.

56. Armistead Wellford, phone interview with author, February 2, 2020.

57. Armistead Wellford, phone interview with author, February 2, 2020.

58. Cline, interview, 2020.

59. Armistead Wellford, personal communication to author, February 2, 2020.

60. Dick Hodgin, phone interview with author, December 3, 2018.

61. Himes, "Calder Sculpts Pool Qs Attack," N19.

62. Jeff Calder, phone interview with author, May 28, 2014.

63. Jeff Calder, phone interview with author, May 9, 2019.

64. Calder, interview, 2019.

65. Calder, interview, 2019.

66. Truly interview, 2018.

67. Ellis, interview, 2017.

68. Schools, interview, 2017.

69. See Joyce, "Panic's Populist Appeal."

70. Rothschild, interview, 2018.

71. Schools, interview, 2017.

72. Rothschild, interview, 2018.

73. See https://widespreadpanic.com/band/.

74. For more on the Athens music scene of the early 1980s, see Rodger Lyle Brown's *Party Out of Bounds.*

75. Schools, interview, 2017.

76. Schools, interview, 2017.

77. Reggie Massey, interview with author, Greenwood, SC, August 12, 2015.

78. Ellis, interview, 2017.

79. Schools, interview, 2017.

80. Dirk Armstrong, phone interview with author, March 8, 2017.

81. Schools, interview, 2017.

82. For more on the phenomenon of audience members wanting to sit in with

the band while they play, see Mike Wesolowski's comments in Emily Edwards (2016, p. 56).

83. Schools, interview, 2017.

84. Schools, interview, 2017.

85. Clayton Sprouse, interview with author, Greenwood, SC, May 3, 2016.

86. Brown seems to be referring to the June 3, 1988 show at Jackson Station when the band played four full sets plus an encore.

87. Clayton Sprouse, email to author, January 13, 2020.

88. Mattie Phifer, phone interview with author, July 30, 2018. Phifer says the band got their name from a Marilyn Monroe movie. She says they stumbled upon it after "brainstorming a lot of things. We were looking for something that was catchy." The line was "about shoes, 'Oh, those are such sensible pumps.'"

89. Phifer, interview, 2018.

90. Catherine Brickley, phone interview with author, September 11, 2018.

91. See Fahey, 2000. Given the history of the blues, and that fact the first blues song ever recorded was "Crazy Blues" (1920) by Mamie Smith, Adia Victoria's recent emergence on the music scene a century later is welcomed. As she writes in her song "Stuck in the South": "Don't know nothin' bout Southern belles / But I can tell you somethin' about Southern hell." Victoria's music blends the exceptional music and clever lyrical work of the best blues music. See Pareless, 2019. Another example of innovation and continuity in the blues tradition can be seen in the outstanding work of Rhiannon Giddens of the Carolina Chocolate Drops. See Sullivan, 2019. The careers of both Victoria and Giddens indicate that, in some ways, blues music may be more alive than ever.

92. Phifer, interview, 2018.

93. Brickley, interview, 2018.

94. The guitarist and backing vocalist for the rock band Heart.

95. Phifer, interview, 2018.

96. Vanderford, interview, 2018.

97. Glenn Phillips, phone interview with author, July 3, 2014.

98. "Everybody was always worn out," the next day says Billy Wirtz, laughing. "You'd be like, 'Oh my God. We played Jackson Station until four in the morning!'"

99. Dik Armstrong, phone interview with author, March 8, 2017.

100. Schools, interview, 2017.

101. Phillips, interview, 2014.

102. Susan Cree, phone interview with author, September 26, 2018.

103. Brickley, interview, 2018.

104. Andrew Rieger, phone interview with author, February 10, 2017.

105. Jeff Calder, phone interview with author, May 28, 2014.

SEVEN : LIVING THE GOOD LIFE

1. "High Time," released in 1970 on the album *Workingman's Dead.*

2. McBride, *Kill 'em and Leave*, 184.

3. King formed a relationship with Mays at Morehouse College. They would remain close until the end of King's life. May delivered the eulogy at Martin Luther King's funeral. See https://time.com/5224875/martin-luther-king-jr-eulogy/.

4. For a powerful introduction to educational inequality in the state, see the documentary *Corridor of Shame: The Neglect of South Carolina's Rural Schools* (2006).

5. See Benson and Dominguez, "The Show Must Go On."

6. Hazel Bryant, interview with author, Liberty, SC, March 6, 2017.

7. Bryant, interview.

8. According to an old flyer, Jackson Station was: "Open earlier in the winter to stoke the stoves. Open later in the evening in summer to avoid the extreme heat. On snow and sleet days, always open, and beer is 65 cents." "Anyone Causing a Disturbance . . ."

9. From an advertisement for Jackson Station in the Greenwood *Index-Journal,* November 26, 1989, 6.

10. Tommy Kidd (*pseud.*), interview with author, Greenville, SC, May 3, 2018.

11. "They would just dote on her," says Gay Coleman, of the way Gerald and Steve related to her daughter. Gay Coleman, interview with author, Greenwood, SC, September 4, 2018.

12. Reggie Massey, interview with author, August 12, 2015.

13. Will Holloway, phone interview with author, September 5, 2015.

14. David Goldman, email to author, January 14, 2015.

15. Reggie Massey, interview, 2015.

16. Michael Rothschild, phone interview with author, September 13, 2018.

17. Dirk Armstrong, phone interview with author, March 8, 2017.

18. Cornelison, "Jackson Station Depot," 5B.

19. Lee and Susan Rush, Email to author, July 17, 2017

20. Dave Schools, phone interview with author, March 14, 2017.

21. Armstrong, interview, 2017.

22. Kidd, interview, 2018.

23. Kidd, interview, 2018.

24. Armstrong, interview, 2017.

25. Brand Stille, phone interview with author, June 16, 2014.

26. Holloway, interview, 2015.

27. Claire St. Donaghy, "Howard's On Main, hosting gathering to remember Starnes Club Forest."

28. Kidd, interview, 2018.

29. Bruce Cobb, interview with author, McCormick, SC, September 4, 2018.

30. Bill Coleman, interview with author, Greenwood, SC, September 4, 2018.

31. Rothschild, interview, 2018.

32. Cornelison, "Jackson Station Depot," 5B.

33. Miller, "The Blues Station," 1D.

34. Graves, "Stars and Bars," 52.

35. Graves, "Stars and Bars," 53.

36. Tinsley Ellis, phone interview with author, February 18, 2017.

37. Ellis, interview, 2017.

38. Ellis, interview, 2017.

39. Roland Tranter (*pseud.*), interview with author, Greenwood, SC, March 6, 2015.

40. Tranter, interview, 2015.

41. Bruce Cobb, interview with author, McCormick, SC, September 4, 2018.

42. Kidd, interview, 2018.

43. Cobb, interview, 2018.

44. Tranter, interview, 2015.

45. Anita Clinton, email to author, December 1, 2018.

46. Harris Bailey, email to author, March 23, 2017.

47. Ellis, interview, 2017.

48. The Reverend Billy C. Wirtz, phone interview with author, February 25, 2017.

49. Scott Cable, phone interview with author, October 24, 2018.

50. Michael Rothschild, email to author, December 1, 2018.

51. Cable. interview, 2018.

52. Henderson, *'Scuse me while I Kiss the Sky,* 69.

53. Cable, interview, 2018.

54. Cable, interview, 2018.

55. "Nappy Brown," *Times,* 63.

56. "Brown's Throat Burning Style. Spanned Five Lyrical Decades."

57. Cora Garmany, interview with author, Pomaria, SC, November 19, 2016.

58. Teddy Roberts, phone interview with author, October 30, 2018.

59. Roberts, interview, 2018.

60. Roberts, interview, 2018.

61. Roberts, interview, 2018.

62. Roberts, interview, 2018.

63. Rothschild, email, 2018.

64. Rothschild, email, 2018.

65. Rothschild, email, 2018.

66. Rothschild, email, 2018.

67. Rothschild, email, 2018.

68. Nappy Brown was posthumously inducted into the North Carolina Music Hall of Fame in October 2015. See http://northCarolinamusichalloffame.org/.

69. Bob Margolin, email to author, October 18, 2018.

70. Bob Margolin, Wirtz and Cable, "Thank You, Nappy Brown."

71. Bob Margolin, email, 2018.

72. Margolin, "Thank You, Nappy Brown."

73. Billy Wirtz says that Nappy came back to the blues because he "wasn't making the money" with Gospel music.

74. Cora Garmany says Nappy would change outfits "two or three times a night."

75. Wirtz, interview, 2017.

76. Garmany, interview, 2016.

77. Cora Garmany says, "He could play his nose. You was swear he was playing a harp. In his songs, he would play his nose. Sure would. How he did it I don't know, but he would do it."

78. Wirtz, interview, 2017.

79. Bob Margolin, email to author, July 3, 2014.

80. Bertram Rantin, "50 Years of Passionate Performing," E11.

81. Garmany, interview, 2016.

82. Reggie Massey, interview, 2015.

83. Reggie Massey, interview, 2015.

84. Rothschild, interview, 2018.

85. Garmany, interview, 2016.

86. Cable, interview, 2018.

87. Cable, interview, 2018.

88. Teddy Roberts says that Nappy Brown liked Jackson Station so much that he thought about buying it. "Nappy wanted to buy it and Cora wanted to buy it. She said she would cook the food."

89. Cable, interview, 2018.

90. Catherine Brickley, phone interview with author, September 11, 2018.

91. Susan Cree, phone interview with author, September 26, 2018.

92. The Lander University men's tennis team won national titles in 1985, 1988, 1991, and 1992.

93. Joe Cabri, interview with author, Greenwood, SC, February 17, 2017.

94. Jack McConnell, phone interview with author, September 21, 2018.

95. Glenn Phillips, phone interview with author, June 3, 2014.

96. Bailey, email, 2017.

97. Debbie Massey, interview with author, Greenwood, SC, September 4, 2018.

98. Wirtz, interview, 2017.

99. Wirtz, interview, 2017.

100. Bryant, interview, 2017.

101. Bryant, interview, 2017.

102. Kidd, interview, 2018.

103. Deborah Milling, phone interview with author, July 8, 2014.

104. Milling, interview, 2014.

105. Deborah Milling, email to author, January 4, 2020.

106. Tersh Harley, email to author, October 27, 2018.

107. Tranter, interview, 2015.

108. McConnell, interview, 2019.

109. Tranter, interview, 2015.

110. David Truly, phone interview with author, September 18, 2018.

111. McConnell, interview, 2019.

112. Milward, *Crossroads*, 86.

113. Though the back deck at Jackson Station was where most people went to imbibe in illicit activity, occasionally this would be found on the front deck, too. "There was pot smoking on the front porch in the 1970s," said Harris Bailey in an email to author, March 23, 2017.

114. Shelia Carlisle, email to author, January 20, 2019.

115. Kidd, interview, 2018.

116. Kidd, interview, 2018.

117. Operation Jackpot refers to a major federal drug investigation, based in South Carolina, in the early 1980s. Spearheaded by future governor Henry McMaster, it resulted in many arrests and the disruption of smuggling networks across the state. For a historical overview, see David Slade, "South Carolina's Operation Jackpot broke new ground for civil asset forfeiture," The *Post & Courier,* June 11, 2017. Available at http://www.postandcourier.com.

118. Kidd, interview, 2018.

119. Wirtz adds that there "not like mountains and mountains [of cocaine]" at Jackson Station. He says, "You weren't sitting there with your teeth grinding at noon the next day, at least I wasn't."

120. Wirtz, interview, 2017.

121. Fletcher, *There is a Light,* 324.

122. Patoski and Crawford, *Stevie Ray Vaughan,* 84

123. Patoski and Crawford, *Stevie Ray Vaughan,* 84.

124. Who Killed Mr. Moonlight?, 308.

125. Tranter, interview, 2015.

126. Tranter, interview, 2015.

127. Recorded by the band Traffic and released in 1971.

128. Dave Schools, phone interview with author, March 14, 2017.

129. Mark Cline interview with author, January 31, 2020.

130. The consensus among interviewees is that Gerald had firearms at Jackson Station. John Sanders says, "I think he had an old pistol and old shotgun. The shotgun stayed by a storage cabinet in the kitchen." John Sanders, interview with author, Hodges, SC, July 25, 2018.

131. Wirtz, interview, 2017.

132. There was also a raid on Jackson Station in 1978, right before the club opened, as noted earlier.

133. Tersh Harley, phone interview with author, October 3, 2018.

134. Tranter, interview, 2015.

135. Truly, interview, 2018.

136. Linn Johnson, interview with author, Greenwood, SC, September 22, 2015.

137. Johnson, interview, 2015.

138. Tommy Kidd, interview, 2018.

139. Harley, interview 2018.

140. John Sanders, interview with author, Hodges, SC, July 25, 2018.

141. Harley, interview, 2018.

142. Harley, interview, 2018.

143. Wirtz claims that, "at the time, Columbia, South Carolina, was the most wide-open town on the east coast one time for drugs. It was floating on a sea of cocaine and crystal. Every club. They didn't even start until two in the morning. They rocked and rolled. And then one of the club owners, they found him in a quarry. He'd been shot. It got ugly. The drugs, unfortunately, can bring in a whole other element of things."

144. Wirtz, interview, 2017.

145. Guran Blomgren also reports that prohibition against "shoot[ing] up" (i.e. intravenous drug use) was also listed on Jackson Station show programs. "We'll Show Them What the Blues Is," 15.

146. Schools, interview, 2017.

147. Jeff Calder, phone interview with author, May 28, 2014.

148. Tinsley Ellis, interview, 2017.

149. Harley, interview, 2018.

150. Anita Clinton, email to author, December 2, 2018.

151. McConnell, interview, 2019.

152. "The G&C Railroad built this building in 1852."

153. "Thanks for taking the time . . ."

154. "Code of Conduct."

155. Truly, interview, 2018.

156. Tranter, interview, 2015.

157. Anita Clinton, email to author, December 2, 2018.

158. Ellis, interview, 2017.

159. Russ Fitzgerald email to author, February 27, 2017.

160. Cobb, interview, 2018.

161. McConnell, interview, 2019.

162. Harley, interview, 2018.

163. David Goldman, email to author, January 13, 2015.

164. Tommy Kidd, interview, 2018.

165. Apart from Mrs. Jackson, most of the staff at Jackson Station were male. However, bar pamphlets do mention two female bartenders—Joy Ogenbach and Mary Beth Arant—at Jackson Station. Maxine Syrkett also worked there shortly before the attack on Gerald Jackson.

166. Benjamin Hawthorne, interview with author, Greenwood, SC, July 18, 2014.

EIGHT : APRIL 7, 1990

1. Roland Tranter (*pseud.*), interview with author, Greenwood, SC, March 6, 2015.

2. The Jackson Station menu was limited but decent. In the early years, according to Dirk Armstrong, one would find "crackers in a sleeve, bags of chips, the hot dog or grilled cheese." In the late 1980s, when they started serving liquor, the kitchen added more nourishing fare like steaks, turkey clubs and cheeseburgers to comply with state food and alcohol regulations. Dirk Armstrong, phone interview with author, March 8, 2017.

3. As Alton Payne (who briefly brought Jackson Station back to life with Bonnie Capps in the mid-1990s) put it, "Everybody's that played here just loves it. The acoustics are the best because of the old wood." See Burns, "Payne Head Engineer," 11.

4. Teddy Roberts, phone interview with author, October 30, 2018.

5. Early on, learning about bands at Jackson Station usually happened through word of mouth. Tinsley Ellis, who was both a performer and a patron at Jackson Station, says, "It was very difficult back then because there was no Internet. To find out who was playing, you had to call there or know. I'm not sure if he ever had a mailing list. It was very cryptic as to who was playing there." Tinsley Ellis, phone interview with author, February 18, 2017.

6. Armstrong, interview, 2017.

7. David Goldman, phone interview with author, June 24, 2014

8. Deborah Milling, phone interview with author, July 8, 2014.

9. McConnell, interview, 2018.

10. McConnell, interview.

11. Cornelison "Jackson Station Depot," 1B.

12. Schools, interview, 2017.

13. Schools, interview, 2017.

14. Schools, interview, 2017.

15. Cornelison, "Jackson Station Depot," 1B.

16. The Reverend Billy C. Wirtz, phone interview with author, February 25, 2017.

17. Goldman, interview, 2014.

18. "May 1989," Jackson Station Concert Calendar. Author's Collection.

19. Andrew Rieger, phone interview with author, February 10, 2017.

20. Deborah Milling, email to author, July 8, 2014.

21. Terry Pierce, email to author, February 28, 2017.

22. Linn Johnson, interview with author, Greenwood, SC, September 22, 2015.

23. Reggie Massey, interview with author, Greenwood, SC, August 12, 2015.

24. Massey, "Letter to SC Department of Probation, Parole, and Pardon Services."

25. Carlton, "These Guys Paid Dues to Spread the Blues."

26. The State of South Carolina v. Terry Daniel Stogner. Transcript of Record, 90-GS-24–839, Greenwood, SC, February 11, 1991, 88.

27. South Carolina v. Stogner, 110.

28. South Carolina v. Stogner, 186.

29. South Carolina v. Stogner, 194.

30. South Carolina v. Stogner, 194.

31. South Carolina v. Stogner, 196.

32. It is not known who drove to Jackson Station. Craig Douglas claimed on the stand that he took the wheel for the nine-mile trip up to Hodges. Douglas said he drove the truck because Douglas "scared [him] when he was sober, much less driving while he was drinking (South Carolina v. Stogner, 197). However, when Stogner testified, he said he was the one who drove from Sports Break to Jackson Station (South Carolina v. Stogner, 255).

33. John Sanders, interview with author, Hodges, South Carolina, July 25, 2018.

34. This account, of Stogner and Douglas getting kicked out of and then sneaking back into Jackson Station, was also mentioned in interviews with other people for this project, including Bonnie Capps, Linn Johnson, Jack McConnell and Nic Massey.

35. In a subsequent conversation, Sanders said the money in question was not actually a "bar tab," per se, but rather a debt owed to Mrs. Jackson. He said it was from a previous concert where Mrs. Jackson had let Douglas in without paying. Sanders implied that Douglas wanted to see another show at Jackson Station even though he had not settled for the last one. Because of this, Sanders says, Mrs. Jackson sent the men packing. John Sanders, phone interview with author, October 11, 2018.

36. John Sanders phone interview, October 11, 2018.

37. Sanders, phone interview, 2018.

38. Sanders, phone interview, 2018.

39. Bonnie Capps, phone interview with author, July 16, 2014.

40. Sanders did not directly witness what happened next. His recollection is based on the account of a group of late arrivals who had just arrived at the club and were said to have observed the altercation.

41. Sanders, interview, 2018.

42. This is the estimate provided by Greenwood neurosurgeon, Dr. Harold Schmidt. See State v. Stogner, 157.

43. Reggie Massey, interview with author, Greenwood, SC, August 12, 2015.

44. Nic Massey, interview with author, Greenwood, SC, February 4, 2016.

45. Sanders, interview, 2018.

46. South Carolina v. Stogner, 84

47. Armstrong, interview, 2017.

48. Armstrong, interview, 2017.

49. South Carolina v. Stogner, 86

50. Mattie Phifer, phone interview with author, July 30, 2018.

51. South Carolina v. Stogner, 107.

52. South Carolina v. Stogner, 43

53. Armstrong, interview, 2017.

54. South Carolina v. Stogner, 98.

55. South Carolina v. Stogner, 103.

56. South Carolina v. Stogner, 109.

57. Phifer, interview, 2018.

58. Sanders, interview, 2018.

59. Sanders, interview, 2018.

60. Tersh Harley, email to author, September 27, 2018.

61. Armstrong, interview, 2017.

62. South Carolina v. Stogner, 98.

63. South Carolina v. Stogner, 81

64. Hazel Bryant, interview with author, Liberty, South Carolina, March 6, 2017.

65. "Interview with Tommy Craig Douglas," Greenwood Country Sherriff Department, interview taken by Deputy Randy Miles, April 7, 1990, 2.

66. "Interview with Craig Douglas," 2.

67. "Interview with Craig Douglas," 2.

68. Search Warrant, Greenwood Country Sheriff's Department. April 7, 1990, signed by T. W. Williams (Judge) and Randy Miles (Affiant).

69. "Interview with Craig Douglas," 2.

70. Elaine Ellison-Rider, "Greenwood Man Gets 10 Years in Ax Assault on Club Owner," *Greenville News*, February 15, 1991, 1A.

71. South Carolina v. Stogner, 47.

72. South Carolina v. Stogner, 47.

73. "Interview with Craig Douglas," 2.

74. "Interview with Craig Douglas," 1.

75. "Interview with Craig Douglas," 1.

76. "Interview with Craig Douglas," 1. The reader is forgiven if, like the author, s/he does not completely follow the mathematical logic in this calculation.

77. "Interview with Craig Douglas," 1.

78. Whether or not there was any "cutting" of Stogner would be a persistent issue in the case. Right after they arrived at Stogner's apartment after driving back to Greenwood, Douglas said he had "looked at [Stogner's] eye, looked at his ears; wasn't cut that bad but he was cut." "Interview with Craig Douglas," 2.

79. "Interview with Craig Douglas," 2

80. "Interview with Craig Douglas," 2.

81. Stogner, search warrant.

82. Stogner, search warrant.

83. South Carolina v. Stogner, 49.

84. "Return," Terry Stogner Search Warrant, Greenwood County Sheriff's Office, April 7, 1990.

85. South Carolina v. Stogner, 49.

86. South Carolina v. Stogner, 51.

87. South Carolina v. Stogner, 51.

88. South Carolina v. Stogner, 52.

89. South Carolina v. Stogner, 53.

90. "Incident Report," Greenwood County Sheriff's Department, April 7, 1990.

91. South Carolina v. Stogner, 191.

92. "Terry Daniel Stogner," FBI Identification Record, United States Department of Justice, Washington, DC. NO-92824213. State of South Carolina v. Terry Stogner, Greenwood County Courthouse, Greenwood, SC.

93. Stogner FBI Record, 1.

94. Stogner FBI Record, 1–2.

95. A small town just south of Greenville, SC.

96. Stogner FBI Record, 2.

97. Stogner FBI Record, 3.

98. Stogner FBI Record, 4.

99. Stogner FBI Record, 4.

100. Blakely, "Letter to Elizabeth Jackson."

101. South Carolina v. Stogner, 60.

102. "Investigative Supplementary Report," Deputy Tony Roberts, Greenwood County Sheriff's Department, April 7, 1990.

103. South Carolina v. Stogner, 65.

104. South Carolina v. Stogner, 131.

105. "Interview with Terry Tinsley," Greenwood Country Sherriff Department, interview taken by Deputy Sherry Scott, April 7, 1990, 1.

106. "Interview with Terry Tinsley," 2.

107. "Interview with Terry Tinsley," 1.

108. "Interview with Terry Tinsley," 3.

109. "Interview with Terry Tinsley," 3.

110. "Interview with Terry Tinsley," 3.

NINE : PICKING UP THE PIECES

1. "With a Little Help from My Friends," from the 1967 album Sgt. Pepper's Lonely Heart Club Band.

2. "Brutal Murder," 1.

3. The State of South Carolina v. Terry Daniel Stogner. Transcript of Record, 90-GS-24–839, Greenwood, SC, February 11, 1991, 155.

4. South Carolina v. Stogner, 159.

5. South Carolina v. Stogner, 155–56.

6. South Carolina v. Stogner, 155–56.

7. South Carolina v. Stogner, 156.

8. Linn Johnson, interview with author, Greenwood, SC, September 22, 2015.

9. Mattie Phifer, phone interview with author, July 30, 2018.

10. Phifer, interview, 2018.

11. Dirk Armstrong, phone interview with author, March 8, 2017.

12. South Carolina v. Stogner, 74.

13. Armstrong, interview, 2017.

14. Johnson, interview, 2015.

15. John Sanders, interview with author, Hodges, SC, July 25, 2018.

16. Bonnie Capps, phone interview with author, July 16, 2014.

17. Clark, *Walking Papers*, xi.

18. "The size and width of the old train depots . . ."

19. Tony Davis, interview with author, Greenwood, SC, August 17, 2015.

20. Reggie Massey, interview with author, Pomaria, SC, November 19, 2016.

21. Randy Miles, interview with author, Greenwood, SC, December 18, 2018.

22. Donaghy, "Jackson Station." As Nic Massey says, "A place like that, that was bringing in the music they were, you know, there really hasn't been anything like that around here, as far as I've seen." Nic Massey, interview with author, Greenwood, SC, February 4, 2016.

23. Capps, interview, 2014.

24. Capps, interview, 2014.

25. Nic Massey, interview, 2017.

26. Nic Massey, interview, 2017.

27. Armstrong, interview, 2017.

28. Johnson, interview, 2018.

29. Eddie Blakely, postcard to David Goldman.

30. "Sensible Pumps to Perform Benefit Show," Friday, June 15, 1990, concert Flyer, author's collection.

31. David Goldman, letter to Rose-Marie Williams.

32. Goldman, letter.

33. Eddie Blakely, postcard to David Goldman.

34. Capps, interview, 2014.

35. Reginald Massey, letter to South Carolina parole board, author's collection.

36. Larry Jackson, personal comment to author, July 24, 2014.

37. Jeff Calder, phone interview with author, May 9, 2019.

38. Jack McConnell says that 90 percent of the time, Gerald could diffuse situations verbally. Only very rarely would he have to lay his hands on a patron. "If he had to, he could," get physical with an unruly customer, says McConnell. However, he says, "That was always a last resort." Jack McConnell, phone interview with author, September 21, 2018.

39. Otis Harvley, interview with author, Hodges, SC, March 17, 2017.

40. Bureau of Justice Statistics. National Crime Victimization Survey, average annual victimization, 2004–2008. See https://www.bjs.gov/index.cfm?ty=tp&tid=44.

41. Thomas Kidd (*pseud.*), interview with author, Greenville, SC, May 3, 2018.

42. Tinsley Ellis, phone interview with author, February 18, 2017.

43. Ellis, interview, 2017.

44. Dave Schools, phone interview with author, March 14, 2017.

45. The Reverend Billy C. Wirtz, phone interview with author, February 25, 2017.

46. Sanders, interview, 2018.

47. McConnell, interview, 2018.

48. David Goldman, phone interview with author, June 24, 2014

49. Tinsley Ellis says Gerald "was indestructible; until they attacked him."

50. Roland Tranter (*pseud.*), interview with author, Greenwood, SC, March 6, 2015.

51. Ellis, interview, 2017.

52. Kidd, interview, 2018.

53. Sanders, interview, 2018.

54. Glenn Phillips, phone interview with author, June 3, 2014.

55. McConnell, interview, 2018.

56. McConnell, interview, 2018.

57. South Carolina v. Stogner, 114–15.

58. Catherine Brickley, phone interview with author, September 11, 2018.

59. Phifer, interview, 2018.

60. Letter from Dr. Charles Petit to "Whom It May Concern," December 18, 1990, Greenwood County Sheriff's Department.

61. Johnson, interview, 2015.

62. David Goldman, journal entry, October 7, 1990.

63. Goldman, journal entry.

64. Goldman, journal entry.

65. David Goldman, email to author, January 14, 2015.

66. Tersh Harley, phone interview with author, October 3, 2018.

67. Harley, interview, 2018.

68. Armstrong, interview, 2017.

69. Harley, interview, 2018.

70. Harley, interview, 2018.

TEN : THE TRIAL

1. The State of South Carolina v. Terry Daniel Stogner. Transcript of Record, 90-GS-24–839, Greenwood, South Carolina, February 11, 1991, 18.

2. Marvin Watson, interview with author, Greenwood, SC, February 5, 2016.

3. South Carolina v. Stogner, 123.

4. After his death, the South Carolina General Assembly would pass a Concurrent Resolution, in which they expressed their "deepest sympathy to the family and many friends of one of the Palmetto State's most prominent and respected leaders." Commenting on Jones' legal skills, the Resolution stated, "Whereas, when it came to prosecuting a case, nobody could touch William T. Jones. He will long be remembered as a master at courtroom rhetoric-many a legal opponent learned that the hard way. They dreaded having to match wits and wisdom with him, and the records show

why. He got the job done, and he did it with a flair that was both effective and appealing. Solicitor Jones was a showman and when he was in court there was never a dull moment. It was a pleasure to see him work." See https://www.scstatehouse.gov /sess113_1999–2000/bills/3274.htm.

5. Ellison-Rider, "Greenwood Man Gets 10 Years," 1A.

6. South Carolina v. Stogner, 2–3, 9.

7. South Carolina v. Stogner, 14.

8. South Carolina v. Stogner, 15

9. South Carolina v. Stogner, 15.

10. South Carolina v. Stogner, 19.

11. South Carolina v. Stogner, 19.

12. South Carolina v. Stogner, 19.

13. South Carolina v. Stogner, 20.

14. South Carolina v. Stogner, 23

15. South Carolina v. Stogner, 24.

16. South Carolina v. Stogner, 24.

17. South Carolina v. Stogner, 24–25.

18. South Carolina v. Stogner, 25.

19. South Carolina v. Stogner, 26.

20. South Carolina v. Stogner, 116.

21. South Carolina v. Stogner, 134.

22. South Carolina v. Stogner, 121.

23. South Carolina v. Stogner, 124.

24. South Carolina v. Stogner, 123.

25. South Carolina v. Stogner, 124.

26. South Carolina v. Stogner, 126.

27. South Carolina v. Stogner, 126.

28. South Carolina v. Stogner, 128.

29. South Carolina v. Stogner, 129.

30. South Carolina v. Stogner, 61.

31. South Carolina v. Stogner, 199.

32. David Porreca, "Trial under Way," 2.

33. South Carolina v. Stogner, 201.

34. South Carolina v. Stogner, 202.

35. South Carolina v. Stogner, 202.

36. South Carolina v. Stogner, 206.

37. South Carolina v. Stogner, 207.

38. Porreca, "Trial Under Way," 2.

39. South Carolina v. Stogner, 208.

40. South Carolina v. Stogner, 208.

41. South Carolina v. Stogner, 208.

42. South Carolina v. Stogner, 208.

43. South Carolina v. Stogner, 211.

44. South Carolina v. Stogner, 211.

45. South Carolina v. Stogner, 212.

46. "Interview with Tommy Craig Douglas," 2.

47. South Carolina v. Stogner, 212.

48. South Carolina v. Stogner, 213.

49. "Interview with Tommy Craig Douglas," 2.

50. South Carolina v. Stogner, 204.

51. South Carolina v. Stogner, 217.

52. South Carolina v. Stogner, 220.

53. South Carolina v. Stogner, 236.

54. South Carolina v. Stogner, 232.

55. South Carolina v. Stogner, 247–48.

56. South Carolina v. Stogner, 257.

57. South Carolina v. Stogner, 257. Later, on page 300 of the Trial Transcript, he said he put the keys in the ignition.

58. South Carolina v. Stogner, 258.

59. South Carolina v. Stogner, 258.

60. South Carolina v. Stogner, 259–60.

61. South Carolina v. Stogner, 260.

62. South Carolina v. Stogner, 261.

63. South Carolina v. Stogner, 267.

64. South Carolina v. Stogner, 263.

65. South Carolina v. Stogner, 261.

66. South Carolina v. Stogner, 261.

67. South Carolina v. Stogner, 262.

68. South Carolina v. Stogner, 262.

69. South Carolina v. Stogner, 262.

70. South Carolina v. Stogner, 263.

71. South Carolina v. Stogner, 263

72. South Carolina v. Stogner, 264.

73. South Carolina v. Stogner, 264.

74. South Carolina v. Stogner, 260.

75. South Carolina v. Stogner, 264.

76. South Carolina v. Stogner, 264.

77. South Carolina v. Stogner, 307.

78. Mattie Phifer, phone interview with author, July 30, 2018.

79. South Carolina v. Stogner, 322.

80. South Carolina v. Stogner, 323.

81. South Carolina v. Stogner, 325.

82. South Carolina v. Stogner, 326.

83. South Carolina v. Stogner, 329.

84. South Carolina v. Stogner, 336.

85. South Carolina v. Stogner, 337.

86. South Carolina v. Stogner, 24.

87. South Carolina v. Stogner, 339.

88. South Carolina v. Stogner, 339.

89. South Carolina v. Stogner, 341.

90. South Carolina v. Stogner, 341–42.

91. South Carolina v. Stogner, 349.

92. South Carolina v. Stogner, 350.

93. South Carolina v. Stogner, 350–51.

94. South Carolina v. Stogner, 351.

95. South Carolina v. Stogner, 352.

96. South Carolina v. Stogner, 352.

97. South Carolina v. Stogner, 352.

98. South Carolina v. Stogner, 353.

99. South Carolina v. Stogner, 356.

100. South Carolina v. Stogner, 357.

101. South Carolina v. Stogner, 361.

102. South Carolina v. Stogner, 361.

103. South Carolina v. Stogner, 363.

104. South Carolina v. Stogner, 364.

105. South Carolina v. Stogner, 365.

106. South Carolina v. Stogner, 366.

107. South Carolina v. Stogner, 366.

108. South Carolina v. Stogner, 372.

109. South Carolina v. Stogner, 373.

110. South Carolina v. Stogner, 375.

111. South Carolina v. Stogner, 376–77.

112. South Carolina v. Stogner, 380.

113. South Carolina v. Stogner, 381.

114. South Carolina v. Stogner, 383.

115. South Carolina v. Stogner, 384.

116. South Carolina v. Stogner, 384.

117. South Carolina v. Stogner, 386.

118. South Carolina v. Stogner, 386–87.

119. South Carolina v. Stogner, 387–88.

120. South Carolina v. Stogner, 388.

121. South Carolina v. Stogner, 388.

122. "No, that's not permissible," said the judge. "Anything else?" South Carolina v. Stogner, 395.

123. David Porreca, "Greenwood Man," 2.

124. Linn Johnson, interview with author, Greenwood, SC, September 22, 2015.

125. Debbie Massey, interview with author, Greenwood, SC, September 4, 2018.

126. Bill Coleman, interview with author, Greenwood, SC, September 4, 2018.

127. South Carolina v. Stogner, 162.

128. South Carolina v. Stogner, 76.

129. South Carolina v. Stogner, 58

130. South Carolina v. Stogner, 129, 135.

131. South Carolina v. Stogner, 67.

132. W. Townes Jones IV, interview with author, Greenwood, SC, September 4, 2014.

133. South Carolina v. Stogner, 339.

134. South Carolina v. Stogner, 24.

135. South Carolina v. Stogner, 20.

136. Robert Tinsley, interview with author, Greenwood, SC, July 15, 2020.

137. Townes Jones interview, 2014.

138. Townes Jones interview, 2014.

139. Terry Tinsley's older cousin, Robert Tinsley, says that Terry was "highly traumatized" by witnessing the attack on Gerald. Terry Tinsley died in 2006 at the age of 40. Robert Tinsley, interview with author, Greenwood, SC, July 15, 2020.

140. Anita Clinton, email to author, March 1, 2017.

141. Watson interview, 2016.

142. Watson interview, 2016.

143. Watson interview, 2016.

144. Watson interview, 2016.

145. Watson interview, 2016.

146. Watson interview, 2016.

147. Watson interview, 2016.

148. Boorda, "I am So Blessed."

149. Glenn Phillips, phone interview with author, June 3, 2014.

150. Tersh Harley, email to author, September 27, 2018.

151. Tersh Harley, phone interview with author, October 3, 2018.

152. Reverend Billy C. Wirtz, phone interview with author, February 25, 2017.

153. Reverend Billy C. Wirtz, phone interview with author, February 25, 2017.

154. Johnson interview, 2015.

155. Watson interview, 2016.

156. "Appeal from Greenwood County," 2.

157. "Appeal from Greenwood County," 4.

158. "Appeal from Greenwood County," 4.

159. "Appeal from Greenwood County," 4.

160. "Appeal from Greenwood County," 4.

161. "Appeal from Greenwood County," 4.

162. "Appeal from Greenwood County," 5.

163. "Appeal from Greenwood County," 5. Emphasis in original.

164. "Appeal from Greenwood County," 5.

165. "Appeal from Greenwood County," 6.

166. "Judgement of the Supreme Court," No. 90-CP-24–674, South Carolina Supreme Court, September 14, 1993. Available at Greenwood County Courthouse.

167. Reggie Massey, interview with author, Greenwood, SC, August 12, 2015.

168. Massey, "Letter to SC Department of Probation, Parole, and Pardon Services."

169. Reggie Massey, interview, 2015.

170. Donaghy, "Jackson Station."

171. Watson, interview, 2016.

ELEVEN : REHABILITATION

1. "Heroes," on the album Heroes (1977) by David Bowie.

2. The State of South Carolina v. Terry Daniel Stogner, Transcript of Record, 90-GS-24–839, Greenwood, South Carolina, February 11, 1991, 156.

3. Mattie Phifer, phone interview with author, July 30, 2018.

4. June 30, 1990. Courtesy of David Goldman.

5. Hazel Bryant, interview with author, Liberty, SC, March 6, 2017.

6. Donaghy, "Jackson Station," 1C.

7. Dirk Armstrong, phone interview with author, March 8, 2017.

8. Catherine Brickley, phone interview with author, September 11, 2018.

9. Bob Margolin, email to author, July 3, 2014.

10. Terry Pierce, email to author, February 28, 2017.

11. Steve "had scored way up, very, very high on the initial entrance exams. Steve was very well read and was very smart." Harley says that the school tried to find a scholarship for Steve, but "it just wasn't feasible for him to work, take care of Gerald, and try to go to school." Tersh Harley, phone interview with author, October 3, 2018.

12. Harley, interview, 2018.

13. Linn Johnson, interview with author, Greenwood, SC, September 22, 2015.

14. John Sanders, interview with author, Hodges, SC, July 25, 2018.

15. Boorda, 2008. "I am So Blessed," 1.

16. Bryant, interview, 2017.

17. Brand Stille, phone interview with author, June 16, 2014.

18. Anita Clinton, email to author, November 30, 2018.

19. Deborah Milling, phone interview with author, July 8, 2014.

20. Bryant, interview, 2017.

21. Harley, interview, 2018.

22. Sanders, interview, 2018.

23. Harley, interview, 2018.

24. Tersh Harley, email to author, September 27, 2018.

25. Johnson, interview, 2015.

26. Robert Tinsley, interview with author, Greenwood, SC, July 15, 2020.

27. Johnson, interview, 2015.

28. Drink Small, phone interview with author, July 17, 2014.

29. Small, interview, 2014.

30. Benjamin Hawthorne, interview with author, Greenwood, SC, July 18, 2014.

31. Harley, interview, 2018.

32. Johnson, interview, 2015.

33. Roland Tranter (*pseud.*), interview with author, Greenwood, SC, March 6, 2015.

34. Recorded by Bessie Smith in 1929 (Columbia Records).

35. Drink Small, interview with author, Columbia, SC, October 17, 2014.

36. Nic Massey, interview with author, February 4, 2016.

37. Bryant, interview, 2017.

38. Boorda, "I am So Blessed," 1.

39. Bryant, interview, 2015.

40. Johnson, interview, 2018.

41. Harley, interview, 2018.

42. Tim Bradshaw, email to author, March 10, 2018.

43. Donaghy, "Jackson Station Owner," 2C.

44. Donaghy, "Jackson Station Owner," 1C.

45. "Artist Claims Fame at Dorn VA," *Art World News*, April 2005, Vol. 1., No. 1, 1, author's collection.

46. Donaghy, "Jackson Station Owner," 1C.

47. Donaghy, "Jackson Station Owner," 1C.

48. Bryant, interview, 2017.

49. Bryant, interview, 2017.

50. Bryant, interview, 2017.

51. Boorda, "I am So Blessed," 1.

52. Donaghy, "Jackson Station Owner . . . ," 2006, p. 27

53. Donaghy, "Jackson Station Owner . . . ," 2006, p. 28.

54. Boorda, "I am So Blessed," 2.

55. Boorda, "I am So Blessed," 3.

56. Boorda, "I am So Blessed," 3–4.

57. A newspaper advertisement in spring 1991 declared, "Under new management! Same Ol' Jackson's With A New Attitude," *Index-Journal*, April 5, 1991, 8.

58. Verver, "Next Stop: Jackson Station," 54.

59. Verver, "Next Stop: Jackson Station," 54.

60. Verver, "Next Stop: Jackson Station," 53.

61. Burns, "Payne Head Engineer," 12.

62. Then known as Bonnie Fisk.

63. Burns, "Payne Head Engineer."

64. Bonnie Capps, phone interview with author, July 16, 2014.

65. Burns, "Payne Head Engineer," 12.

66. Burns, "Payne Head Engineer," 12.

67. Burns, "Payne Head Engineer." 12.

68. Capps, interview, 2014.

69. Tinsley Ellis, phone interview with author, February 18, 2017.

70. See "At Area Clubs," *Index-Journal,* February 22, 1996.

71. David Truly, phone interview with author, September 18, 2018.

72. *Index-Journal,* July 31, 1997, 19.

73. *Index-Journal,* September 25, 2003, 13.

74. Scott Cable, phone interview with author, October 24, 2018.

75. Harley, interview, 2018.

76. "Gerald Thomas Jackson."

77. "Steve was a horrible chain smoker," notes Tersh Harley. "I mean, I'm talking, one after the other."

78. Harley, interview, 2018.

79. Reggie Massey, phone interview with author, January 29, 2016.

80. Terry Pierce, email to author, February 28, 2017.

81. Bryant, interview, 2017.

82. Terry Pierce, email to author, February 28, 2017.

83. Daniel Prince, interview with author, Greenwood, SC, September 16, 2016.

TWELVE : JACKSON'S 'TIL DAWN

1. Harris Bailey, email to author, March 23, 2017.

2. For a good introduction, see Michael Broadway, Robert Legg, and John Broadway, "Coffeehouses and the Art of Social Engagement," *Geographical Review* 108, no. 3 (2018): 433–56.

3. A couple of years ago, the author had a new hot water heater installed in our house. The plumber noticed my guitars and the conversation turned to music. I asked him about Jackson Station. He said he knew the place and that he "used to go there when it was a biker bar." Yet Jackson Station was never just a biker bar. Bikers went to Jackson Station throughout the entire time it was open. In making such a statement, the plumber was presumably differentiating himself from other types of people who would have gone to the bar for other reasons.

4. Bob Margolin, email to author, July 3, 2014.

5. C. Rauch Wise, comment on Tribute Wall, September 17, 2010. Available at http://www.blythfuneralhome.com/obituary/Gerald-Thomas-Jackson/Columbia -SC/823713.

6. Larry Acquaviva, *Nobody Cares You are Here: The Panic Years—Part I,* 49–50.

7. John Milward comments, "Blues fans are forever worrying about the health of the genre, but in fact, the music and the context in which it has been heard has been in constant flux for the past one hundred years." See *Crossroads,* vii.

8. Miller, "The Blues Station."

9. Armistead Wellford, phone interview with author, February 2, 2020.

10. Miller, "The Blues Station," 1D.

11. For more on Sheila Carlisle and Arhooly, see Edwards, *Bars, Blues, and Booze*; and Limnios, "Sheila Grady Carlisle: Over the Rainbow."

12. Sheila Carlisle, email to author, January 30, 2019.

13. Sheila Carlisle, email to author, January 30, 2019.

14. Russ Fitzgerald, email to author, December 7, 2018.

15. Bonnie Capps, phone interview with author, July 16, 2014.

16. Reverend Billy C. Wirtz, phone interview with author, February 25, 2017.

17. Dave Schools, phone interview with author, March 14, 2017.

18. Thompson, The New Mind of the South, 173.

19. Thompson, New Mind of the South, 173.

20. Tersh Harley, phone interview with author, October 3, 2018.

21. "Carlos Santana Reflects on Woodstock." Available at https://www.pri.org /file/2019–08–02/carlos-santana-reflects-original-woodstock.

22. "Carlos Santana Reflects on Woodstock." Available at https://www.pri.org /file/2019–08–02/carlos-santana-reflects-original-woodstock.

23. Acquaviva, Nobody Cares Who You Are, 48–49.

24. Michael Rothschild mentions that though there are opportunities for musicians to play at festivals these days, it is often harder for them to "connect the dots." He says older artists like Tinsley Ellis have to a certain extent been "grandfathered in," but the "younger acts . . . have a little tougher time." Michael Rothschild, phone interview with author, September 13, 2018.

25. Spera and Dicolo, "Tipitina's."

26. See Wray, Cultural Sociology.

27. One notable difference, however, is that Jackson Station was more inclusive and universalistic in orientation (in that it accepted everyone) whereas many of the music festivals today are aimed towards this or that "tribe." As such, the audiences at many music and art festivals are often quite homogeneous. It was precisely the heterogeneity of the Jackson Station crowd that made it so interesting as a music venue and social establishment.

28. Burrows, From CBGB to the Roundhouse, 91.

29. Robert Tinsley, interview with author, Greenwood, SC, July 15, 2020.

30. With some friends from New College, the author spent one unforgettable night at Benny's Blues Bar (located at the corner of Valence and Camp) at Mardi Gras in 1991. It was that experience that introduced him to the power of live blues music.

31. Reggie Massey, interview with author, Greenwood, SC, August 12, 2015.

32. David Truly, phone interview with author, September 18, 2018.

33. Tinsley Ellis, phone interview with author, February 18, 2017. Mattie Phifer of the Sensible Pumps concurred with these sentiments. "I don't think I could [stay up all night] today," she said. "Back then it was a grand adventure." Mattie Phifer, phone interview with author, July 30, 2018.

34. Ellis, interview, 2017.

35. David Truly, phone interview with author, September 18, 2018.

36. Freddie Vanderford, phone interview with author, September 5, 2018.

37. For a discussion of such spaces in other places and times, see Bunzl, "Between Oppression and Affirmation."

38. Reverend Billy C. Wirtz, phone interview with author, February 25, 2017.

39. There were still limits to the extent of their disclosure. In a 1992 interview with Jeffrey Verver, Steve Bryant was simply described as "former manager and long-time Jackson Station aficionado" (p. 53). There was no mention of his relationship with Gerald.

40. Uribe, "Foreword," xiii.

41. Wirtz, interview, 2017.

42. Deborah Milling, phone interview with author, July 8, 2014.

43. Deborah Milling, email to author, July 8, 2014.

44. See Frank Beacham, *Whitewash: A Journey through Music, Mayhem and Murder,* 2007.

45. Edwards, *Bars, Blues, and Booze,* 231.

46. Edwards, *Bars, Blues, and Booze,* 231.

47. Edwards, *Bars, Blues, and Booze,* 232.

48. David Goldman, email to author, October 27, 2019.

49. Beacham, *Whitewash,* 18.

50. See Cornelison, 1B. The photograph was taken by Frank Pearce.

51. As it would be for the next thirty-two years, finally being taken down from the South Carolina State House grounds in July 2015.

52. David Goldman, email to author, February 4, 2020.

53. https://www.merriam-webster.com/dictionary/liberty.

54. Verver, "Next Stop: Jackson Station," 54.

55. See Edwards, 2016.

56. Verver, "Next Stop: Jackson Station," 54.

57. Tinsley, interview, 2020.

58. "Thoughts without content are empty, intuitions without concepts are blind." Immanuel Kant, *Critique of Pure Reason.* Available at https://plato.stanford .edu/entries/kant-judgment/supplement1.html.

59. Mattie Phifer said that in her experience many people misunderstand blues music, believing it to be "sad music." This is not the case. "It's music that takes your troubles away. Makes you feel good."

60. Richard Wright, "Foreword," ix.

61. Russ Fitzgerald, interview with author, Greenwood, SC, March 9, 2017.

62. South Carolina v. Stogner, 355.

63. Glenn Philips, phone interview with author, June 3, 2014.

64. Blomgren, "We'll Show Them What the Blues Is," 15.

65. This can be a heavy burden to bear. As Russ Fitzgerald said, "You don't pick one of those things up [i.e., a guitar] because you are happy and well–adjusted. You don't . . . When you do the wild-man, electric blues thing . . . you do it because there is something that is . . . not right. There is a, some pull, the void, is pulling you . . . Jackson's kind of clarified that. You'd go there and you'd watch these guys and many of them were very fine musicians, but you'd realize, you know, there's something off here."

66. For a point of reference, see the song "P-Funk Wants to Get Funked Up" (1975) by Parliament on their album Mothership Connection. It contains the lyric, "So sit back, dig, while we do it to you in your eardrums."

67. Shows that, ironically, can now be streamed online and watched from the comfort of one's living room.

68. Schools, interview, 2017.

69. Bruce Cobb, interview with author, McCormick, South Carolina, September 4, 2018.

70. Edwards, *Bars, Blues, and Booze*, 4.

71. He says that there was a "big counter-culture" in Greenwood at the time. Tim Bradshaw, phone interview with author, April 7, 2018.

72. David Truly, phone interview with author, September 18, 2018.

73. Roland Tranter (*pseud.*), interview with author, Greenwood, South Carolina, March 6, 2015.

74. David Goldman, email to author, November 3, 2019.

75. Schools, interview, 2017.

76. Ellis, phone interview with author, February 18, 2017.

77. Acquaviva, 49.

78. Benjamin Hawthorne, interview with author, Greenwood, South Carolina, July 18, 2014.

79. Cornelison, "Jackson Station Depot," 5B.

80. Massey, "Letter to SC Department of Probation, Parole, and Pardon Services."

81. David Goldman, email to author, January 24, 2019.

82. See the 2015 documentary, *Keith Richards: Under the Influence,* directed by Morgan Neville.

83. For an introduction, see Rüdiger Safranksi, *Martin Heidegger: Beyond Good and Evil* (Cambridge, MA: Harvard University Press, 1999).

84. Ellis, interview, 2017.

APPENDIX : MUSICIANS AT JACKSON STATION

1. Before his death, Reggie Massey shared with me a large plastic box of booking folders from Jackson's Station. These folders (which are now in the possession of his son, Nic Massey) contain information about various musical acts (e.g., booking contracts and promotional materials). Reggie had received the box from Steve Bryant. It is clear that most of the artists with information in the box played Jackson's Station. Others may or may not have played the club. It is likely that they did play Jackson Station, but it is impossible to know for sure. These artists include: the Adjusters, the Alligators, Bachelors of Arts, the Dusters, Eddie "Guitar" Burns, Government Cheese, James Cotton, the Paralyzers, Roger Wilson and Low Overhead, Southern Culture on the Skids, and Studio B. Most of the information about shows at Jackson Station is from the mid-to late 1980s. There is not as much information about bands

that played Jackson Station from 1982 to the mid-1980s. It is likely that much of the band information (i.e., contracts, flyers, calendars) from those days was lost or went missing after the attack on Gerald and when different people took over the depot.

2. This show is noted but no set list is available at Widespread Panic fan-site, Everyday Companion. See http://www.everydaycompanion.com/setlists/19870417a .asp.

3. The show is not listed at Everyday Companion. See *Index-Journal,* June 11, 1987, p. 6.

4. The show is not listed at Everyday Companion. See *Index-Journal,* August 20, 1987, p. 6.

5. Everyday Companion incorrectly lists the band playing at the New Deli in Greenville, North Carolina, on this date. However, there is a concert flyer and advertisement in the *Index-Journal* (p. 6) from March 17, 1988, showing that Widespread Panic played Jackson Station on March 18. There is a recording of the band playing in Greenville, South Carolina, the night before.

6. The set list for this show is available at Everyday Companion. See: http:// www.everydaycompanion.com/setlists/19880401a.asp.

7. The set list for this show is available at Everyday Companion. See: http:// www.everydaycompanion.com/setlists/19880603a.asp.

8. The set list is for this show is available at Everyday Companion. See: http:// www.everydaycompanion.com/setlists/19881007a.asp.

9. The set list for this show is available at Everyday Companion. See http:// www.everydaycompanion.com/setlists/19881118a.asp.

10. The show is not listed at Everyday Companion. See *Index-Journal,* April 6, 1989, p. 6.

Bibliography

Acquaviva, Larry. *Nobody Cares Who You Are: The Panic Years—Part I.* Atlanta, GA: Deeds Publishing, 2018.

"An Old Map," *Index-Journal,* May 26, 1926.

"Annual Midwinter Ball Set," *Index-Journal,* January 21, 1967.

"Another Atrocious Murder," *Intelligencer* (Anderson, SC), July 26, 1866.

"Anyone Causing a Disturbance . . ." Jackson Station Depot. Bar pamphlet. ca. 1980. Author's collection.

"Appeal from Greenwood County Court of General Sessions." *State of South Carolina v. Terry Daniel Stogner.* Case No. 90-GS-24–839. April 26, 1993. Microfiche available at South Carolina Supreme Court, Columbia, SC.

"Artist Claims Fame at Dorn VA." April 2005. *Art World News,* vol. 1, no. 1. Dorn VA Hospital. Author's collection.

Beacham, Frank. *Whitewash: A Southern Journey through Music, Mayhem, & Murder.* New York: Booklocker, 2007.

"Beer Prices." Jackson's Station Depot. Bar Pamphlet. ca. 1981. Author's collection.

Benson, Adam, and Damian Dominguez. "The Show Must Go On: Drag Show Fundraiser for Humane Society Moves to Abbeville." *Index-Journal,* March 6, 2019.

Blakely, Eddie. Letter to Elizabeth Jackson. April 7, 1990. Greenwood County Sheriff's Office.

Blakely, Eddie. Postcard to David Goldman. June 3, 1990. Courtesy of David Goldman.

Blomgren, Guran. "We'll Show Them What the Blues Is." *Dagens Nyheter* (Stockholm), March 11, 1984. Translated from the Swedish by Garreth Piekarski.

Bonner, Raymond. "When Innocence Isn't Enough," *New York Times,* March 4, 2012.

Boorda, Dina G. "I am So Blessed." Letter sent to Dorn VA Hospital, 2008.

Bouie, Jamelle. "The Trump Strain in American History." *New York Times,* July 29, 2019.

Broadway, Michael, Robert Legg, and John Broadway, "Coffeehouses and the Art of Social Engagement," *Geographical Review* 108 (2017): 433–56.

Brooks, Leslie. "Jenkins says federal agent framed him," *Index-Journal,* May 22, 1979.

Brown, August. "The Story of LA club Jewel's Catch One and its pioneering owner finds its way to Netflix." *Los Angeles Times,* May 2, 2018.

Brown, Rodger Lyle. *Party Out of Bounds: The B-52s, R.E.M., and the Kids Who Rocked Athens, GA.* Athens: University of Georgia Press, 2016.

Brown, Tanya Ballard. "The Origin (and Hot Stank) of the Chitlin Circuit." *National Public Radio*, February 16, 2014. https://www.npr.org/sections/codeswitch /2014/02/16/275313723/the-origin-and-hot-stank-of-the-chitlin-circuit.

"Brown's Throat Burning Style Spanned Five Lyrical Decades." *Canberra Times*, October 7, 2008.

"Brutal Murder." *Abbeville Press and Banner*, October 12, 1865.

Bunzl, Matti. "Between Oppression and Affirmation: Historical Ethnography of Lesbian and Gay Pasts." *Anthropological Quarterly* 68 (1995): 121–28.

Burns, St. Claire. "Payne Head Engineer at Jackson Station," *Index-Journal*, January 25, 1996.

Burrows, Tim. *From CBGB to the Roundhouse: Music Venues through the Years.* New York: Marion Boyars, 2009.

Calt, Stephen. *I'd Rather be the Devil: Skip James and the Blues.* Chicago, IL: Chicago Review Press, 2008.

"Carlos Santana Reflects on Woodstock." *The World*, August 1, 2019. Available at: https://www.pri.org/file/2019-08-02/carlos-santana-reflects-original-woodstock.

Carlton, William. "These Guys Paid Dues to Spread the Blues," *News Sentinel*, August 7, 1986.

"Carols at Hodges." *Index-Journal*, December 18, 1963.

Chandler, Jerome Greer. "Their Brother's Keepers: Medics & Corpsmen in Vietnam," *Air Force Medical Service,* January 11, 2018. Available at: https://www.airforce medicine.af.mil/News/Display/Article/1413458/their-brothers-keepers-medics-corps men-in-vietnam/.

Clark, Francesco. *Walking Papers.* New York: Hyperion, 2010.

"Code of Conduct," Jackson Station Depot Bar Pamphlet. ca. 1980. Author's collection.

Cornelison, Jimmy. "Jackson Station Depot." *Greenville News*, February 11, 1983.

"Deaths and Funerals—M. Edgar Jackson." *Index-Journal*, January 19, 1959.

"Deaths and Funerals—Elizabeth Jackson." *Index-Journal*, November 21, 2001.

DeLune, Clair. *South Carolina Blues.* Charleston, SC: Arcadia Publishing, 2015.

"Discharges," *Index-Journal,* November 6, 1975.

Donaghy, St. Claire. "Jackson Station Owner Master's Another Outlet for His Creativity." *Index-Journal*, July 2, 2006.

Donaghy, St. Claire. "Kinfolk still Kicking after 30 Years." *Index-Journal*, November 28, 2009.

Donaghy, St. Claire. "Howard's On Main hosting gathering to remember Starnes Club Forest." *Index-Journal*, April 15, 2018.

"Door Charges," Jackson's Station Depot. Bar pamphlet. ca. 1981. Author's collection.

Edwards, Emily D. *Bars, Blues, and Booze: Stories from the Drink House.* Jackson: University Press of Mississippi, 2016.

Ellis, Mike. "Rail Depot Closes Permanently for 95-year-old Hodges Landmark." *Greenville News*, June 1, 1965.

Ellison-Rider, Elaine. "Greenwood Man Gets 10 Years in Ax Assault on Club Owner." *Greenville News*, February 15, 1991.

"Extracts from a Trip to the South." *Abbeville Press and Banner*, February 19, 1869.

Fahey, John. *How Bluegrass Destroyed My Life*. Chicago, IL: Drag City Incorporated, 2000.

Fletcher, David. *There is a Light that Never Goes Out: The Enduring Saga of the Smiths*. New York: Three Rivers Press, 2012.

"Gerald Jackson." *Index-Journal*, August 6, 1969.

"Gerald Jackson." *Index-Journal*, August 27, 1969

"Gerald Thomas Jackson" (October 10, 1946–September 4, 2010). Blyth Funeral Home. Available at: https://www.blythfuneralhome.com/obituaries/Gerald-Thomas-Jackson?obId=2135915#/obituaryInfo.

Goldman, David. Letter to Rose-Marie Williams, July 29, 1990. Courtesy David Goldman.

Graves, Beth Arnold. "Stars and Bars: Where the Music Makers go to Hear Music Being Made." *Southern Magazine*, September 1988, 52.

Grazian, David. *On the Make: The Hustle of Urban Nightlife*. Chicago: University of Chicago Press, 2011.

Greenwood County Sherriff's Office. "Interview with Terry Tinsley." Interview taken by Deputy Sherry Scott, April 7, 1990.

Greenwood County Sherriff's Office. "Interview with Tommy Craig Douglas," Interview taken by Deputy Randy Miles, April 7, 1990.

Haskins, David J. *Who Killed Mr. Moonlight? Bauhaus, Black Magick and Benediction*. London: Jawbone, 2014.

Hayes, Carey. "Hodges Depot: From Pitchfork Ben's Podium to a Nightclub." *Greenville News*, June 5, 1975.

Henderson, David. *'Scuse Me While I Kiss the Sky*. New York: Atria Books, 2008.

"High School Junior Prom is Scheduled Next Friday." *Index-Journal*, April 19, 1966.

Himes, Geoffrey. "Calder Sculpts Pool Qs Attack." *Washington Post*, August 19, 1987.

"Hodges Program." *Index-Journal*, December 23, 1963.

Hogan, Maura. "The Last Best Party." *Charleston City Paper*, December 12, 2018.

"Horrible Crime at Hodges" *Intelligencer* (Anderson, SC), November 27, 1895.

Hughes, Conor. "Second Home: Harvley's Has Been the Place to Go for many Regulars for Many years." *Index-Journal*, July 30, 2017.

Hughes, Langston. *The Dream Keeper and Other Poems*. New York: Alfred A. Knopf, 1994.

"I'm thinking of a clever way . . ." Jackson Station Depot. Bar pamphlet. ca. 1981. Vol. 2. No. 4. Author's Collection.

Jackson, Vince. "In era of segregation, Littlejohn Grill was social center for Black people in Clemson." *Independent-Mail*, July 1, 2009.

Joyce, Mike. "Raucous Reunion of the 'Old School." *Washington Post*, June 16, 1989.

Joyce, Mike. "Panic's Populist Appeal." *Washington Post*, August 15, 1991.

Kantrowitz, Stephen. *Ben Tillman & the Reconstruction of White Supremacy.* Chapel Hill: The University of North Carolina Press, 2000.

Lauterbach, Preston. *The Chitlin' Circuit and the Road to Rock 'N' Roll.* New York: W. W. Norton, 2011.

"Liberal with the People's Money," *Edgefield Advertiser*, October 28, 1868.

Limnios, Michael. 2014. "Sheila Grady Carlisle: Over the Rainbow." Michael Limnios Blues Network. Available at: http://blues.gr/profiles/blogs/north-Carolina-singer -shelia-grady-carlisle-talks-about-the-blues.

"Local Boys to Attend T & I Convention." *Index-Journal*, March 12, 1964.

Lollis, Tom. "Faith Healer Leroy Jenkins Plans Museum in His Old Home." *Index-Journal*, May 12, 1977.

Margolin, Bob, Billy Wirtz and Scott Cable. "Thank You, Nappy Brown." September 2008. Available at: https://forums.stevehoffman.tv/threads/nappy-brown-rip .162012/.

"Marriages and Engagements." *Index-Journal*, September 22, 1943.

Massey, Reginald. Letter to SC Department of Probation, Parole, and Pardon Services, August 24, 1994. Author's collection.

"May 1989," Concert Calendar. Jackson Station Depot. Author's collection.

Mays, Benjamin E. *Born to Rebel: An Autobiography.* Athens: University of Georgia Press, 2003.

McBride, James. *Kill 'em and Leave: Searching for James Brown and the American South.* New York: Spiegel & Grau, 2016.

Miller, Michael. "The Blues Station: Hodges Club Rocks All Night." *The State*, July 7, 1989.

Milward, John. *Crossroads: How the Blues Shaped Rock 'N' Roll (and Rock Saved the Blues).* Boston, MA: Northeastern University Press, 2013.

"Music Program to be Tonight at West Hodges." *Index-Journal*, November 17, 1959.

"Nappy Brown." *The Times* (London), October 1, 2008.

"162 Pupils Had Top Attendance Records." *Index-Journal*, June 6, 1958.

"$1400 Raised by Northside Pancake Event." *Index-Journal*, October 24, 1961.

Pareles, Jon. "Adia Victoria Wants to Make the Blues Dangerous Again." *New York Times*, February 27, 2019.

Patoski, Nick, and Bill Crawford. *Stevie Ray Vaughan: Caught in the Crossfire.* New York: Back Bay Books, 1993.

Porreca, David. "Greenwood Man Gets Maximum Sentence in Assault with Bush Ax." *Index-Journal*, February 13, 1991.

Porreca, David. "Trial Under Way in Assault on Hodges Nightclub Owner." *Index-Journal*, February 12, 1991.

Price, Megan. "Remembering Lander President Emeritus Larry A. Jackson." November 9, 2017. Available at: https://www.lander.edu/node/6406.

"Progress of Improvement in the District—Improvement at Hodges." *Abbeville Press and Banner*, November 2, 1871.

Rantin, Bertram. "50 Years of Passionate Performing." *The State*, September 27, 2002.

Rusavskiy, Vitaliy. "Face of Defense: Navy Corspman Serves to Help Others," U.S. Department of Defense. July 13, 2018.

Sheehan, Jim. "An Afternoon Ride in the Country (On a 120-Year-Old Train Station?)." *Independent-Mail* (Anderson, SC), June 8, 1975.

Simon, Ellis B. "Cabaret Crowd May Hear 'All Aboard' at Jackson's Station Depot by Next Spring." *Index-Journal*, December 4, 1975.

Sims, Horace. "At the Museum." *Index-Journal*, June 9, 1985.

Slade, David. "South Carolina's Operation Jackpot broke new ground for civil asset forfeiture." *Post & Courier*, June 11, 2017.

"South Carolina Deaths." *Index-Journal*, December 31, 1946.

Spera, Keith, and Jerry Dicolo. "Tipitina's bought by members of New Orleans funk band Galactic." *New Orleans Advocate*, November 30, 2018. Available at: nola.com.

"Stage Notes." Jackson Station. Bar pamphlet. March 1989. Author's collection.

State of South Carolina v. Terry Daniel Stogner. *Transcript of Record*, 90-GS-24–839, Greenwood, South Carolina, February 11, 1991. Microfiche available at South Carolina Supreme Court, Columbia, South Carolina.

"Student Assistants Are Selected." *Index-Journal*, September 25, 1965.

Sullivan, John Jeremiah. "Folk Like Us." *New Yorker*, May 20, 2019.

"Talent Show." *Index-Journal*, April 3, 1965.

"Terry Daniel Stogner." FBI Identification Record, United States Department of Justice, Washington, DC. NO-92824213. Available in Clerk of Courts Office, Greenwood County Courthouse, Greenwood, SC.

"Testimony of W.K. Tolbert in the Contested Election Case." *Abbeville Press and Banner*, February 26, 1869.

"Thanks for taking the time . . ." Jackson Station Depot. Bar pamphlet. ca. 1981. Author's collection.

"The Condition of the State." *Charleston Daily News*, December 1, 1868.

"The G&C Railroad built this building in 1852." Jackson Station Depot. Bar pamphlet. ca. summer 1981. Author's collection.

"The size and the width of the old train depots." Jackson Station Depot. Bar pamphlet. ca. 1981. Author's collection.

"Their Posters Won." *Index-Journal*, April 19, 1962.

Thomas, Vicki. "Hodges Depot: The Center of Hodges Life Years Ago to Get a Facelift." *Index-Journal*, June 6, 1975.

Thompson, Tracy. *The New Mind of the South*. New York: Free Press, 2013.

Uribe, Virginia. "Foreword." In *Growing Up Gay in the South*, edited by James Sears, xi–xiii. New York: Harrington Park Press, 1991.

Verver, Jeffrey. "Next Stop: Jackson Station." *Sandlapper: The Magazine of South Carolina*, Mid-year, 1992.

Wade, James H., Jr. *Greenwood County and Its Railroads, 1852–1992*. Greenwood, SC: The Museum, 1993.

"We at Jackson Station thank you folks . . ." Jackson Station Depot. Bar pamphlet. ca. 1981. Author's collection.

"We have a new addition to our gallery . . ." Jackson Station Depot. Bar pamphlet. ca. 1981. Author's collection.

"West Hodges Pupils to Give Musical Play." *Index-Journal*, April 28, 1960.

Williamson, Joel. *After Slavery: The Negro in South Carolina During Reconstruction, 1861–1877*. Chapel Hill: University of North Carolina Press, 1965.

Wilson-Giarratano, Gail. 2014. *Drink Small: The Life and Music of South Carolina's Blues Doctor*. Charleston, SC: The History Press.

Wray, Matt, ed. *Cultural Sociology*. New York: W. W. Norton, 2014.

Wright, Richard. "Foreword." In *Blues Fell This Morning: The Meaning of the Blues*, edited by Paul Oliver, vii–xii. New York: Horizon Press, 1960.

Index